W9-BWV-849

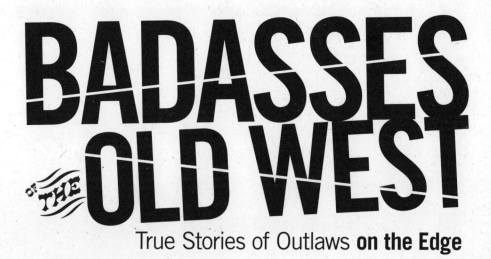

BADASSES OF THE OLD WEST

True Stories of Outlaws **on the Edge**

Edited by **Erin Turner**

TWODOT

GUILFORD, CONNECTICUT
HELENA, MONTANA

AN IMPRINT OF GLOBE PEQUOT PRESS

To buy books in quantity for corporate use
or incentives, call **(800) 962-0973**
or e-mail **premiums@GlobePequot.com.**

A · T W O D O T® · B O O K

Copyright © 2010 by Morris Book Publishing, LLC

ALL RIGHTS RESERVED. No part of this book may be reproduced or transmitted in any form by any means, electronic or mechanical, including photocopying and recording, or by any information storage and retrieval system, except as may be expressly permitted in writing from the publisher. Requests for permission should be addressed to Globe Pequot Press, Attn: Rights and Permissions Department, P.O. Box 480, Guilford, CT 06437.

Text contributions by Jan Cleere, Charles L. Convis, Elizabeth Gibson, T. D. Griffith, Barbara Marriott, Sean McLachlan, Jan Murphy, Michael Rutter, Robert Barr Smith, R. Michael Wilson, Jim Yuskavitch.

TwoDot is an imprint of Globe Pequot Press.

Library of Congress Cataloging-in-Publication Data is available on file.

ISBN 978-0-7627-5466-3

Printed in the United States of America.

10 9 8 7 6

CONTENTS

Introduction

The American frontier was about as tough a place as anyone can imagine. The indigenous Native American tribes had their own laws and rules, but no jurisdiction over white settlers. While many of the settlers were good, religious people moving west to start a new life, the wide open spaces of America's reaches attracted some pretty unlawful types as well. The wild land that comprised the American West attracted the worst kind of people—outlaws, murderers, rapists, and robbers—many on the run and looking for places to hide while they continued to break the law. Violence became epidemic and a way of life for most, making these new territories of the United States a very dangerous place to live for the newcomers who came to settle there looking for a better life. Collected here are some of the stories of these villains, who despite their outrageous crimes and way of living, certainly contributed to the history of the American people.

OLD TOM STARR

Implacable

In the fall of 1843, Tom Starr, two of his brothers, and Arch Sanders raided the house of a Cherokee political rival. Not content with murdering only the rival, the Starrs also killed his wife and a traveler staying the night at his house. Worst of all, after the brothers set fire to the house, a child ran out of the flames. A Cherokee acquaintance of Tom Starr's later passed along the story as Tom told it to him: "[A] little boy about five years old came running out and begged him not to kill him, and Tom . . . just picked him up and threw him in the fire. He said he didn't think God would ever forgive him for that and I said I didn't think He would either."

If Tom didn't already have a reputation as a holy terror, he surely did after murdering the pleading child. With a price of $1,000 on each of their heads, Tom and his brothers ran for cover across the Arkansas, but they were far from through. Over time he, his brothers, and their followers are thought to have killed at least twenty men. And Tom himself said it was a good many more.

Old Tom was a formidable figure, intimidating just to look at. He was big, six foot five, and a powerful man. He wore his black hair down his shoulders, generally had his eyelashes plucked, and often sported a rawhide necklace, tastefully hung with the earlobes of men he had killed. He was remorseless and unforgiving, tough and grim, and a terrible enemy, but he was born of a violent time in Cherokee country, when deep-seated loyalty was perhaps the most valued quality in a man next to courage. Old Tom had more than his share of both.

Back in 1836 and 1837, a number of Cherokee families traveled west from their ancestral homelands in Georgia, preferring to move in their own time and at their own pace rather than be driven west by U.S. troops. Those who did not leave their homes then would later be herded along what became known as "the Trail of Tears." After the Removal Treaty had been signed in 1835, only one question remained: When would the Cherokee Nation move to the new lands to the west?

In 1833 the Starr clan, led by Tom's father, James, was among the early immigrants to Indian Territory. A larger group of eastern Cherokees arrived in the territory in 1838, and the tribe split into two groups. One was the treaty party: the signers of the treaty and their supporters. The others, led by principal chief John Ross, formed a larger group, forcibly removed from their ancestral lands by the U.S. government. Because they had vehemently objected to the voluntary relinquishment of those lands, they were known generally as the antitreaty party. For a while there were actually two governments, and a great deal of bad blood between the two groups.

The old chief, John Ross, proposed a constitution that would unify all the settlers under a single government. Those who had settled in the territory earlier replied that "the newcomers in coming into a territory which already had an organized government accepted that government; and accordingly, since the Western Cherokees had received and welcomed their brother emigrants, the two people were already united."

The bitterness was a recipe for trouble, and in 1839 the antitreaty faction's anger boiled over. A group of Cherokees hostile to the treaty men met in secret. To them assassination seemed to be the simple solution to their hatred for the men who had signed the detested treaty. So antitreaty militants murdered leaders of the faction that had signed away the old lands. They even dragged one from his sickbed, slashing the fingers of his wife when she tried to protect her husband.

In another case killers approached and asked their victim for medicine for a sick friend. He started toward his house to get it, and the reward for his kindness was a tomahawk buried in his face, followed by more hacking and chopping and several bullets pumped into his body.

The assassins also planned to kill James Starr, but he was warned in time to escape. He found temporary protection at Fort Gibson. He would shelter there several times, in later days, as violence became epidemic in the Goingsnake District of eastern Indian Territory.

Tom Starr and three more of James's sons, Bean, Washington, and Ellis, were the heart of the family. Along with a cousin, Suel Rider, the brothers went on the attack. The last straw for the Starrs came when some thirty of the Ross opposition struck the Starr homestead and shot down James as he washed his face before breakfast.

They then murdered his crippled fourteen-year-old son, Buck, and would have killed three younger boys except that their mother and grandmother wrapped their arms around them. An early resident of the area, a doctor, later said that James's wife faced the murderers and calmly told them when Tom heard of the murders of her husband and son that he would settle with them.

Unwilling to kill the Starr women, the raiders then moved down the road and shot down Rider in his own front yard. One of the Ross men then dismounted and stabbed Rider in the heart. They next attacked Washington Starr on the road. He was very badly injured, but he still managed to find cover and escape. As the killers were busy trying to do away with Washington, one of James's younger sons, Creek, ran to Tom's house, some two miles away, with news of the murders.

Victory had gone—temporarily—to the antitreaty men: When James was buried, only the women of the family could safely attend the funeral. But the killers had missed Tom Starr, which would prove to be a fatal mistake, for Tom would never forget the injury to his family. A month or so later, after young Buck had died of his wounds, Tom told his wife, Catharine, "I will get every man who killed Buck and Pa. I will not stop killing until I do, and I will never be taken alive."

When Tom said something, he generally meant every word of it, and he and his surviving brothers got to work quickly. Stan, the Cherokee who had stabbed the wounded Suel Rider as he lay on the ground, was soon a corpse himself. Tom Starr and a band of supporters sent one Wheeler Fought into a local Indian dance where Stan was enjoying himself. The plan was to have Fought fill Stan with booze and later tell him that a jug of whiskey was hidden in a fallen tree.

The tactic worked, for later in the evening, a drunken Stan thought of the jug and rode his horse toward the tree. As he did, Starr's band shot him out of the saddle and then stabbed him to death, just as he had killed Rider. Fought's loyalty to the treaty party cost him his own life. Once the antitreaty party found out that he had lured Stan to his death, Fought was also killed.

Tom not only shed the blood of his enemies but also delighted in ravaging their property. He was fond of stealing the opposition's slaves and selling them farther to the south, and he coveted their livestock, too. Not long after his first murders, the Starr brothers were jumped by a posse of Indian police while driving stolen mules and horses toward the Texas line. Bean Starr was killed in the ensuing fight, and later Starr cohort Charles Smith—himself the son of a murdered treaty signer—fatally stabbed a lieutenant in the Indian police unit that had killed Bean. Smith did not last long himself, hunted down by the police and killed while resisting arrest.

The violence continued. Early in 1845 another signer of the treaty was also murdered, and the son of an ex-chief was killed during a council at Fort Gibson. An April 1846 letter to Stand Watie, later a Confederate brigadier, gives some of the flavor of the times:

> *You will doubtless recollect that . . . the murderer of James Starr was killed and scalped and that Fought was caught for decoying him and has since been hung. Since that time Oto Cornsilk has been killed. . . . Barrow Justice has been caught, tried and was hung yesterday. . . . John Brown & his company caught a horse thief and they killed him . . . rumored that he and his company . . . have cut up another man . . . in his own house. I forgot to mention that another man was killed at Ellis Harlan's. . . . I think there is now to be no end to bloodshed, since the Starr*

*boys & the Riders have commenced revenging the death of their
relatives.... Murders in the county have been so frequent until
the people care little about hearing these things.*

In November of 1845 a group of disguised riders burned down the home of
Return Meigs, the chief's son-in-law. Two Cherokees who had seen the arson-
ists were murdered, but Meigs said the raiders were the three surviving Starr boys
and Ellis West. Within days more violence erupted, leaving eleven men dead and
another eighteen wounded. More bloodshed ensued, and the U.S. Army sent dra-
goons into Cherokee country to restore some semblance of order. More killings
followed, however, and more members of the treaty party fled into Arkansas.

The burning of Meigs's house and the murder of the two witnesses to the
arson were the last straw for the antitreaty contingent. In 1846 President James
Polk at last stepped in to deal with the simmering mess in the Cherokee country.
By now there were no fewer than three separate groups vying for power. Polk
suggested that perhaps the Cherokee country should be split into three separate
political entities, and a bill to that end appeared in the House.

Nobody liked his radical suggestion, and the Cherokees uneasily became
one nation. Part of the accord was a general pardon for all Cherokees for all
offenses and crimes, a provision especially valuable for the Starr clan.

Tom Starr moved into the rugged southwestern corner of the Canadian
District near Briartown—now in Muskogee County—in the great bend of the
South Canadian River. When the Civil War broke out, he went off to war as a
scout for Stand Watie's Confederate brigade, in opposition to tribal Union supporters, called "pin Indians" (from their custom of wearing crossed pins on their
shirts as a symbol of support for the Union). At least a couple of accounts assert
that Tom "fought alongside" and was visited by the odious Missouri bushwhacker
William Quantrill, although this seems, at best, a very remote possibility.

The war did little to ease the old hatreds that split the Cherokee Nation.
Stand Watie, as a Confederate brigadier, wrote his wife in the autumn of 1863,
commenting casually on more killing, and on the burning of the opposition
chief's home. "Killed a few pins in Tahlequah," he wrote. "They had been holding council. I had the old Council House set on fire and burned down."

After the war Tom went back to his civilian enterprises. According to legend his business consisted mostly of whiskey running—forbidden by federal law
in the Indian nations—and trafficking stolen cattle and horses. He also operated
the first ferry on the South Canadian River.

By now he presided over a small army of kinfolk: his eight sons and two
daughters and all their offspring. Old Tom's empire also included an extensive
collection of in-laws: Even if lawmen had tried to ride into Starr country to arrest
Tom, they would have needed a battalion to smoke him out.

Starr's home was a friendly place for ex-bushwhackers, including the Younger boys and, it is said, the James brothers. Such men, moving fast and keeping to the brush, could always find a meal and safety with Tom Starr. It was during this postwar period that the Starr empire got its name of "Younger's Bend."

Stories about Old Tom were legion. One tells of a $500 bet on a horse race between Starr and a transient gambler. Seeing Starr was not carrying a gun, the gambler, with more hubris than good sense, made the mistake of threatening Starr, saying no matter which horse won, he would just take the money. Understandably, that irritated Starr, and he told the gambler so.

It is hard to imagine a professional betting man being that stupid, especially if he knew Tom's reputation. Still, according to legend, when Tom's horse won, the gambler reached for his gun. Old Tom grabbed his bowie and threw it so hard that it pierced the gambler's body and stuck in the ground.

Other tales of Tom Starr are somewhat less grim. There's the story of how he outwitted and unhorsed an entire company of soldiers who had been sent to capture him. Cutting down a section of telegraph wire, he stretched it across the road about waist high and led his pursuers into it. While the soldiers picked themselves up and recovered their horses, Starr went his way chuckling. This tale is about as likely as the Easter Bunny, but it's typical of the mythology that inevitably grew up around any larger-than-life figure . . . and Tom Starr surely was that.

Whatever other illicit doings Old Tom may have been up to, late in life he seemed to favor booze running as his source of pocket change. For a while all went well, but in time his luck ran out. In June 1884 he was charged under federal law with running five gallons of whiskey into Cherokee country, and in December 1885 he was arrested on a warrant for selling four gallons more. Then in 1886 he was caught smuggling another gallon into Indian Territory and jailed at Fort Smith in lieu of a $300 bond.

When the Fort Smith grand jury met, it indicted him on the 1885 and 1886 offenses, and in November 1886 Tom appeared before Judge Isaac Parker of the Western District of Arkansas. Tom made the decision to plead guilty, probably not a wise idea, and Judge Parker gave him a year in prison on the first count and a consecutive six-month sentence on the second one. By the end of November, Tom was behind bars in the federal prison at Menard, Illinois. He would languish at Menard until early in 1888.

Maybe prison took something out of Tom Starr's free spirit. Maybe he had just been too long on the back roads of violence and anger to be happy on the placid paths of peace. In any case he did survive his erstwhile daughter-in-law, Belle, murdered from ambush near her Younger's Bend home in 1889.

Back from prison, Tom lived on at Younger's Bend in failing health, until he died in 1890. He was gone, but he would not be forgotten.

THE UNDISTINGUISHED CAREER OF BILL DALTON

Surly Amateur

Bill Dalton's henchman turned his Winchester on Longview City's Marshal Matt Muckleroy and blasted him in the belly. Muckleroy was fortunate, however, for the round caromed off some silver dollars the lawman carried in a pouch in his pocket, split, and did no permanent damage. He eventually recovered from his wound. More serious was the wound of a saloon keeper, J. W. McQueen, hit as he ran into the alley at the beginning of the firefight. The shot that slammed into McQueen's body seemed for a while to be a mortal wound, but he too eventually recovered.

Another citizen, Charles Leonard, who was merely walking through the "court house yard," was hit in the left hand. Other accounts say that mill hand Charlie Learn—presumably the same man—was murdered near the courthouse fence. Bill had finally realized his dream of being a real bandit leader. It wouldn't last long.

There is a myriad of tales about Bill, probably as many as there are about his more infamous brothers. He came from California, where he lived at a place he called a ranch outside Paso Robles. Born in Missouri in 1865, he married in California and fathered a couple of children.

All kinds of wonderful myths surround his life there, including tales that he was wealthy, that he served in the legislature, that he fathered a child out of wedlock down in Hugo, Oklahoma, and that he had a covey of mistresses. All of these are false except the possibility that he may have been wealthy. Even so, he certainly detested what he considered the "Establishment," especially the Southern Pacific Railroad, which many farmers believed was corrupt and oppressive in its dealings with ordinary people.

Bill also had a real talent for resurrection, mostly at the hands of newspapers. At various times during his relatively short outlaw season, the public read about his demise. In late summer of 1893, he apparently died at Ingalls. Rising from the grave, he was killed at Sacred Heart Mission in the spring of 1894. A whole regiment of lawmen shot him yet again before he was well and truly extinguished in the summer of 1894. Though by now he was buried in California, he revived and was captured in New York in 1896. One book even concluded that he committed suicide in Wyoming.

But most of Dalton's carnage took place in Oklahoma. At first he joined up with veteran outlaw Bill Doolin, who had rallied a new gaggle of outlaws assembled from survivors of the old Dalton aggregation. The Doolin Gang, as the new group was called, promptly became a thorn in the side of honest men. It grew, according to some estimates, to as many as twelve or fourteen men.

In the wild 1893 shoot-out with the Doolin Gang in the outlaw town of Ingalls, Oklahoma Territory, three deputy U.S. Marshals were killed. All but one of the gang members galloped to safety and went on with their nefarious doings, although Arkansas Tom Jones (aka Roy Daugherty) was captured during the Ingalls fight and sent to prison.

The papers deluged their readers with the usual flood of misinformation, including the news that Dalton had killed Lafe Shadley, one of the lawmen. In fact, it appears that Shadley and the other two lawmen were killed by Arkansas Tom, sniping from his room at a hotel. Various reports had Dalton shot once or maybe twice, along with Bitter Creek Newcomb and somebody called Dynamite Bill. Dalton was portrayed as the leader of the gang.

While the gang lasted, they were a terror. On January 23, 1894, for example, Doolin and Tulsa Jack Blake, backed up by Bitter Creek Newcomb, struck the Farmers' and Merchants' Bank of Pawnee, Oklahoma Territory. They got only $300 on this raid because the bank's time lock was still set, but they temporarily kidnapped the cashier, releasing him only when they were well clear of the town.

Less than two months later, Doolin and Dalton, with other gang members waiting outside town, kidnapped the station agent at Woodward in the wee hours, took him to the station, and forced him to open the Santa Fe safe. They got away with some $6,500 on this raid, a considerable sum for the time.

In the aftermath of the Woodward robbery, lawmen circulated a detailed description of Bill Dalton: "Twenty five years old, five feet ten inches tall, weight 170 pounds, two weeks growth of beard, slouch hat with high crown and crease in top, pants in boots, checkered handkerchief about his neck, dark suit, sack coat, dark complexion."

The depredations of the Doolin Gang at last inspired Chief Justice Frank Dale of the Territorial Supreme Court to call in Marshal Evett Dumas Nix and issue some famous instructions, practical if somewhat unjudicial.

"Marshal," said Judge Dale, "I have reached the conclusion that the only good outlaw is a dead one. I hope you will instruct your deputies in the future to bring them in dead." The gang's days were numbered.

During a robbery of a store at tiny Sacred Heart, Dalton and Bitter Creek Newcomb shot down a tough elderly shopkeeper who strongly objected to being robbed by couple of hoodlums. In return the old man put a bullet into Bitter Creek. It was after Sacred Heart that Doolin and Dalton parted ways. The reason they rode their separate trails may have been Dalton's ambition to lead his own gang, or maybe it was the intelligent Doolin's conviction that Dalton was too much of a loose cannon to ride with any longer.

On his own Dalton decided to recruit some guns to help him and try his wings as an independent operator. He started with bank robbery. Although Dalton had a world of arrogant self-confidence and an overactive mouth to go with it, it does not appear that he ever amounted to much as an outlaw leader.

Still, Bill Dalton's name was well known, and a bewildering collection of newspaper stories reported him and his gang in a variety of places as far apart as Wagoner, Oklahoma Territory; Kendallville, Indiana; and Washington, D.C. According to the *Cherokee Advocate,* they had "over fifty murders to their credit."

Dalton left his wife and children at a farm owned by Houston Wallace. It was a shabby place near the little town of Elk, down in the neighborhood of the city of Ardmore, Oklahoma. Now an independent operator, Dalton turned his attention to Texas, where he had not been reported as visiting so far. The target was the First National Bank of Longview, located in that little town in the eastern part of the state. Dalton put together a collection of unimpressive bad men, including one Jim Wallace, brother of Houston Wallace. Jim Wallace took the "nom de robber" of George Bennett.

To Wallace, Dalton added a couple of other eager criminals, usually identified as the two Knight (possibly Nite) brothers, Jim and Big Asa, Other sources reported that the other outlaws were local sawmill hand Jim Jones and one Will Jones. Or maybe one of them was George Bennett, or perhaps Tom Littleton, or even Charles White.

These additional amateur hard cases, whoever they were, would give Dalton his very own gang. This dubious aggregation was a very far cry from the Daltons of other days, or the old, bold James-Younger Gang, but ever-cocky Bill Dalton must have figured his new confederates ought to suffice to knock over a little country bank.

Dalton did a simple reconnaissance of the town alone—maybe doing some solitary fishing in the Sabine River or maybe, as other sources say, wetting a line with the rest of his gang. Now the gang was ready to seize their jackpot. One or two stayed with the all-important horses in an alley behind the First National; Dalton and the fourth man went inside. Dalton had ready a curious note, written in pencil on the back of a poster; he handed it to the cashier, Tom Clemmons:

> *Home, May 23*
> *The First National Bank, Longview*
> *This will introduce to you Charles Speckelmeyer, who wants*
> *some money and is going to have it. B and F.*

Clemmons did not take the note seriously. He thought it was some sort of charity appeal and was ready to donate something. But then he found himself looking down the muzzle of Dalton's Winchester and realized he had big trouble. While Dalton held Clemmons and other bank men at gunpoint, another robber, probably Big Asa, pushed through a door behind the counter area and quickly scooped up whatever money he could find. The haul included, as the *Daily Oklahoman* reported, "$2000 in ten-dollar bills numbered 9, and nine $20 bills numbered 20, and a quantity of unsigned bank notes."

A bank officer scuffled briefly with one of the bandits, and everyone else in the bank intelligently took this opportunity to run out the back door and disappear. The outlaws herded Clemmons and his brother J. R. in front of them out of the bank.

Dalton's plan began to unravel when the local law spotted his gang outside the Longview bank and grew suspicious. Or maybe, as the Longview *Morning Journal* later reported, the alarm might have been given by a businessman, John Welborne. It seems one of the bandits had invited him in, but Welborne wasn't having any part of all those guns. He ran off down the street shouting that the bank was being robbed.

However the word passed around the town, armed citizens converged from all directions, and a wild firefight broke out in the alley. The outlaws inside the bank cleared out in a hurry. They tried to drive the bank employees with them toward their horses, using them as human shields, but their hostages were having none of this and ran away in another direction.

The shooting in the alley rose to a roar as the outlaws traded shots with an assortment of angry citizens and peace officers. George Buckingham, a bartender, grabbed a pistol and ran to the sound of the guns; he was one of the first citizens on the scene, and his reward was a slug in the face from Wallace's rifle. Buckingham died before he could fire a shot.

By all accounts Wallace was shooting a saddle gun from the hip and was, as citizen P. T. Boyd said much later, "a dead shot with his Winchester Special." The weapon was afterward found to have sights made of bone. "The story," said a later president of the bank, "and I don't doubt the truth of it, is that the piece of bone is from a human skull; from the head of one of Bennett's [Wallace's] victims."

Wallace seemed to be doing most of the shooting, and most of the damage, but he was running out of luck. After Muckleroy went down, his deputy, Will Stevens, stood his ground in a shower of outlaw bullets and got a round into Wallace. Or maybe, according to another citizen, the fatal round came from a hardware merchant, who in later years refused to be identified by the press.

[He s]tuck his single-action Colt .45 through an open window
of a near-by brick building. He leveled down on Bennett

> *[Wallace] just as the desperado turned to drop City Marshal*
> *Muckelroy [sic] . . . [T]he man with the .45 wouldn't shoot*
> *until Bennett [Wallace] turned again to face him. The bandit*
> *saw that menacing Colt as he turned and both of the men fired*
> *at about the same time.*

The unidentified merchant is quoted as saying, perhaps a trifle pompously, that he "could have gotten Bill Dalton and one of the Nite boys from my place in the window . . . but they had their backs turned . . . and I wouldn't shoot even a murdering bank robber in the back." But later newspaper accounts of the fight state that Wallace was shot in the back, and it's hard to imagine any Westerner having such scruples in the midst of a firefight in which his fellow citizens were being shot.

Or maybe the shooter was somebody else altogether. Local attorney Claude Lacy got credit for the shooting, said a retired city judge:

> *Claude was in the saloon next to the bank when the shooting*
> *started and he ran to the door. . . .[O]ne of Bennett's [Wallace's]*
> *bullets shattered the glass in the door and forced him to run in*
> *the other direction, into a feed store. . . . [T]he windows at the*
> *back of the store looked out on the alley and Claude got behind*
> *some sacks of feed and drilled Bennett in the back. . . . At least,*
> *he always got credit for shooting him first but the man was hit*
> *from all directions.*

Whoever fired the fatal round, or rounds, Wallace went down, dying, and the rest of the gang took to their heels.

Across the Oklahoma line lawmen recovered the outlaws' horses, the animals exhausted from being pushed too hard. However, Dalton and his two remaining cronies stole more horses near Stringtown and turned west toward the Muddy Boggy, riding into the Chickasaw Nation. And there, on May 29, the trail apparently ended.

But the officers did not stop looking. They were as sick of arrogant outlaws as Judge Dale was, and the Longview bank had offered a $500 reward for the robbers. The Longview citizenry had chipped in another $200, making a tidy reward for lawmen accustomed to facing great danger for miserable pay. There were various newspaper reports that members of the gang had been captured, none of which were accurate. But at last, in early June, the patient officers got a break.

In Ardmore the perennially impoverished Houston Wallace bought provisions, including ammunition, to the tune of some $200. The store owner, uneasy at such unusual purchases by Wallace, took the bills to the U.S. commissioner. He wired Longview and quickly learned that the $10 bills were part of the loot from the bank robbery. Wallace may have bought a wagon as well, which would have further aroused suspicion.

Deputy U.S. Marshal Seldon Lindsey followed Wallace to the express office. There, accompanied by two women who kept their sunbonnets pulled close around their faces, Wallace presented a package pickup order. The express agent produced the package, but Wallace refused to sign a receipt for it. Lindsey then arrested all three on suspicion of introducing liquor into Indian Territory—a federal offense—and the box was broken open forthwith. Sure enough, it contained nine quarts of red-eye.

Wallace caved in quickly. "The whiskey is not mine," he said. "It's for some people who are staying with me." The women would not say much at all, beyond giving the unenlightening names of Smith and Pruitt. They even refused to say where they lived, but Lindsey drew his own conclusions. Wallace was forthwith consigned to the local jail, and the two women were placed under guard.

The deputy marshal headed for Wallace's farm. Six other deputy U.S. Marshals rode out in two groups, joined by two local officers, and they surrounded the place, which was a two-room shanty. The eight took their places early in the morning on June 8.

As the officers encircled the Wallace farmhouse, Deputy U.S. Marshal Loss Hart worked his way toward a ravine in back of the house. The ravine provided the only obvious escape route, since it was the only path away from the shack that had any useful cover. Before Hart could get all the way to the ravine, a man emerged onto the house porch, saw Lindsey, and dashed back inside. He immediately reappeared, jumping out of a back window, and this time he had a pistol in his hand. As he sprinted for the deep ravine that would give him cover, Hart shouted at him to halt, but the man turned and raised his pistol to shoot at the lawman. Oklahoma City's *Daily Oklahoman* put it well, albeit a little dramatically:

> *A .44 ball, hot from the deputy's Winchester, tore into his body at the waistband near the right rear suspender button, and with two convulsive leaps he fell.*
>
> *Bill Dalton, the notorious desperado and bandit, met his death on the 8th inst. at Elk, I. T. C. L. Hart, a deputy marshal of the Paris district, fired the shot that sent the spirit of the outlaw to its home. . . . Hart . . . called on him to halt. Dalton half turned around, tried to take aim while running, and just then the officer shot. Two jumps in the air were the only motions made.*

The *Fort Worth Gazette* reported Dalton went down before the "unerring aim" of Loss Hart, "[a] .44 Winchester hole at the pants band on the right side of the spinal column, near the hip, shows where the little messenger of justice had rid the country of the worst outlaw who ever stole a horse or shot a man in the Southwest."

Inside the tiny house the officers found six terrified children, and bolts of silk cloth stuffed with numerous crisp bills and a Longview bank sack. A couple of the children told the officers their names were Dalton. After an initial denial of any relation to Bill Dalton, one of the two women arrested in Ardmore the day before at last broke down when she saw Dalton's body. She then confirmed she was his wife.

Although poor Adeline Dalton had still another sorrow to bear, most people rejoiced at Dalton's passage. As did the *Daily Oklahoman:* "Stretched out on a pine board in the rooms of Undertaker Appolis on Caddo street . . . Bill Dalton . . . lies stiff and cold . . . a .44 Winchester hole at the pants band on the right side of the spinal column . . . and that small piece of lead has rid the country of the worst outlaw who ever stole a horse or shot a man."

From a photograph Houston Wallace identified his brother as the bandit deputy Stevens killed at Longview. There was no trace of the Knight brothers at Ardmore. They had evaded pursuit this time, but they were headed for the same bitter end that awaited every man who rode with the Doolin-Dalton outfit. It took more than a year for fate to catch up with the Knights, but at last the two brothers—and a criminal cohort, one Jim Crane—were run down and killed on the Charles Schneider ranch along Bear Creek in Menard County, Texas.

What remained of Bill Dalton was shipped off to sunny California, where it was duly planted in Merced County. A newspaper story from Ardmore reported the departure under a heading that solemnly announced, MR. DALTON CONTINUES DEAD. And amazingly, to the editorial disgust of various newspapers. "[A] burning shame," said the *Daily Ardmorite*. A federal grand jury much later indicted Loss Hart and the rest of the lawmen with him for the murder of Dalton, "the worst outlaw ever to . . . shoot a man." The officers were released on their own recognizance, and there is no record that they were ever tried.

So perished the last of the outlaw Daltons, joining the long line of Oklahoma hoodlums killed by peace officers. And others were still to die under the guns of the law. Of the several members of the Dalton-Doolin Gangs, the swaggering hard cases with the jaunty nicknames and the larger-than-life reputations, just one outlaw—aside from Emmett Dalton—died of natural causes. This man, Little Bill Raidler, debilitated by his old gunshot wounds, did not long survive his release from prison. The last man to go was Arkansas Tom Daugherty in 1924, back in the robbing business after stretches in prison and even a spell of honest employment. With his death in Joplin, Missouri, thoroughly ventilated by lawmen's bullets, passed the last of the old gang.

It is not recorded that there was any widespread mourning.

BOB ROGERS

Psychopath

Jess Elliot was a lawyer and Cherokee constable, and he was in Catoosa to serve legal papers. He ended up in a Catoosa saloon, and there he met Bob Rogers. Both men had been drinking, and they soon locked horns.

Their falling-out soon escalated into a fistfight, which Rogers clearly won. With Elliot on the saloon floor, other men stopped the fight. Rogers left, and Elliot was persuaded to stay in the bar and recuperate until he could ride. Elliot rested up a little, then went outside, mounted, and rode off.

He did not get far, for Rogers was lying in wait for him. Rogers charged into the constable and knocked him out of the saddle, then dismounted and drew his knife. Rogers cut Elliot's throat, making three horrible gashes, and left him in the roadway.

Elliot bled to death in less than half an hour, as other men, including a doctor, tried to save him. When Elliot died, they stayed with the body, building a fire and sending one of their number to fetch Deputy Marshal John Taylor. But before Taylor could reach them, Rogers suddenly appeared out of the night. While the horrified townsmen looked on, Rogers rode through the fire, ran off the doctor and the other men, and then kicked and stomped the lifeless body of his victim, rummaged through Elliot's papers, and rode off into the gloom.

Marshal Taylor trailed Rogers as far as Sapulpa, but there the trail went cold. After his ghastly outrage against Elliot, nobody could doubt that Rogers had a crazy streak, or that he would ride on to other devilment.

Rogers's career outside the law started in a small way with horse theft. He lifted about a dozen of somebody else's animals in the territory, drove his booty over into Arkansas, and sold them. Deputy Marshal Heck Bruner didn't have to spend much time pursuing Rogers before he duly dragged him back to Fort Smith to face the formidable federal judge, Isaac Parker.

Because of Rogers's youth—he was nineteen the first time he met Parker—Parker decided to be lenient in this, Rogers's first offense. He gave the young man a prison sentence, but suspended it and put Rogers on probation.

During his customary sentencing lecture, Parker gave Rogers some good advice, as he often did with bad men who appeared before him. "This is your first offense, lad," the judge said kindly. "If you continue in this path of life, death may be the penalty." It was very good counsel indeed, but Rogers paid no attention to it at all and quickly returned to his burgeoning career of larceny. In the fall of 1891, he was charged with assault with intent to kill a lawman but released on bond.

He was not tried for this offense, and for a time he remained near Catoosa where he met Jess Elliot. As sure as sunrise, after the Elliot murder Rogers returned, and he had put together his own little gang, a collection of scum nearly as bad as he was. Two of them were the brothers Kiowa and Dynamite Jack Turner, the latter already wanted for murder in Colorado. The other hoodlums were Willis Brown and one Bob Stiteler. It is said that the gang struck out to emulate the Daltons, and for a little while their criminal career went reasonably well. In a period of two months in 1893, they managed two successful robberies, one on the Katy railroad line and a second on the Kansas and Arkansas Valley road near the Seminole switch. They also hit a bank at Mound Valley up in Labette County, Kansas.

They had a brief collision in the summer of 1893 with able deputy marshal Heck Bruner and a posse out west of Vinita. Most of the gang managed to escape the ambush, but the lawmen killed both Rogers's brother Sam and one Ralph Halleck.

Then, just before Christmas of 1893, they tried a job on a Katy train north of Vinita, but the engineer put the hammer down and dashed through the ambush. Frustrated, the gang opened fire as the train rushed past them, hitting the fireman in the jaw. But their bonanza was long gone.

On the same day, however, they managed to get this business of train robbery right. This time it was an Arkansas Valley train, which the gang successfully diverted onto a siding crowded with freight cars. The boys must have figured that their luck was with them again.

By and large, things had started reasonably well for the gang, in spite of losing men to the relentless Bruner. But Rogers and Stiteler incautiously paid a visit to Rogers's brother-in-law, Henry Daniels. They in turn were visited by Deputy Marshal W. C. Smith.

Rogers was warming his feet before Daniels's fire when he looked up to see the bad end of Smith's revolver. The officer sent Rogers's brother-in-law upstairs to bring Stiteler down, and Stiteler was forthwith arrested. But before Smith could get his quarry out of the house, Rogers hit him in the head and Stiteler disappeared into the night. The law went a-hunting, and the unfortunate Stiteler was back in custody before daybreak. But Rogers was long gone to rejoin the remains of his gang. The law pressed on with its search.

In January 1894 Deputy Marshal Heck Bruner led a posse to the gang's overnight camp on Big Creek, and a gunfight erupted. Caught by surprise, the gang came in a bad second. Kiowa was killed and Willis Brown was severely wounded, hurt so badly that he would die at Vinita on the return trip to Fort Smith. Dynamite Jack, despite his ferocious name, surrendered. But once again, Rogers disappeared.

Early in 1895 Rogers seems to have tried his hand at running booze into Indian Territory, a federal offense. Warrants were also issued for him on charges of robbing two men, C. W. Adams and William Wiley. Rogers's fortunes had sunk very low by now. At last he ran out of luck altogether, just a week after robbing Wiley.

Rogers had been elusive for a long time, but he chose to stay in his regular stomping grounds rather than ride away. Nor could he avoid the law forever, not with the expert hounds of the marshal service baying on his back trail.

On March 13, 1895, the law finally caught up with Rogers. He was staying overnight with his father near Horseshoe Mound. Ironically, the place was only some twenty miles south of Coffeyville, Kansas, scene of the Dalton Gang's disaster less than three years before. After midnight a large posse led by Deputy Marshal Jim Mayes stashed its horses in a thicket and surrounded the Rogers house. Once his men were in position, Mayes and eight others approached the front of the building.

The elder Rogers appeared on the porch to ask what they wanted, and Mayes told him bluntly, "We want your son. The house is surrounded and he can't escape this time. Light a lamp." Rogers's father had no choice but to follow Mayes's orders, and the posse entered. Their quarry was upstairs. "Come down, Bob," Marshal Mayes called, "and surrender."

The reply was vintage Rogers, "Come and get me."

Three of the lawmen, led by Deputy Marshal W. C. Daniels, went up the stairs to bring Rogers down. Rogers met the three deputies at the head of the stairs. He had a revolver in each hand, but Daniels bravely challenged him. "Drop those guns," he said, and a sane, sensible man probably would have done just that.

But this was Bob Rogers, who apparently was neither sane nor sensible, and he opened fire on the lawmen point-blank. Daniels went down immediately with a bullet through the heart, and a second deputy, Phil Williams, took a serious arm wound. Williams fell backward into the third lawman, and the two tumbled together back down the stairs.

The rest of the lawmen opened a furious fire on the house, driving somewhere between two and three hundred rounds through the board walls of the building. The bombardment continued until the house was riddled with holes and some of the rafters were virtually cut in two, but Rogers was still unhurt. The posse then sent the elder Rogers into the house to summon his son to surrender, but Rogers would not listen, even to his father. He defiantly retorted, "I'll give up after I am killed."

Mayes's response was more rifle fire. Rogers remained miraculously unwounded, though his father was said to have been hit—in the big toe, of all places. But then Rogers called out to the posse men, offering to surrender "if you let me bring my gun."

This dubious offer must have sounded risky to Mayes and his men, but it was better than trying to send anybody back up those deadly stairs. Mayes agreed that Rogers could bring his rifle with him but cautioned the outlaw to keep the muzzle of the weapon pointed down.

The marshal and his men sensibly took cover behind a stack of poles in the yard and waited for Rogers to appear. When their quarry walked out the door, Mayes stood up behind the poles. Rogers stopped and asked a strange question, "Do you have a warrant for me?"

"No," said the Marshal, "and [we] don't need one."

Which was perfectly true.

At which Rogers raised the muzzle of the Winchester, but this time he never got off a shot. The whole posse opened up on him as one, and Rogers went down full of holes. He had been hit by twenty-two bullets and two shotgun loads.

So ended the bizarre and brutal career of Bob Rogers.

All of eastern Oklahoma could sleep more soundly.

JESSE EVANS

The Escape Artist

For Jesse Evans, trouble was a family affair. Born in Missouri in 1853, Evans moved to Kansas in 1871 with his family. And on June 2 of that year, the members of the Evans family were arrested for passing counterfeit money. Some went to jail, but Jesse was lucky—he was fined $500 and released. On his own, he left Kansas, stayed briefly in Texas, then crossed the border into New Mexico Territory.

Evans signed on as a wrangler for cattle baron John Chisum and worked his way up to the position of foreman. It was while he was working for Chisum that he met Billy the Kid, who would become an icon of the western outlaw. Both Billy and Evans left Chisum's employ at about the same time. Evans and his gang members, known as the "boys"—Tom Hill, Frank Rivers, and Frank Baker—began working for J. J. Dolan and L. G. Murphy, supplying stolen cattle for their government contracts. Dolan and Murphy were cattle brokers and partners in one of the town's mercantile stores. Much to their dismay, a new mercantile store had been opened by Englishman John Tunstall and Scotsman Alexander McSween, newcomers to town. Tunstall also owned a ranch, and Billy the Kid went to work for him as a wrangler. Tunstall and McSween became the bitter enemies of Dolan and Murphy, and that rivalry put Billy and Evans in opposite camps.

On New Year's Day of 1876, Evans got into serious trouble when the men he was celebrating with decided to shoot up the local dance hall in Mesuilla. Their indiscriminate shots killed three soldiers from the 8th Cavalry stationed at Fort Selden. Despite the level of violence involved, no warrants were issued.

Eighteen days later, Evans was involved in another killing. Evans, Samuel Blanton, and a man named Morris were at a saloon in Las Cruces where they met Quirino Fletcher. Fletcher bragged about having killed some Texans in Chihuahua, Mexico. The idea of this Mexican killing Texans was more than the trio could tolerate. In a fit of anger, they took justice into their own hands and killed Fletcher, leaving his body in the street. The corpse lay untouched until sunrise the next morning, when Fletcher's family arrived and claimed it. Evans pleaded not guilty to the charge of murder and was ultimately acquitted.

In 1877 Evans's cattle rustling came to the attention of Albert J. Fountain, a local cattleman and political activist, who was trying to uncover proof of a connection between rustling in the Lincoln area and the Santa Fe Ring. On July 18

Fountain departed the courthouse with warrants for the arrest of Evans and several prominent citizens. Fountain started for home with his young son. Father and son disappeared along the route and were never seen or heard from again. Evans was suspected in the disappearance, but there was no evidence to tie him to the event. Nonetheless, he was quickly building a reputation as a man with a gun for hire—a dangerous gun.

That summer in 1877, Evans and the boys kept busy rustling livestock from several Lincoln County ranches. On one raid they took Tunstall's horses. When Tunstall found his livestock in Evans's care, he swore out a warrant for Evans's arrest. However, Sheriff Brady, a man who unofficially worked for Dolan, did nothing to serve the warrant. Tunstall's foreman took matters into his own hands. Forming a posse, he tracked down Evans and his boys and captured them. This time, Sheriff Brady had no choice but to lock up the outlaws.

In jail Evans bragged to the other prisoners that they would not hold him long. Tunstall agreed with Evans. He described the pathetic conditions of the jail, saying that the shackles were filed, the log walls had holes, and no attempt was being made to secure the prisoners. On the night of November 16, Evans, Baker, and Hill walked out of the Lincoln County jail and went back to work for Dolan. No one was surprised.

On February 18, 1878, Dolan sent Evans and his boys on an errand. Dolan claimed that Tunstall owed him money, and he placed an attachment on Tunstall's property. A group of horses that had been stolen by Evans and his gang and then rescued by Tunstall were initially excluded from the attachment. However, Sheriff Brady received a new set of orders, presumably from Dolan, to get the horses. Hearing that Tunstall was driving them to his ranch from a holding site, Brady organized a posse to collect the horses, deputized John Matthews to lead it, and included Evans and his boys in the posse.

Jesse Evans and two of the boys rode ahead of the twenty-man posse. It was a clear, crisp February afternoon, and the trail of Tunstall's horses was easy to follow. Tunstall had gathered his small herd and, along with Billy the Kid, Robert Widenmann, Dick Brewer, and John Middleton, set out for his ranch. Billy and Middleton trailed the horses. Tunstall led the small drive with Widenmann and Brewer taking care of the middle. When the procession flushed some wild turkey, Tunstall told his hands to go after them while he waited with the herd. That's where Evans found him.

Evans, Hill, and William Morton crested the ridge and saw Tunstall and his horses, all alone, at the bottom of the canyon. "We're not going to hurt you, Tunstall," shouted Evans.

Tunstall rode toward the three men. They threw up their guns, resting their rifles on their knees, waiting for Tunstall.

"Not yet," Evans whispered, "wait until he gets nearer."

As Tunstall rode closer, Morton brought his rifle to his shoulder and fired. The bullet hit Tunstall in the chest. As he pitched forward, Evans moved toward the fallen Tunstall, retrieved his revolver, and shot him in the head. It took all three of them to load Tunstall's body on the back of his horse. Leading the horse, they moved about a hundred yards away from the trail into the trees. Morton and Hill dumped the body on the ground. Turning toward Tunstall's horse, one of them pumped a bullet into the animal's head, killing it instantly. The only eulogy they offered was, "that ought to teach the sidewinder not to buck Murphy and Dolan."

When the rest of the posse arrived, Evans explained that Tunstall's killing was an act of self-defense; Tunstall had gone for his gun when he spotted them. Some of the riders quietly questioned that story, but they turned their horses and headed back to town. Later, other members of the posse told a story of being too far back to see anything. The self-defense proclamation stood, mainly because of the corruption of the Lincoln County sheriff, who was in the pocket of Dolan and Murphy.

What Evans did not realize was that his killing of Tunstall opened the gates and let hell enter Lincoln County. The murder of Tunstall was just the opening salvo in the violence that became the Lincoln County War.

The Lincoln County War was not truly a cattle war or a land war, although in some ways it was a war for both. Ultimately, it was a war for economic supremacy. Until John Tunstall and his partner Alexander McSween showed up, J. J. Dolan and L. G. Murphy had owned the only mercantile store in the Lincoln County area, a huge land section in eastern New Mexico Territory. In addition, they held false claims to thousands of acres of land and sold them illegally to unsuspecting settlers.

Dolan and Murphy had control over the government's Indian contracts, the local farmers' crops, and settlers in Lincoln County. And during the 1800s Lincoln County was the largest in the New Mexico Territory, covering about one-quarter of the region. That was a sizeable chunk of land to control.

Not only did Murphy and Dolan have a monopoly on goods and contracts, they also controlled the local law enforcement and had strong ties to the Santa Fe Ring.

For years the federal government had complained about the poor quality of goods that Murphy and Dolan delivered on their Indian contracts. They also believed the outfit was charging them exorbitant prices. It was not until Tunstall came to town and established his ranch and mercantile store that the government and the locals had a choice. Another element colored the relationship between Dolan and Murphy, Tunstall and McSween. The Irishmen emigrated from their home country and were of working-class stock. Tunstall came from a posh English family, and McSween was a lawyer with Scottish parents.

At the time ethnic bigotry was unlabeled but overt. In a letter to his parents, John Tunstall described Sheriff Brady as "an Irishman, a slave of whiskey and a man I think very little of, he is a tool." He used Brady's ethnicity as a slight.

The animosity between the owners of the two stores started soon after Tunstall's arrival. It did not take long before both sides armed themselves with men who had guns and knew how to use them. And there were a number of rough men around the territory with suspect pasts, men who were willing to lend their guns for a cause, if the price was right. In this case the price was right for Evans and his boys.

The coroner's inquest on Tunstall's murder concluded that Jesse Evans, Frank Baker, Thomas Hill, George Hindman, James J. Dolan, and William Morton shot Tunstall. Eyewitnesses identified them all as being involved in the murder. These outlaws were all members of "The House," a name given to the supporters of Murphy and Dolan. Members of the opposite faction who supported Tunstall and McSween were called "The Regulators."

When the constable, Atanacio Martinez, went to arrest Tunstall's murderers, Sheriff Brady refused to let him serve the warrants and in fact arrested Billy the Kid and Fred Waite, who accompanied the constable. When they asked Brady why he arrested the men, he replied, "Because I had the power." During the next five months, threats, shootings, illegal arrests, and confrontations boiled tempers in Lincoln. In early March, Dick Brewer and a posse of McSween sympathizers arrested Morton and Baker at the Dolan cow camp near the Pecos River. Unfortunately, the two never stood trial; they were shot, killed, and buried on the trail to Lincoln. Some say they tried to escape; others say that the Dolan faction had them killed so they "wouldn't talk."

Meanwhile, Evans and his pal Tom Hill were going on about their business—the business of robbing, rustling, and stealing, that is. They raided a sheep camp belonging to John Wagner, a German immigrant. While they were busy looting, the shepherd unexpectedly returned. Grabbing a rifle Hill had left leaning against a tree, Wagner shot and killed Hill and wounded Evans.

Evans escaped but decided to turn himself in at Fort Stanton, where he could get the medical attention he needed. If accused of the Tunstall murder, he planned to blame the now-dead Tom Hill. The military jailed Evans when he showed up at Fort Stanton; however, it wasn't long before Evans bribed a guard and was once again free.

On April 1 the two factions moved closer to war when Billy the Kid and other Tunstall loyalists ambushed and killed Sheriff Brady and George Hindman. The list of men responsible for the murder of Tunstall was getting shorter.

After Brady's death George Pippin became sheriff. He immediately made it clear that he was a Dolan-Murphy man by arresting McSween on a trumped-up charge of assault. The charge was ridiculous, and McSween was quickly released.

In mid-April of 1878, a grand jury of the Supreme Court of the territory finally indicted Jesse Evans, George Davis, Miguel Seguero, and Frank Rivers for the murder of John Tunstall. Evans was the only one of the group who could be located. He was arrested, and a bond was set at $5,000—an easy sum for Evans and his powerful friends to raise. Once again, Evans was a free man.

The federal government in Washington was aware that things were spinning out of control in the territory and sent Judge Frank Warner Angel, a special investigator, to look into the Tunstall murder and the operations of the Dolan and Murphy group. Angel reported that "there is no doubt that Wm. Morton, Jesse Evans and Tom Hill were the only persons present and saw the shooting, and that two of these persons murdered him. . . . " Since Morton and Hill were dead, that left only Evans to face the charges.

Things in Lincoln County came to a head on July 14, 1878. The Regulators set up several fortified places and sealed off the east end of town. Sheriff Pippin sent for his men, who were out of town trying to locate McSween and his cronies. They came in the west end of town and set up their defenses.

The battle lasted for five days. The first four days saw few casualties: a dead man from The House, a dead horse, a dead mule, and the accidental wounding of a young man who got in the way of the fight. It was on the evening of July 19 that Pippin's group made its move: They set the McSween stronghold on fire.

McSween waited until early morning, and as flames engulfed the building, he attempted to escape into the darkness. As he darted out the front door, he met a barrage of bullets and was killed instantly.

By the end of the fighting, men from both sides of the war were dead: McSween, Morton, Baker, McCloskey, Hill, Sheriff Brady, Hindman, Roberts, Brewer, and Middleton. Billy the Kid and Jesse Evans, who fought on opposite sides of the battle, sustained only minor wounds. And with both Tunstall and McSween now dead, the Lincoln County War ended.

The next morning some of Dolan's men broke into the Tunstall store. When the store clerk showed up, he found Evans in his underwear trying on a new suit of clothes he had picked off the rack.

In December 1878 Billy the Kid decided to return to Lincoln and make peace with Jesse Evans. He set up a meeting with Dolan and Evans. After dark Evans met Billy the Kid in the middle of the street. "I ought to kill you right now," Evans told Billy. The Kid did not scare easily, though, and he recognized the statement for bluster on Jesse's part.

Jesse and Billy agreed to end their fighting and to not testify against the other. There was quite a group of tough men in town that night. Both men brought friends with them for support. After Billy and Evans agreed to a truce, the group decided to celebrate. Billy, a nondrinker, was soon the only sober one.

Evans had a new member of his gang, a young, foolish kid by the name of Billy Campbell. Campbell was not around for the Lincoln County War and deeply regretted the lost opportunity to prove his manhood.

In the middle of the celebration, Huston Chapman walked out of his house. Chapman was an abrasive, aggressive man. Campbell put his pistol on Chapman's chest and said "dance." Chapman was not going to let this rabble bully him. There was some scuffling and some insults and then Dolan, standing behind Chapman, fired at the same time as Campbell. Chapman staggered and fell to the ground.

There are two versions of what happened next. Some report that the two gunmen fired so closely together that they set off a powder keg near Chapman. Others report that someone poured whiskey on Chapman's body and set fire to it. The results were the same: Chapman was burnt to a cinder.

The Chapman murder is what finally convinced the territorial governor to do something about the lawlessness in Lincoln. He instructed the commander of Fort Stanton to round up thirty-five desperados. Included on the list were Billy the Kid, Tom O'Folliard, Dolan, Campbell, and Evans. Billy the Kid and O'Folliard managed to give the authorities the slip. Dolan, Campbell, and Evans were not so lucky. Authorities arrested them and hauled them into jail.

Billy the Kid, now completely disgusted with Evans and not trusting him, worked a deal with the governor, giving testimony against Evans for the promise of amnesty. His testimony helped indict the trio. However, the three did not spend much time as the guests of the county. They escaped from the Fort Stanton jail during the night of March 19, 1879, and a freed Evans lit out for Pecos County, Texas.

For four months Evans kept to his ways: stealing cattle, robbing stores, and following a lawless and unrepentant life. On July 3, 1880, the Texas Rangers got information on Evans's hideout. The pursuit of Evans resulted in the death of two Rangers; one of them, Red Bingham, was shot by Evans; the other by an unidentified outlaw Evans was riding with.

It took the Rangers nine days, but they finally captured Evans and locked him in the "bat cave," a dungeon blasted out of rock in the jail. Evans would never break out of this cell; the cave was beneath the sheriff's office, and a trapdoor covered with heavy timbers was the only way in and out.

On October 9, 1880, the state of Texas sentenced Evans to ten years in the state prison in Huntsville, Texas, for the murder of Bingham. But just two years later, Evans worked his magic one final time. He escaped from a road gang in May 1882 and disappeared.

But Jesse Evans was too bad a man and too colorful an outlaw to be forgotten. Over the years, rumors popped up about him. Some say he was seen in Tombstone, Arizona Territory, in 1882 or 1883. Others believed he went to live on a relative's ranch and left the house only at night. The best rumor involved a man named Bushy Bill Roberts and concerned the strong physical resemblance between Billy the Kid and Evans. Both were small in stature, standing less than five foot seven and weighing around 150 pounds. Both had fair hair and light complexions. However, their personalities were quite different. Evans was surly, unfriendly, and almost illiterate. Billy the Kid was an avid reader, wrote a fine hand, loved to sing, and was friendly and outgoing.

Bushy Bill claimed to be Billy the Kid. While Bushy knew much about Billy, there were many factual holes in his claim. However, the only Anglo in the Lincoln County War not accounted for was Evans. And Bushy Bill knew too many details about the war to have just read about it. He had to have been in Lincoln at the time. That leads some to think that Bushy Bill was really Jesse Evans. Now wouldn't that be something—Jesse Evans making the ultimate escape, removing his identity by impersonating his old friend and enemy Billy the Kid?

"DIRTY" DAVE RUDABAUGH

The Dirtiest Outlaw of All

Dave Rudabaugh didn't have much use for water. He didn't use it to wash, brush his teeth, or clean his clothes, and he sure as hell was not going to drink it. Give him the pure fire of whiskey anytime. Dirty Dave came by his nickname honestly.

Maybe that explains why he was such a drifter—he was a hard man to be around for any length of time. People always knew when Dirty Dave was coming; his scent preceded him.

However, not everyone saw Dave as an unkempt character. In 1882, a *Denver Tribune* reporter described him in these flattering terms:

> He is thick set and athletic in build; is about five-feet nine-inches in height. He is suave and very gentlemanly in his deportment. He has brown hair, hazel eyes and a heavy mustache of a shade of brown lighter than that of his hair.
>
> He is fluent in speech, mildly argumentative in disposition, and has that peculiar faculty of being able to obtain news and facts where others would fail. This is a faculty which he uses advantageously in his search for express news on railroads.
>
> He is as brave as a lion and a natural born organizer. He gathers a gang and has it in working condition within a few days. He is always clear-headed, has the cunning of a fox, and never falls into a position of unnecessary danger through the recklessness of bravery or dissipation.

Considering Dirty Dave's criminal activities, this article was obviously the writing of a very creative reporter. About the only thing he got right was the description of Rudabaugh's lush mustache.

Rudabaugh was born in Illinois in 1854. His father was killed in the Civil War, and Rudabaugh grew up poor and uneducated. By the time he was twenty-six, he had a variety of lawless occupations on his resume—cattle rustling in Texas, train robbery in Kansas, and gambling wherever he managed to find a deck of cards and a seat for his unwashed body. To balance out the bad, he sometimes worked with the law instead of against it. However, most of his law enforcement activities were with sheriffs whose honesty was questionable.

Rudabaugh wasn't big on loyalty. On several occasions he turned against his partners, giving evidence to the law to save his own skin. They say that these unprincipled characteristics paired with his accuracy with a gun earned him the fear of the notorious Billy the Kid.

Dirty Dave was not a big planner or thinker. It was this unpredictability that set off a series of events that proved to be his downfall.

When the citizens of Dodge City, Kansas, decided to clean up their town, Las Vegas in the New Mexico Territory became the destination for many of Dodge's unsavory characters. In 1880 Las Vegas was as wild as any western town could be, and the Dodge City gang members took control. They terrorized the residents and elected themselves as town officials. The gang consisted of Justice of the Peace H. G. Neill, also known as Hoodoo Brown; Marshall Dutchy Goodlet; and Constable Dave Mather. Dirty Dave, Tom Pickett, and J. J. Webb were hired on as special officers. These "lawmen" were frequently involved in murder, train robberies, and cattle rustling.

Easy money was always a lure for the Dodge City boys, and one day Webb, with the help of Dutchy Goodlet, decided to relieve Michael Keliher, a visiting traveling salesman, of the large amount of cash he was carrying. They enlisted the aid of a railroad worker named Boyle. The plan was for Boyle to pick a fight with Keliher while the two were drinking; Webb and Goodlet would rush in, arrest Keliher for disturbing the peace, and relieve him of his cash. The plan went terribly wrong; in their excitement to get the job done, Webb and Goodlet barged into the saloon and killed Keliher.

Much to the surprise of Webb and Goodlet, their pals Mather and Dave Rudabaugh arrested them for murder. Mather was so disgusted with the outcome of these events that he quit the police force and left town. Rudabaugh decided to take a more hands-on approach by freeing J. J. Webb from jail. Just because the "law" required him to put his pals in jail didn't mean he believed they should stay there—and with that in mind, he decided to spring them.

It was in the early morning hours of April 30, 1880, when Rudabaugh and John "Little Allen" Llewellyn hired a carriage and told the driver to wait in front of the jail. It was a typical carriage with slow horses in the traces. Why Rudabaugh picked this means of transportation considering what he planned to do is a puzzle.

Rudabaugh and Llewellyn entered the jail and asked to see Webb. The jailer, Antonio Lino-Valdez, allowed Rudabaugh to pass a newspaper to Webb, but when the men told him to hand over the cell key, he refused. Llewellyn shot and killed him. Tossing the keys in Webb's cell, both Rudabaugh and Llewellyn made a run for it.

J. J. Webb did some quick thinking. If he ran, the law would hunt him down; if he stayed, his pending appeal to the Supreme Court might make him a free man. He decided his best strategy was to stay put.

The two gunmen jumped into the waiting hack and ordered the driver to take them to East Las Vegas. There they kicked the driver out, and Rudabaugh took the reins. The first thing they did was to stop at Houghton's Hardware Store and help themselves to a pair of six-guns and two rifles.

In the meantime a hastily mounted posse of four men gathered to pursue the outlaws. Unfortunately, the posse ran out of ammunition and had to head back to town before they caught the culprits. A larger posse was soon organized, mounted up, and went on the chase. After traveling twenty-five miles, they came to a sheep camp where they found the abandoned carriage and its horses. The outlaws had stolen two fresh and faster horses, leaving their nags and the carriage with a Mexican shepherd. Here the town posse lost the trail of the murderers.

Rudabaugh and Llewellyn were on the run; their attempted rescue of Webb a complete failure. The jailer was dead, his murderers gone, and J. J. Webb still in jail. They rode hard and long on their flight for freedom. Llewellyn was not a well man, and the ride was taking its toll. He complained constantly about his tuberculosis and rheumatism. He begged Rudabaugh to end his suffering. One day out on the open range, Rudabaugh put a bullet in Llewellyn's head and buried him along the road to Alkali Wells.

From there Dirty Dave made his way to Fort Sumner, New Mexico, and joined Billy the Kid's gang. He soon became the Kid's right-hand man.

Back at the jail, Webb was having second thoughts about his appeal. Suspecting that vigilantes were sizing up his neck, he made a decision to seek freedom. He and five other prisoners picked the jail lock and escaped. Webb headed for a hideout with fellow prisoner and mule thief George Davis.

Meanwhile, the hunt was on for Billy the Kid. Sheriff Pat Garrett heard the Kid was in the Dedrick ranch house at Bosque Grande on the Pecos River. On November 26, Garrett and his posse surrounded the house. The trap didn't catch Billy, but they did get Webb and Davis, who were hiding in the house. Both were hauled back to the San Miguel jail.

Garrett continued his hunt for the Kid's gang, which now included Rudabaugh along with Billy Wilson, Tom Pickett, Tom O'Folliard, and Charlie Bowdre. Garrett and Frank Stewart, from the Canadian River Cattlemen's Association, received a tip to check Fort Sumner.

Garrett and his posse were settled in the fort and waiting when the six horsemen came in, slowly riding through the snow. The trap was sprung. Garrett and his men opened fire, hitting O'Folliard, a lead rider. O'Folliard fell and his horse galloped off. The remaining five outlaws turned and hightailed it out of the fort, disappearing in the snowstorm, which had increased in intensity.

During the confrontation Rudabaugh's horse was hit, but he rode it until it dropped dead then double-mounted behind Billy Wilson. Back at the fort the posse laid the wounded O'Folliard on a blanket near the fire and settled down to a game of cards. O'Folliard died thirty minutes later.

Stewart and Garrett decided to hold off on going after the outlaws until the storm abated. When the storm blew itself out on December 24, they picked up the trail and followed it to an abandoned sheep camp called Stinking Springs, where the outlaws were hanging out.

The camp got its name from a nearby sulfa spring that gave off an odor of rotten eggs. After living with Dirty Dave, the gang hardly noticed the smell.

The outlaws had sought shelter in an abandoned rock house without a door. Billy the Kid's horse was in the house; the other three tied up outside.

The posse arrived at Stinking Springs, and as dawn broke, a man fitting the Kid's description stepped into the doorway. Garrett gave the signal, and the man was riddled with bullets. He staggered, said, "I wish . . . ," and then fell dead in the snow. It was then that the posse realized they had shot Charlie Bowdre.

The four inside the shelter settled in to defend themselves, and throughout the morning and early afternoon, the lawmen and the outlaws traded shots.

Garrett noticed that one of the outlaws' horses was slowly moving toward the doorway. When the horse was halfway inside, he fired a quick shot, killing it. The horse now blocked the doorway, the only entrance in or out of the shelter. The lawmen shot the tethers of the other two horses, who immediately galloped off.

By late afternoon Billy and his remaining gang realized their position was hopeless. They were cold, hungry, and without mounts. A white cloth appeared in the doorway, and after receiving assurances, Dave Rudabaugh came out for a talk. He suggested that the outlaws would surrender if promised food and a safe passage to jail. Garrett and Stewart agreed, and the four prisoners were loaded onto a wagon for the journey to the San Miguel County jail.

On Christmas Day of 1880, the lawmen and what was left of Billy the Kid's gang stopped in Puerto de Luna for a holiday dinner at the home of Roman Catholic priest Alexander Grzelachowski. And on December 26, Billy's gang arrived at the Las Vegas jail.

Both the *Las Vegas Gazette* and *Optic* ran stories on the capture, detailing the excitement of the town as the prisoners rode down the main street. A few days later the *Optic* printed an article describing the four outlaws. Dirty Dave's description read as follows:

> *Dave Rudabaugh looks and dresses about the same as when in Las Vegas, apparently not having made any raids upon clothing stores. His face is weather-beaten from long*

*exposure. This is the only noticeable difference. Radubaugh
[sic] inquired somewhat anxiously in regard to the feeling in
the community and was told that it was very strong against
him. He remarked that the papers had published exaggerated
reports of the depredations of Kid's party in the lower country.
It was not half as bad as had been reported.*

The prisoners were taken to the railroad station for their train trip to Santa Fe, where they would await trial in the city jail. A large, angry crowd met them at the depot. They wanted Rudabaugh to stand trial in town for the murder of the San Miguel jailer. Las Vegas Sheriff Romero tried to get Rudabaugh off the train and return him to the county jail.

According to a report in the *Optic,* "The engineer of the outgoing train was covered by guns and ordered not to move his engine." However, Rudabaugh was in the hands of a U.S. Marshal and "they were in duty bound to deliver him to the authorities in Santa Fe."

Rudabaugh went on to Santa Fe where some of his old running mates, including Webb, were awaiting trial for the robbery of two stagecoaches and the attempted robbery of a train, both near Las Vegas.

Rudabaugh went into court to testify in Webb's defense. Rudabaugh admitted that he was the head of the gang that robbed both stages and that Webb was not part of either robbery. His statement won an acquittal for Webb. It also helped free the other men held in connection with the robberies.

Rudabaugh never gave the names of the men who participated in the robberies. Many believed they were the Dodge City boys—"Mysterious" Dave Mather, Joe Carson, and other members of Hoodoo Brown's police force, including Doc Holliday. All this was speculation. There was no proof.

The next day the court indicted Rudabaugh on three charges of robbing the U.S. mail, including two stagecoach robberies and one attempted train robbery. He pleaded guilty to all charges.

On February 26, Rudabaugh's robbery sentence was suspended, and he was ordered returned to San Miguel County for trial in the death of jailer Antonio Lino-Valdez. An indictment for first-degree murder was waiting for Rudabaugh in Las Vegas.

Rudabaugh had no desire to take his chances in Las Vegas. The time had come for Dirty Dave to seek freedom. Along with Billy the Kid and Billy Wilson, he developed a cunning plan.

The *Santa Fe New Mexican* gave a full report in early March 1881:

*Yesterday afternoon it was discovered that the Kid and his
gang had concocted and were stealthily carrying out a plan by*

*which they hoped to gain their freedom and escape the fate that
awaits them. And very fortunate it was that the discovery was
made just when it was, for a night or two more would have
sufficed for completion of the well laid scheme. It appears that
Sheriff Romulo Martinez fearing that the four desperate men,
the Kid, Rudabaugh, Billy Wilson and (Edward M.) Kelly,
would ere long make a desperate effort to get out, had promised
to pay one of the prisoners if he would assist the guard in
keeping watch, and yesterday the fellow informed him that the
men were trying to dig out. Sheriff Martinez, accompanied
by Deputy Marshall Neis, at once proceeded to the jail, and
entering the cell, found the men at supper. They examined the
room and found that the bed ticking was filled with stones
and earth, and removing the mattress discovered a deep hole.
Further investigation showed that the men had dug themselves
nearly out, and by concealing the loose earth in the bed and
covering the hole up with it had almost reached the street
without awakening the suspicion of the guard. Last night they
were closely guarded and heavily ironed, and today further
precautions will be taken.*

Afraid of vigilante action in Las Vegas, Rudabaugh requested a trial in Santa Fe. On April 22 a Santa Fe court found him guilty of murder and sentenced him to hang in Las Vegas on May 20. Rudabaugh immediately appealed his sentence. The authorities sent him to the Las Vegas County jail to await the results.

In September, still waiting for his appeal trial, Rudabaugh attempted to escape jail by picking the lock. The attempt failed when he awoke one of the guards asleep in the hallway.

Then, on the morning of December 3, 1881, the guards discovered that seven prisoners had escaped through a nineteen-by-seventeen-inch hole in the stone wall of one of the cells. After almost a year of incarceration, Dave Rudabaugh and his friend J. J. Webb were free. That morning Rudabaugh and Webb hopped a train and left Las Vegas. Four months later, Webb died of smallpox in Winslow, Arkansas.

Five years later Dirty Dave was working and walking the streets of Hidalgo de Parral, Mexico. The town suited him. It was at the end of Chihuahua, a barren, hilly, rugged place that even Mother Nature seemed to disdain. What made it a town at all was the silver that had been discovered and was being mined in the surrounding hills. Silver brought life to the village—as well as brothels, cantinas, and gaming halls. These in turn brought unsavory characters into town, including Dirty Dave, who began making his living at the card tables.

His disposition and his dishevelment hadn't improved in his five years in Hidalgo de Parral. If anything, he was more unpleasant and dirtier. He insulted everyone, abused the Mexicans, and was a dangerous man to challenge.

On February 18, 1886, he was at his usual station playing cards at the cantina. Although he did not understand Spanish, he did know that the natives were being particularly insulting and obnoxious. One of the players suddenly stood, and reaching for his pistol, accused Dirty Dave of cheating. Rudabaugh shot him right between the eyes. Another player took a shot at him but missed, and Rudabaugh proceeded to plug him through the heart. No one in the cantina paid much attention to the gunfight, since it was not an unusual occurrence.

Rudabaugh had had enough for the night. He left the cantina and went for his horse—but it was nowhere in sight. Cursing a blue streak, Rudabaugh headed back to a now-darkened cantina. The street around him was strangely deserted and barricaded.

Rudabaugh knew then that he was a marked man. All his senses went on alert, and he pulled out his gun and cautiously continued toward the cantina. But for all his caution, the life of Dirty Dave Rudabaugh—the man no jail could hold, a member of Billy the Kid's gang, and a feared outlaw—was coming to an end. "Come out and fight," he roared to the night. His answer was a rifle shot, then another, and another. "Coward!" he screamed—and fell dead.

Townspeople poured into the street. Legend has it that one man wielded a sword and neatly severed Dirty Dave's head from his body. For hours the head was paraded around the town. Then, the crowd went to the cemetery, dug a hole, and dumped in the head and body.

The dirtiest outlaw came to a dirty end: a bundle of bones, blood, and dirt in a shallow, unconsecrated grave.

BILLY THE KID

The Killing of the Kid

Billy the Kid is on the run, living in his saddle, and hiding out with some of the sheepherders around Fort Sumner. He's begging for meals—but there is never enough to eat. It's late evening, July 13, 1881, and a hungry and saddlesore Billy rides into Fort Sumner to see his lover and to spend some time with his Mexican friends at the fort. Near midnight he rolls out of bed, not bothering to put on his shoes. Pete Maxwell has butchered a steer, and beef sounds mighty appealing to the hungry Kid. Off the table he grabs his six-shooter and picks up a butcher knife to cut himself a steak.

In stocking feet he pads across the porch to Maxwell's bedroom for the key to the meat locker. He passes two strangers sitting on the edge of the porch near the doorway to Maxwell's room, open to catch the evening breeze. Billy wonders who the men are and what they are doing at Maxwell's Fort Sumner house. *"Quiénes son usted?"* he asks them—who are you? *"Amigos,"* they reply.

Although they identify themselves as friends, his concern about the strangers grows. He slips past them and enters Maxwell's bedroom. As he enters the room, he turns and approaches the bed, softly questioning, "Who are the men outside, Pete? Who are they?" Maxwell doesn't answer.

Sheriff Pat Garrett is sitting next to Maxwell's bed, but the deep shadows of the room hide him from Billy's sight. Garrett sees the slim figure as it enters the darkened room. When he hears the voice, he knows he has his man. Garrett makes a slight move for his gun. Perhaps Billy sees the movement, or perhaps he senses that someone besides Maxwell is in the room. Instinctively he steps back, but he doesn't shoot, even though he has his six-gun in hand. That hesitation costs Billy his life.

Garrett quickly snaps off a shot that throws Billy's body to the side. Billy lurches backward and falls. Garrett's first shot hits Billy in the chest; his second hits the wall. Then Garrett hears the moan. In the grip of terror, he runs from the room, followed by Pete Maxwell. "I've just killed Billy the Kid," he shouts. "I've killed him."

Deputies Kip McKinney and John Poe are waiting outside on the porch. Garrett explains to them what happened, but the men doubt that the infamous Kid is actually dead. To prove it, Maxwell gets a candle and holds it up to the bedroom window. There on the floor, in the flickering candlelight, the deputies see the body. It is the first time they have ever actually seen Billy the Kid. McKinney is a New Mexico man, and Poe is a cattle detective for the Canadian River Cattlemen's Association who has recently been deputized by Garrett.

A crowd of locals, drawn by the gunshots, begins gathering around the ranch house. Deputy McKinney enters the bedroom and sees a woman cradling the body. When Garrett reenters the room, he finds McKinney kneeling next to her.

Many of the Mexicans living at the fort are friends of Billy's. With real sorrow, they begin to remove the body and prepare it for burial. Gently they carry it across the street to a carpenter's shop. Billy the Kid is laid out on a long, simple wooden table while the carpenter builds his coffin.

One of the local men in the crowd is Justice of the Peace Alejandro Saguaro. He gathers several men together and informs them they are now a coroner's jury. However, before the jury can view the body, Garrett writes a report and thrusts it into the hands of the jury members, telling them to sign it. They do so and return the paper to Garrett.

The following day, Milnor Rudulph rides into Sumner to report the death. Another coroner's jury is formed. This jury supposedly views the body, writes out a report in Spanish, and gives it to Garrett to be filed.

That afternoon, the Kid is buried in the fort's cemetery next to his friends and fellow outlaws, Tom O'Folliard and Charles Bowdre.

Garrett had begun his search for Billy the Kid three months before that July night, but the trail had turned cold and Garrett had become discouraged. He became increasing convinced that Billy had run for the Mexican border.

It wasn't a whim that sent Garrett to Pete Maxwell's ranch house to track Billy. It was a lead from John Poe. Poe had heard talk from old friends that Billy the Kid was hanging around Fort Sumner. Rumor had it that Billy had a Mexican girlfriend there, and Sheriff Garrett was willing to follow any lead.

He and his deputies rode into Fort Sumner that night of July 13, 1881, to question Pete Maxwell about Billy's whereabouts. Garrett figured that as a friend, Maxwell would cooperate and give him information on Billy.

Garrett and the two deputies arrived outside Maxwell's house about nine o'clock at night. They hid in the peach orchard for several hours, waiting for another deputy. About midnight they decided their wait was futile, and the three approached the house. Garrett told his deputies to remain outside while he checked with Maxwell. The deputies positioned themselves near the rail that ran around the porch

Billy the Kid was no stranger to Garrett. During the Lincoln County War days, Garrett and Billy had been friends. Garrett spent a considerable amount of time in Lincoln at the gaming tables, where he met and frequently played poker with the Kid. Kid was nicknamed Little Casino; Pat, who was over six feet tall, Big Casino. After they left Lincoln they went their separate ways. Garrett cleaned up and became a law enforcer, while Billy continued his lawlessness.

During his outlaw career Billy the Kid had been captured and jailed but escaped. While breaking out of jail, he killed two deputies; afterwards, Lew Wallace, the governor of New Mexico Territory, offered a $500 reward for his capture. Garrett, a new sheriff in the territory, was seeking to make a name for himself; that and the lure of $500 made him determined to end the career of the infamous outlaw.

Six days after Garrett shot the Kid, he rode into Santa Fe to claim the reward from acting Governor W. G. Ritch (Governor Wallace had left New Mexico to accept a post as the U.S. ambassador to Turkey). Ritch wanted to look over the records pertaining to the reward before paying. On July 23 Ritch informed Garrett that he would not pay the reward. He claimed it was a personal offer made by the former governor, and the territory was not bound to honor it.

People around the state begin raising money to reward Garrett. On August 6, Garrett was given $1,300 by the residents of Dona Ana County and $600 by Santa Fe County. Finally, in 1882, he was awarded $500 from the New Mexico Territory.

But not everyone believed that Pat Garrett's action was an act of justice; some saw it as cold-blooded murder. And indeed, the shooting was not the result of a chase, a gunfight, a challenge, or even an attempted capture. In shooting Billy the Kid, it was believed that Garrett had violated the *duello*—one of the unwritten codes of the Old West. The duello mandated that gunfighters either warn their victims or give them a chance to draw before firing. Garrett did neither.

Garrett may have convinced himself that he was ridding the people of a dangerous villain. But at the time of the shooting, more than 60 percent of the territory's citizens considered Billy a hero and a victim, not a villain. And they now believed that their hero, their icon of the Old West, had been murdered—killed without a fighting chance. But had he been?

Deputy Kip McKinney, who accompanied Sheriff Garrett to the fort that night, didn't think so. He told a different story about the night the Kid was killed. McKinney's story matches Garrett's—except, according to McKinney, Billy hadn't been killed. He believed that Billy survived his gunshot wound, and that a man who had died the night before, a Mexican, was buried at the fort in place of Billy the Kid.

Although the two deputies believed Garrett when he told them that the man lying dead was Billy the Kid, they later changed their minds and maintained that the Kid had lived. And the deputies weren't the only old westerners who believed that Billy had survived. A man named Collins said he helped carry the body that Garrett claimed was Billy the Kid to the grave, but he insisted it was not actually Billy. Caesar Brock, an acquaintance of both Billy and Garrett, said that they killed a Mexican and buried him, pretending that he was the Kid. And rumor has it that Billy roamed around the New Mexico Territory for a long time after his supposed death. Some say he traveled from ranch to ranch looking for work, never saying who he was or from where he hailed. Eventually, he headed for Mexico with his lover.

But if Billy the Kid was not killed on the night of July 13, why would Pete Maxwell, Pat Garrett, and the Mexicans who lived at the fort go along with the hoax? Publicly, Garrett insisted on the truth of his story and hired Marshall Ashmum Upson to write a book about the event, entitled *An Authentic Life of Billy the Kid*. The book, filled with lies and half-truths, was an abysmal failure for Garrett. Interestingly, there is no record of Pete Maxwell's account of that night. And Garrett never filed any of the coroner's jury findings.

Money is always a great motivator, and $500 in the 1800s was a considerable amount for anyone, including a sheriff. Also, it has been suggested that Billy's girlfriend was actually related to Garrett and Maxwell. Perhaps the reward and family ties were enough for Garrett and Maxwell to fake Billy's death. As for the residents of Fort Sumner, Billy was a good friend to the Mexicans at the fort. For him they would keep their silence.

As for Garrett, his life was never easy after the incident. He was known as "the man who killed Billy the Kid." He lost a reelection for sheriff and was denied several other government appointments. He spent his late years on his New Mexico ranch fighting a running battle with goatherders, and his end came in a most inglorious way. In 1908 he was shot to death while relieving himself by the side of the road.

Over the years there have been attempts made to end the controversy over Billy the Kid's death. Most recently, in New Mexico, researchers planned to dig up the supposed graves of Billy the Kid and his mother and compare their DNA. Unfortunately, a flood at Fort Sumner in 1990 washed away the tombstones, making it uncertain which plot was Billy's, so the excavation never happened. And in 2006, Tom Sullivan, a former Lincoln County sheriff, and Steve Sederwall, who was once mayor of Capitan, New Mexico, dug up a grave in Prescott, Arizona, that they claimed was Billy the Kid's. They hoped to compare bone DNA with bloodstains on the table where Billy was laid out. Their attempt failed.

And so the debate goes on. Was Billy the Kid killed by Pat Garrett at Fort Sumner on July 13, 1881, or did the Kid escape? More than a hundred years later, there are still no definitive answers to the mystery of the death of Billy the Kid.

CHARLES BROWN

Savage Killer Swings by His Neck

Following a night of heavy drinking, poker playing, and running up substantial losses, Charles Brown quietly sliced the screen door of his former employer's business, lifted the latch, slipped into the popular Deadwood restaurant, and began searching for valuables. As he entered the bedroom of Mrs. Emma Frances Stone, at the back of the restaurant, in the dead of night, he heard her soft snoring and saw her small dog sleeping on the bed next to her.

Drunk and broke, Brown tried to jimmy the lock of a trunk within which he knew the woman stored valuables. When his pocketknife proved ineffective, he returned to the kitchen and retrieved a butcher knife and a meat cleaver. As he tried to pry open the top of the trunk, the small dog began to growl. Fearful it would awaken Mrs. Stone, Brown grabbed the animal and snuffed out its life before it could bark. When the commotion roused the woman, Brown struck a single savage blow with the meat cleaver that hit Mrs. Stone above the bridge of her nose and nearly cleaved her head in half. Panicked, the killer threw a pillow over the slain woman's head; nabbed a gold watch, some jewelry, and coins; and fled the establishment.

As he left the scene of the grisly murder, Brown woke his seventeen-year-old grandson by marriage, Ralph Walker, who was sleeping in a room nearby, and the two hopped into Brown's wagon and rode in darkness to his home near Whitewood.

When the sun rose about 5:15 on the morning of May 16, 1897, it signaled the start of the day for waitress Maggie Hudson. Her first customer was Leon J. Libby, and he wanted eggs with his meal. The order required that Maggie retrieve the eggs from storage in the small apartment where her boss, Mrs. Stone, often slept while her husband was out of town. Not wishing to awaken her employer at such an early hour, Maggie quietly opened the door and entered the room. The bloody scene she encountered made her flee for help.

Scurrying back to the dining room, Maggie asked Mr. Libby to confirm her suspicions. "Libby then entered the storeroom and a short investigation soon satisfied him that Mrs. Stone was dead and had been murdered," the *Deadwood Weekly Pioneer* reported on May 20, 1897. "Hastily leaving the room he told Miss Hudson to allow nobody to enter and then went out in search of a policeman."

When informed of the crime, Chief M. J. Donovan and Sheriff Matt Plunkett immediately suspected Ralph Walker and Charles Brown, the latter of whom had recently left the employ of Mrs. Stone. Both Brown and Walker were black, so the police were perhaps racially motivated in directing attention to the two men. But both had also been seen leaving town in Brown's wagon in the early morning hours of the murder. Without delay three law officers headed for Brown's house, where they found and arrested the two men without incident, handcuffed them together, and transported them back to Deadwood.

To law enforcement officers Charles Brown was a known commodity. A year earlier, they had arrested the man for what today would be described as a domestic dispute, but which in the latter part of the nineteenth century was treated far differently by the press. In a sad display of journalism, the *Daily Pioneer Times* of Deadwood used racial epithets to report on February 6, 1896, that Charles Brown had "amused himself Saturday night" by "thumping" the Chinese woman with whom he was living. And when the court ruled on the matter a few days later, the newspaper stated, "The evidence was positive against Brown, and he was fined $15 for the fun he had Saturday night. . . ."

As news of the vicious murder of Mrs. Stone spread through the Deadwood community, it set off a wave of recriminations against Brown and his suspected accomplice. When it was learned that law enforcers were returning the suspects to Deadwood, the cry of lynching went up and the townsfolk demanded revenge.

Forewarned about the potential vigilantes, the sheriff elected to split the suspects up. He placed Brown in the custody of a deputy and deputized four other trustworthy men on the spot. He kept custody of the teenaged Walker and led the suspect right through town to the jail without incident. Meanwhile, the five deputies with Brown took a more circuitous route to the jail, staying to the backstreets and railroad tracks. As they closed in on downtown, they encountered small bands of men with hate in their eyes.

"Only a short distance had been gone when the posse found itself confronted by a mob of several hundred," according to the *Times*'s account. "Cries of 'hang him!' 'get a rope' and other like expressions, indicative of the temper of the crowd, were heard on all sides."

But the honorable men selected by the sheriff were not to be deterred in their mission. "It was then that the officers drew their weapons, and on a double-quick hustled Brown into jail," said the *Times*. "Even after they had been locked up, the mob continued to linger about the jail and courthouse, apparently only waiting for someone to take the lead and make a rush to get at the prisoners."

As the excitement died and the mob disbanded, law officers began gathering evidence in the crime. Police identified and arrested eight "colored" witnesses, as the *Times* reported, and others as possible accomplices and jailed them all. Doctors examined the victim's body and determined the death had been caused by wounds inflicted with a sharp instrument such as an ax. Workers at the restaurant noticed that a large cleaver and carving knife were missing from the kitchen. A search of the creek bed closest to the murder scene yielded a meat cleaver and a butcher knife.

While Brown sat in jail awaiting arraignment, he must have pondered how the course of his life had brought him to his present predicament. Brown was born a Missouri slave on March 1, 1843, the property of a Colonel Halliday. Brown's mother died when he was nine, and the young man was sold to a neighboring slaveholder with a brutal overseer. As an eighteen-year-old, Brown had witnessed the start of the Civil War, and when he was nineteen, President Lincoln issued the Emancipation Proclamation. But as he lived in a Confederate state that denied him and his fellow slaves any measure of freedom, the war and proclamation meant relatively little to Brown.

In the midst of the Civil War, Brown, now twenty years old, was sent to St. Louis, sold to a Frenchman, and had his name changed to Isadore Cavanaugh. After accompanying his owner to California, Brown became a freeman. Brown's release from his master meant independence and adventure. He traveled to Portland, Oregon, then sailed around South America's Cape Horn to New York City while working on a merchant vessel. He signed on as a servant to a Captain Taylor, a cavalryman, and accompanied him across the Atlantic Ocean to Liverpool, England, before returning to New York.

Brown's exploits took him to Chicago, New Orleans, and Mexico, before he found steady work as a cattle driver in Texas. On his final drive Brown found himself at Fort Randall, on the Missouri River in the Dakota Territory. He married in March 1872 at age twenty-nine, then settled in Sidney, Nebraska, before seeking work five years later in Wyoming and Colorado. By 1879, three years after its settlement, Brown and his wife were living in Deadwood, where he would stay for the remainder of his days.

When his wife left him, Brown was devastated, and he spiraled downward, living what he later admitted to a newspaper reporter was "not a righteous life." He had frequent run-ins with the law; they culminated in his arrest for the cold-blooded murder of Mrs. Emma Stone, wife of Col. L. P. Stone.

While Brown contemplated his crime behind bars, the citizens of the Black Hills paid their respects to the family of his victim, filling a local church for the funeral and singing soulful hymns that included "Asleep in Jesus," "Nearer My God to Thee," and "Shadow of a Mighty Rock." "The sobs and groans of the husband and daughter filled each heart present with grief and sorrow so intense as to be almost beyond description, and the thoughts that went out toward the author of the cause of their agony were bitter ones," the *Deadwood Weekly Times* reported on May 20. The account went on to describe the attack on Mrs. Stone as a "terrible, cowardly, cold-blooded tragedy."

When Brown was finally arraigned in circuit court before Judge A. J. Plowman, newspaper reporters were aghast that the "negro" defendant didn't just plead guilty and expedite the entire judicial process. As it would eventually play out, it was quick enough. "The courtroom was crowded, as the report had been going that Brown, the accused, was going to plead guilty, thereby merely devolving upon the court the unpleasant task of passing sentence," the *Times* noted. "A sense of disappointment was predictable when the ebony-hued suspect said, 'not guilty.'" Judge Plowman set trial for June 10, a scant twenty-six days after the crime had taken place.

With W. L. McLaughlin and Thomas E. Harvey appointed as his counsel, the trial of Charles Brown began June 10, with jury selection and without a single challenge from the defense. The *Times* noted the next day, "It was plain to be seen, then, that the defense did not intend to pursue a vigorously fought case."

Although no one had actually witnessed the crime, prosecutors left little doubt of who had performed the dastardly deed. In sobbing testimony the victim's husband identified his dead wife's gold watch, as well as the knife and cleaver purportedly used in the murder. "It was a pathetic scene and there were but few dry eyes in the vast audience," the *Times* stated. "Brown was not affected in the least, however, but sat as unconcerned and indifferent as could be."

Walker gave damaging testimony against his grandfather, but the government's star witness turned out to be lead police chief Thomas J. Sparks. He told the court that Brown had called him to his jail cell the Wednesday prior to the trial and made a full confession, exonerating all others still implicated in the crime. With Sparks's testimony completed, the trial was handed over to defense attorney Harvey.

"Mr. Harvey arose and the courtroom was hushed to breathless silence, while the suspense was intense," according to the June 17 *Deadwood Weekly Pioneer*. "The defendant's counsel had not offered any evidence, had made but one objection to evidence submitted by the state and not more than three or four witnesses were cross-examined."

The defense attorney then thanked the court and the citizens of South Dakota for their concern and courteous treatment. In light of the defense's submission, prosecutors cut short their closing remarks, and Judge Plowman charged the jury and sent them out for deliberations. They were back in twenty minutes. The verdict, unsurprising to even the defendant, was guilty of murder as charged and fixing the penalty at death.

On his final day of life, Brown approached his impending death with surprising calm, grace, and dignity. In a statement by him published by the *Times* on July 14, the date of his execution, Brown apologized for his crime, affirmed his renewed faith in God, and asked for forgiveness. "I have admitted to man, and before God, that I have killed Emma Frances Stone," he wrote in his final statement. "I am sorry of it, and of all my sins I ask God to forgive me. I feel that He has forgiven me, and now that I have admitted the truth to man, I feel satisfied in the strength of the Lord Jesus Christ to depart from this world as a Christian."

After a breakfast of toast and eggs, a prayer with a Catholic priest, and a last smoke on his favorite pipe, Brown walked firmly into the crowded courtyard clutching a crucifix. After a final prayer, the condemned man was asked if he had anything to say.

After Brown's hands and legs were strapped and a black cap was pulled over his head, the noose was adjusted around his neck. At 10:29 a.m., Sheriff Plunkett pulled the lever, and Brown dropped six feet to his death.

BUD STEVENS

Acquitted of Murdering a Cattle King's Son

Dode MacKenzie had the world at his feet when he walked into a LeBeau, South Dakota, bar in December 1909. The son of a millionaire cattle baron living in a time when a million dollars meant something, Dode was as handsome as he was cocky. And some just didn't take too kindly to that. Even so, when he was gunned down by a bully of a bartender, it heralded a new legend and signaled the end of a small town.

In the late 1800s and early 1900s, fueled by foreign investment and millions of acres of belly-high sweetgrass, Texas cattlemen began moving massive herds to the outback of South Dakota, Montana, and Canada. In a few short decades, cattle blackened the plains as the bison once had. One of the major operators, the Matador Land and Cattle Company, had begun modest operations in Texas in 1878 with a herd of eight thousand head. However, as English and Scottish investors poured money into capital stock, the Matador benefited from low expenses, good grass, and high beef prices and blossomed. By 1882 when Scottish investors incorporated the company, it had a value of $1.25 million and held ownership of 100,000 acres of rangeland, privileges to another 1.5 million acres, 40,000 head of cattle, and 265 horses.

In 1890 Murdo MacKenzie became manager of the Matador, upgraded the herd, and began leasing northern pastures for maturing the company's purebred steers. He would later be labeled "the most influential of American cattlemen," by President Theodore Roosevelt. Under MacKenzie's guidance the Matador secured five hundred thousand acres of rangeland on South Dakota's Cheyenne River Indian Reservation and three hundred thousand acres on the Pine Ridge Indian Reservation. He acquired nearly one million more acres in Montana, Texas, and Saskatchewan, Canada.

Born in County Ross, Scotland, on April 24, 1850, MacKenzie received an education, worked as an apprentice in a law office, and served a decade as an assistant factor for the Balnagown Estate of Sir Charles Ross. In 1876 he married Isabella Stronach MacBain and the couple had five children. In 1885 MacKenzie became manager of the Prairie Cattle Company in Trinidad, Colorado, where he moved his growing family. Six years later, he was offered the manager's position at the prestigious Matador Land and Cattle Company.

As the Matador's vast operations grew, MacKenzie had the opportunity to assign his sons select positions within the company. For son David George MacKenzie—"Dode" to his friends—the assignment came in north central South Dakota. Thanks to the Matador, the tiny town of LeBeau had become one of the largest cattle shipping points in the United States. A snub-nosed ferry boat shuttled back and forth across the muddy Missouri, hauling cattle from the western ranches to the LeBeau terminal for rail shipment east. Cattle herded from Texas, New Mexico, and Colorado also were fattened up on the fertile rangelands before being shipped to market.

Despite its later success LeBeau had extremely humble beginnings. Established in 1875 by French fur trader Antoine LeBeau, it initially served as a trading post on the east bank of the Missouri near the mouth of Swan Creek, some seventy miles upstream from Pierre. As sodbusters flocked to the prairie, LeBeau grew, and by the early 1880s, the town had 250 residents and 60 buildings.

But with the arrival of the Matador herds in 1907, LeBeau witnessed its own renaissance. As the central shipping point, LeBeau enjoyed a surge in commerce but also had to cope with the law-enforcement challenges that came with this success. As dusty cowpunchers assembled with enough pay in their pockets to gamble freely, raise a little hell, and drink enough to drown out the taste of the trail, saloons, hotels, and bawdy houses were soon catering to all these new customers.

One of LeBeau's most frequent and popular visitors was Dode MacKenzie. After leaving college and following in his father's footsteps, he spent a season working cattle in the Texas Panhandle, then came north to the Cheyenne pastures in the summer of 1909. The *Mobridge Tribune* would later describe him as tall, rugged, and handsome, "a man's man" adored by women, but who preferred hanging out with cowboys in a saloon to a stodgy social life. LeBeau's deputy sheriff admitted that a nick in his ear came while Dode was shooting out lights in a honky-tonk. Dode also reportedly shot at the heels of dancing girls in another joint.

Manager of the Matador's herds on the Cheyenne River Indian Reservation, Dode was often described as lacking his father's reserve. Strident, hotheaded, and a heavy drinker, Dode quickly made a name for himself in a town whose officials often looked the other way in view of the MacKenzie family's power over the northern range and the prosperity the Matador had brought to LeBeau. But that too would change.

The summer of 1909 brought a cattle season unlike any other. That fall, more than 150,000 head were loaded on boxcars at LeBeau, destined for eastern markets. Money flowed as freely as the watered-down whiskey served in the local saloons, such as the most popular run by one-eyed Phil Dufran. Former Matador employee Benjamin F. "Bud" Stevens, also called Stephens and Stephenson, now manned the bar at Dufran's saloon, and he and Dode had a history of bad blood that went back all the way to Texas.

When Dode rode into LeBeau on the morning of December 11, 1909, trailed by a bunch of his cowboys, all of them were intent on quenching their thirst and celebrating a great season. Those with Dode said he got a bit boisterous, but he didn't have a drink and wasn't looking for trouble. Later testimony would contradict this version, however, claiming that Dode was gunning for Stevens and that the bartender had been informed of that fact and had armed himself accordingly. "To spice the monotony of a dull Saturday morning some town punks told Bud Stephens he had better have his gun ready as Dode MacKenzie was coming in to get him," according to the *Walworth County Record,* published in nearby Selby, South Dakota. "So Bud had his gun in easy reach when Dode came in the door just before noon."

At about 11:30 a.m. on that Saturday morning, the thirty-one-year-old Dode sauntered into the saloon accompanied by two of his cowboys, Walter MacDonald and Ambrose Benoist. Behind the bar stood an agitated Stevens, a fifty-five-year-old man who had been discharged in Texas by the Matador. Dode and his boys walked to the bar, where an argument ensued between Stevens and the rancher. When Stevens taunted Dode, the younger man told the bartender he would have no trouble with him in the bar, but if he, Stevens, would like to take it up on the street outside, Dode would only be too happy to oblige.

Stevens's response was immediate and extreme. Retrieving a cocked .45-caliber Colt from beneath the bar, he aimed it straight at Dode MacKenzie's chest and pulled the trigger. "Dode crossed his arms over his chest, turned and started toward the door when another shot was fired," an eyewitness told the newspaper. "The bullet entered the left arm, went through the body and grazed the right arm. Before Dode reached the door he was shot again in the back. He stumbled out of the door, half-circled on the sidewalk, then fell to the ground."

Friend Jack Wilson was the first to reach him. "Did he hit you, Dode?" Wilson asked. "Yes, he did," came a faint reply. Fred Richmond took one look at the downed cowboy and said, "My God! Dode is dying." Hearing Richmond make the remark, Dode reached his hand out to him, which Richmond grasped. With three bullets lodged in his body, Dode gasped, "Oh! Oh!" and was gone.

A doctor, C. L. Olson, arrived and quickly realized Dode's condition extended beyond his area of expertise. Three decades later, Olson would still remember that historic day. "When Dode MacKenzie was killed I was just across the street in my office and I reached him just as he had collapsed on the sidewalk, being aroused by the shooting," Olson had said in a later interview. "With another man, I do not recall his name, I rendered what service was indicated. He was beyond all help and was unable to make any statement."

When it was clear Dode was dead, Matador cowboys gingerly scooped up the body of their boss and took him to a nearby house. A coroner was called, telegraphs were dispatched, a box was secured, and the friends of Dode MacKenzie, who one would suspect would be hankering for a lynching, instead respectfully attended to the young man's remains. There would be time enough for justice.

Shortly after the shooting, a Deputy Sheriff Peterson had visited Dufran's saloon, arrested Stevens, and secured the pistol with which Stevens had killed Dode. Enlisting the aid of town leaders, the deputy had Stevens held while he found a team and a wagon to transport him to the county seat of Selby.

In the wake of the violence, messages were sent to Murdo MacKenzie, Dode's father, and to James Burr, bookkeeper at the Matador Ranch. The elder MacKenzie left at once for LeBeau, but when it became apparent he would not reach the town in time for the coroner's inquest, he instead arranged for a special train to convey the remains of his boy back to Colorado.

On Sunday, a day after Dode's death, a Sheriff Hoven and U.S. Attorney Smith arrived in LeBeau and interviewed witnesses. That night, in his Selby jail cell, Stevens was informed for the first time that Dode had died. "When he was told, he turned ghastly pale and for the first time appeared to be deeply moved."

A few days later, a coroner's inquest was held and witnesses described details of the tragedy. The coroner's jury found that MacKenzie came to his death at the hands of Stevens and recommended the suspect be remanded to circuit court for trial. Held without bail, Stevens quickly hired attorneys P. C. Morrison of Mobridge and E. B. Harkin of Aberdeen to defend him against the charges.

Two days after Christmas 1909, and just two weeks after the murder, Stevens found himself in court for his preliminary hearing. Testimony left no doubt that he had shot Dode MacKenzie and that he would be using an argument of self-defense when they went to trial. He wouldn't have to wait long.

On Tuesday, March 22, 1910, Stevens went on trial in Selby for the murder of the cattle king's son. Jury selection was made in one day, and the prosecution completed its case the next. On Thursday the defense began presenting a long list of witnesses to prove that MacKenzie had made threats against the aging Stevens, and that Dode had purchased a gun shortly before the shooting. On Friday both sides made closing arguments, with prosecutors calling for justice for the deceased. When it was defense counsel's turn, Harkin "delivered the most comprehensive and logical argument that has ever been presented here," the *Walworth County Record* reported. "His words impressed the jury and at times tears rolled from the eyes of some of them."

The case was given to the jury at 11:00 a.m. Saturday. After four hours of deliberation, they were back with their verdict: not guilty. When informed of the verdict, Stevens was overcome with emotions and silently shook the hand of each of those on the jury.

Freed by authorities but still fearing retribution from Dode's friends, Stevens fled to Mobridge, where he was still in hiding a week later. But the real reckoning for the demise of Dode MacKenzie would come soon and involve the fate of more than one man; it would sound a death knell for an entire town.

After burying his handsome son, Murdo MacKenzie (for whom the town of Murdo, South Dakota, would be named) set about burying a whole community. For the acquittal of Bud Stevens, the Matador outfit immediately boycotted LeBeau and soon ceased all operations on the Cheyenne River Indian Reservation. As the town dried up, so did the revenues of the Chicago, Milwaukee, and St. Paul Railroad and it soon abandoned plans to bridge the river and lay track westward.

In the summer of 1910, just four months after Stevens walked free, a raging fire burned more than half of the buildings on LeBeau's Main Street. All evidence pointed to arson. Fire hoses throughout the small town had been cut and flammable chemicals were discovered in the smoldering walls of burned-out buildings.

Cattle baron Murdo MacKenzie would live another three decades following his son's untimely death, serving as founding president of the American Stock Growers Association and managing a Brazilian cattle operation before ultimately returning to Denver and once again leading the Matador. He died on May 30, 1939, and was buried in Denver.

Had Murdo MacKenzie lived longer, he may have gained some perverse satisfaction in knowing that the charred remains of the town he blamed for the death of his son would one day be hidden beneath the silent waters of Lake Oahe, formed as a result of a flood control project on the Missouri River.

WILLIAM QUANTRILL

Terror of Civil War Missouri

The morning of August 21, 1863, dawned clear and warm. The residents of Lawrence, Kansas, woke from their sleep and started going about their daily rounds. Men and boys did chores while their wives or mothers prepared breakfast. The town lay quiet, and the Civil War seemed far away. If a few noticed the rising column of dust to the east, they probably thought it was some merchant wagons coming to trade, or a column of Federal troops passing through.

Actually, that column of dust was being kicked up by more than four hundred raiders from Missouri, rebel "bushwhackers" led by the greatest guerrilla chieftain of them all, William Clarke Quantrill.

The bushwhackers had always dreamed of hitting Lawrence. For years it had been the center for the state's abolitionist movement and was the home of Senator James Lane, one of the state's most prominent "Jayhawkers," antislavery guerrillas just as brutal as the bushwhackers. But the town lay forty miles west of the heavily patrolled state line. That Quantrill and his men made it there undetected is a tribute to their skill at hit-and-run warfare.

For days the Missourians had ridden west, dodging Union patrols and burning with hatred. Shortly before, a building in Kansas City used as a prison for many of the guerrillas' female relatives had collapsed, and some had died. William Anderson, one of Quantrill's lieutenants, lost a sister in the accident. A rumor spread that Union soldiers had undermined the building on purpose, and from then on Anderson rode into battle muttering his sister's name, killing everyone he could while foaming at the mouth. He became known as "Bloody Bill."

Despite its obvious potential as a target, there were no trained soldiers in town on the day of the attack. All of them were away, ironically enough, hunting bushwhackers.

The guerrilla horde thundered toward town. Just to the east of Lawrence lived the Reverend S. S. Snyder, a United Brethren Church minister and recruiter for the Second Colored Kansas Volunteers. He sat outside milking a cow when the little army galloped past. Two of the guerrillas rode into his yard and shot him dead.

Soon they poured into town, breaking into separate groups and riding up all the streets. As people poked their heads out windows, they saw men everywhere. Confusion reigned. Many of the guerrillas wore captured Federal uniforms, a favorite disguise, but as the air filled with gunshots and screams it became clear this was no Union army.

A large group headed toward the camps of the Fourteenth Kansas Regiment and Second Colored Regiment, both of which were made up of raw recruits who had not yet been issued guns. The bushwhackers slaughtered more than a dozen of them as the rest fled in panic.

Quantrill, a pistol in his hand, stood up in his stirrups and screamed to his men, "Kill! Kill and you will make no mistake. Lawrence should be thoroughly cleansed, and the only way to cleanse it is to kill! Kill!"

Quantrill led a group to the Eldridge House hotel, the finest in town, and hustled the guests outside. The guerrillas robbed the men, and if any gave the least sign of resistance, they gunned them down. Then they set fire to the building.

It wasn't the only place to burn. Quantrill had assembled a list of known Unionists. Detachments of guerrillas sought out their homes and shot the men in front of their families before torching the place.

All around town flames leapt into the air as more and more houses became engulfed. Dead bodies lay in the streets, boys as young as twelve beside men in their sixties, while bushwhackers looted homes and stores or drank themselves nearly unconscious.

Strangely, no women were seriously harmed. Quantrill had given strict orders about this. In the nineteenth century, chivalry still reigned, at least most of the time. "Bloody Bill" Anderson and some of the other guerrillas would, as the war dragged on and became ever more savage, soon count women among their lengthening list of victims.

But not in Lawrence. In fact, many Kansas women stood up to the guerrillas, dousing the flames as soon as Quantrill's men lit them, or hiding their menfolk and refusing to reveal their whereabouts.

As pandemonium spread, some citizens gathered rifles and hid in brick houses, fortifying the windows and doors with piles of furniture and firewood and sniping at any guerrilla who dared approach. Looking for easier prey, the bushwhackers hurried off to other parts of town.

One guerrilla, a Baptist preacher named Larkin Skaggs, tore down an American flag and tied it to a rope attached to his saddle. Then he rode up and down the street, dragging the flag behind him in the dirt.

After getting bored with this, Skaggs went after Judge Samuel Riggs, near the top of Quantrill's list. In 1860, Riggs had indicted Quantrill for several offenses, for which he was probably guilty. When Skaggs found Riggs and pointed his pistol at him, Riggs knocked it to one side and took off running. Skaggs urged his horse after the judge, but Riggs's wife grabbed onto Skaggs's bridle. Skaggs rode around, trailing the woman on the ground like the American flag and beating at her with his pistol, but she refused to let go until her husband got away.

Soon most names on Quantrill's list had been checked off, except for the name on top. The Jayhawk leader Jim Lane had fled into the countryside wearing only his nightshirt. Quantrill himself showed up at his home to kill him, but found only his wife. He cavalierly allowed Mrs. Lane to retrieve some of the family possessions before setting fire to the house, saying: "Give Mr. Lane my compliments. Please say I would be glad to meet him."

Mrs. Lane was not impressed, and replied: "Mr. Lane would be glad to meet you under . . . more favorable circumstances."

Lane was no coward; he was gone only long enough to get a horse, a gun, and a few men before riding back into town, perhaps hoping for those more favorable circumstances.

It was too late. The guerrillas had already left.

Just after nine in the morning, lookouts warned Quantrill that the Federal cavalry was on its way, and he ordered his lieutenant William Gregg to round everyone up and head back to Missouri. Despite some being so drunk they could barely make it into their saddles, Gregg gathered all of them . . . save one.

Skaggs still rode around town, too drunk to notice everyone else had left. He occasionally stopped to take potshots at fleeing civilians or to steal something, but it took a while for the fact that he was alone to penetrate his bleary brain. When he finally figured it out, he galloped off in panic, and straight into a posse of Kansans riding in the other direction. They disarmed him, and it wasn't long until a local boy named Billy Speer shot him. A Delaware Indian named White Turkey pegged him with an arrow and scalped him. Townspeople hanged his body from a tree and peppered it with bullets.

It was a hollow vengeance. About two hundred corpses littered the street, and much of the town lay in ruins.

More vengeance was coming. Soon a sizeable force of Federal soldiers (this time with weapons), angry locals, and farmers from the surrounding area caught up with Quantrill's band and gave it a running fight all the way back into Missouri. At least forty guerrillas died in the pursuit.

Still the Unionists weren't satisfied. Lawrence was the worst atrocity against civilians in the war. Gen. Thomas Ewing, commander of the District of the Border, issued General Order Number 11 to stamp out guerrilla activity in the region once and for all. It ordered all civilians living in Jackson, Cass, and Bates Counties, and part of Vernon County, to vacate their homes. If they could prove their loyalty, they could live near one of the military bases; everyone else had to leave the area. His men enforced the order with ruthless efficiency, burning homes and looting property on the least excuse, or no excuse at all. Tens of thousands of men, women, and children became impoverished refugees overnight, and the area was known as "The Burnt District" for years afterward. The savage raid on Lawrence led to an equally savage reprisal.

Nothing in Quantrill's childhood hinted that he would become the Civil War's most notorious guerrilla. Friends remembered him as quiet and intelligent but an avid hunter and a good shot. He was born in Ohio in 1837, the eldest child of Thomas Quantrill, a tinker and school principal who often beat his son in public for no apparent reason. His father also got into several scrapes with neighbors and embezzled school funds. At sixteen William followed in his father's footsteps and became a schoolteacher. That same year his father died, and it is doubtful William shed many tears over his grave.

William soon set out to make his fortune, settling in Kansas in 1857 at a time when the territory was the center of the debate over the expansion of slavery, with proslavery bushwhackers and abolitionist Jayhawkers fighting for control. Quantrill worked on a farm for a while and the following year signed on as a teamster for the U.S. Army during its expedition to suppress the Mormon rebellion in Utah. The experience began to change him. The teamsters were a rough lot, inclined to gamble, drink, and fight, and Quantrill gained a reputation as an avid gambler and a quick draw.

The following year he set out with eighteen associates to Colorado in search of gold, but the party ran out of food in the Rockies, suffered attacks by Indians, and got caught in a blizzard. Only he and six others survived. Like virtually everyone else who went to the Colorado gold rush, he didn't strike it rich and was soon back in Kansas working as a teacher.

Quantrill had transformed from a quiet schoolboy to a tough young man. By 1860, the struggle between bushwhackers and Jayhawkers on the Missouri-Kansas border had become worse, much of the fighting simply masking outright banditry. Quantrill saw an opportunity for easy money. He stopped writing to his family and friends in Ohio, something he had continually done in all the years he'd been away. He simply left his old life behind.

He and his friends made money by kidnapping free blacks in Kansas and selling them as slaves in Missouri, or stealing slaves in Missouri and ransoming them back to their owners. They also stole horses and cattle, and while they claimed to be proslavery bushwhackers, they didn't mind stealing from proslavery men too.

Once the American Civil War started in April 1861, Quantrill saw a grand opportunity for more raiding. But he would now have to formally pick a side, and he picked the South.

Quantrill joined the Missouri Confederate army of General Sterling Price, seeing action at the battles of Wilson's Creek and Lexington before leaving during the Confederate retreat to Neosho. Quantrill returned to the Blue Springs area of Jackson County and soon gathered a group of bushwhackers. His education and intelligence, not to mention his ability with guns and horses, made him the obvious leader. Starting with only about a dozen men, his band grew as he became more and more successful at robbing Union farmers and ambushing Federal patrols and supply wagons.

By early 1862 he had become one of the most successful guerrillas in Missouri. When the Union army declared that guerrillas would be treated as bandits and not soldiers and would be executed rather than imprisoned, Quantrill and his men became even more determined. For the most part they stopped taking prisoners. What had started as a government tactic to reduce guerrilla action by striking fear into their hearts only made the war more savage.

Riding the best horses they could steal, and carrying rifles as well as several revolvers each, the guerrillas could outrun and outfight Union troops, who only carried single-shot muskets and rode government nags of indifferent quality. Since many Union troops in Missouri came from as far away as Iowa or even Colorado, and the guerrillas were generally local boys, the rebels knew the terrain better. They knew which farmers they could trust and where to find isolated campgrounds deep in the brush. Still, Quantrill and his men found themselves in many tight spots, sometimes getting surrounded as they rested at what they thought was a safe house and having to fight their way out.

Despite all this activity, Quantrill managed to find time to get a girlfriend, Sarah "Kate" King, an attractive farm girl whom he introduced as his wife although there is no definitive proof they ever married. Kate claimed she was only thirteen when she fell in love with the guerrilla. Back in the nineteenth century people married a lot younger, but even so Kate felt obligated to say in a later interview that she "looked sixteen."

As time went on, Quantrill and his men acted less like Confederate guerrillas and more like bandits. They robbed stagecoaches and civilians, accumulating vast amounts of loot while only occasionally remembering to attack Union troops. Not even Southern sympathizers felt safe from them. The raid on Lawrence was only the culmination of long months of lawlessness.

When autumn stripped the leaves from the bushes that hid their campgrounds, the guerrillas would head to Texas for the winter to loaf around, get drunk, spend and gamble their stolen money, and cause trouble. Confederate officials became increasingly annoyed. Numerous complaints from locals about getting robbed by the guerrillas made the local Confederate commander, Brig. Gen. Henry McCulloch, first try to reason with the guerrillas, then try to get them to join the regular army, and finally to try and kick them out of the region. Nothing worked. Eventually he arrested Quantrill, but the guerrilla escaped.

At the same time, Quantrill was having increasing difficulty controlling his own men. Some of his lieutenants, such as "Bloody Bill" Anderson and William Gregg, split away from the group to head up their own commands. In the summer of 1864, another of his men, George Todd, overthrew him. Todd had nursed a long-standing grudge against Quantrill for not giving him more authority, and finally his patience broke. The two were playing cards one night when Quantrill accused him of cheating. Todd whipped out a pistol and told him to leave camp. Quantrill had no choice but to obey. Only a few men followed him.

Not even Quantrill could satisfy the fractious bushwhackers for long. Some of his men, like Gregg, were appalled by the massacre at Lawrence and the increasing lack of discipline. Others, like Anderson and Todd, simply wanted more power for themselves.

Leading about twenty men, Quantrill returned to Missouri. He did a bit of raiding and helped out during General Price's final invasion of the state in late 1864, but when that invasion failed, he took it as a signal that the Confederate cause was lost. He and a few men headed to Kentucky, slipping across the heavily guarded Mississippi River in the dead of night. A surviving member of Quantrill's band claimed they planned to ride all the way to Washington and assassinate Abraham Lincoln. It is doubtful even Quantrill would be so bold. More likely he simply wanted to get away from the West, where he was known to everyone and hated by almost as many.

Like Missouri, Kentucky was full of bushwhackers, and the Union commander for the state, Gen. John Palmer, swore to stamp them out. He started a "Secret Service" to track down all guerrillas, made up of men as lawless and deadly as the guerrillas themselves. He assigned one of them, a thief and murderer named Edwin Terrell, the task of hunting down Quantrill.

Quantrill acted cautiously in Kentucky. He and his men wore Federal uniforms and passed themselves off as a Union patrol, one of their favorite tricks. Needing fresh mounts, they rode into Harrodsburg on January 29, 1865, to "requisition" some horses. The citizens grumbled, but everyone believed the men to be actual soldiers. It wasn't until a real Union officer objected to having his horse taken that their cover was blown.

"I have been a soldier for two years and you shall not take my horse," the officer complained when he saw a guerrilla sitting atop his prized gray mare.

When the man made no move to dismount, the officer added, "If this horse leaves this stable, it will be over my dead body."

The guerrilla whipped out his pistol, said, "That is a damned easy job," and shot the officer in the face.

Quantrill's men galloped out of town, swept through nearby Danville to steal more horses, and split up. Union cavalry set out in hot pursuit, discovered where one group of a dozen guerrillas had hidden in a house for the night, and killed four before the rest surrendered.

In the following days Quantrill became melancholy and desperate and talked increasingly of death. He continued to do his duty as a guerrilla, however, cutting telegraph lines and attacking a Union wagon train. While this helped the war effort, it also revealed his location.

On May 10, Terrell finally caught up with Quantrill at the farmhouse of a Southern sympathizer. Quantrill and twenty-one men were resting when their lookout saw a long line of riders carrying rifles crest the ridge in front of the barn. As usual, Quantrill and his men vaulted into their saddles, prepared to make one of their famous breakouts. Banging away with their pistols, they galloped away from the farm.

Quantrill, however, was not among them. His horse was a new "acquisition," and it hadn't gotten used to gunfire yet. It panicked and Quantrill couldn't get into the saddle. He ran down the path, calling for two of his men to wait for him, but before he could reach them a bullet hit him in the back, breaking his spinal cord and paralyzing him. He fell face first into the mud.

Quantrill struggled for life for almost a month. He received numerous visitors, including a Catholic priest who converted him, and several ladies. He gave instructions that his stolen loot be given to Kate, although apparently she never received it. He finally passed away on June 6. He never sent a message to the family he had turned his back on.

The butcher of Lawrence was dead.

FRANK AND JESSE JAMES

Legendary Bandits

It had been a good day at the Kansas City Exposition. As night fell, a huge crowd headed for the gates after enjoying a day listening to brass bands, watching trick riders, trying to guess what bushel of corn or fat hog would win the farming contests, and stuffing themselves at the concession stands. It was September 26, 1872, and Missouri was at peace. The economy was improving after the long years of the Civil War, and everyone just wanted to have a good time. Well-fed and content, the crowds headed toward home.

But three riders rode through the throng in the other direction. Murmurs and a few laughs scattered through the crowd when people noticed the men wore checkered bandannas over their faces. Were they entertainers, or local kids up to some prank?

One man dismounted in front of the ticket booth, and to everyone's amazement the other two pulled out pistols and aimed them at the hundreds if not thousands of people around them. Anyone who had been laughing stopped immediately.

The man strode over to the ticket booth, reached his arm through the window, and grabbed the cash box. The ticket seller shouted a protest and ran out of the booth to grapple with the robber. One of the riders fired a shot, but the ticket seller ducked and the bullet hit the leg of a young girl standing nearby. The robber leapt into the saddle and the three rode off, the crowd parting before them in panic.

Kansas City had just been visited by the James gang.

Frank and Jesse James were born to Robert and Zerelda James on a farm near Kearney, Clay County. Robert was a highly educated Baptist minister and one of the founders of William Jewell College in Liberty. In 1850, he left his young family and set out for the gold fields of California, where he soon died. Zerelda kept the farm going and eventually married Dr. Reuben Samuel.

Despite having lost their father, the James boys seem to have had a happy childhood. They loved their new stepfather and lived on a prosperous farm tended by slaves, but they must have been aware of the growing tensions in the region. Pro- and antislavery factions fought it out along the border with Kansas to determine whether the territory would become a slave or free state.

Abolitionist Jayhawkers often raided border counties in Missouri, and the James brothers probably knew some of their victims.

This fierce border war, known as "Bleeding Kansas," was the prequel to the Civil War, which started in 1861. By then Frank was eighteen and Jesse just fourteen. Frank promptly enlisted in the pro-Southern Missouri State Guard and fought in the early Confederate victories at Wilson's Creek and Lexington. While things seemed to be going well for Missouri secessionists in 1861, they would be kicked out of the state the following year after a series of bloody engagements that gave the Union control of Missouri. Except for several large raids, no Confederate army would ever set foot in Missouri again.

But the fight was far from over. Frank had contracted measles and been left behind during the Confederate retreat from Lexington. Union troops captured and paroled him, making him take an oath not to fight the Union before allowing him to go home. He lived there peacefully until in 1863 the Missouri government required all able-bodied men to enroll in a Union militia. This was too much for Frank. While he would take an oath not to fight, he would never fight for the North. Local authorities arrested him for failing to join up, but he managed to escape from the Liberty jailhouse and ended up joining the guerrilla band of William Clarke Quantrill. He would spend the rest of the war roving the countryside, making hit-and-run raids on Federal outposts and destroying train tracks and telegraph wires. Quantrill's wasn't the only guerrilla band operating in Missouri, and these innumerable groups of bushwhackers would be the main rebel resistance in the state for the rest of the war. While the Union had taken Missouri, they had a great deal of trouble holding it.

Unfortunately for the James family, everyone knew Frank had broken his oath and was fighting for the South once again. They might have also suspected that Zerelda and Jesse paid close attention to Federal troop movements and ran messages for the bushwhackers. One day in May 1863 the Union militia showed up at the James farm. This would have probably been the same outfit that Frank would have joined if he could have stomached fighting for the North. The militia questioned Dr. Samuel about Frank's whereabouts, and when he said he knew nothing, they put a noose around his neck, threw the rope over a branch of one of the trees in his yard, and strung him up. Jesse tried to intervene, but they whipped him until he lay limp and bleeding on the ground. The militiamen, laughing and teasing Jesse's stepfather, let him drop and then hauled him up again. Eventually they had enough fun and dragged Dr. Samuel off to jail, leaving Jesse moaning from the welts on his back. The authorities then brought Zerelda to court and forced her to take a loyalty oath.

After this treatment, the young Jesse asked to join Quantrill's guerrillas too, but they rejected him as too young. They also weren't impressed when he shot off the tip of his finger while cleaning a pistol, screaming "dingus!" As a good

Baptist boy, he wouldn't swear even when losing a finger. For the rest of the war, "Dingus" would be his nickname among the bushwhackers.

Jesse finally got a chance to join his big brother in the spring of 1864. By that time Frank rode with "Bloody Bill" Anderson, leader of a faction that had split away from Quantrill's outfit.

Jesse didn't get to stay with his brother long. That summer he snuck into the yard of a Unionist farmer to steal a saddle, and the man shot him. The bullet pierced Jesse's chest and passed right through his body. This laid Jesse up for two months, but as soon as he could get back on his horse, he rode off to rejoin his brother, just in time for "Bloody Bill's" greatest killing spree. The band carved a crimson path through the state in support of Gen. Sterling Price's raid in the autumn of 1864. Both brothers nearly got killed in a failed attack on a Federal blockhouse in Fayette, and went on to Centralia, where Anderson's band slaughtered twenty-two unarmed Union soldiers on furlough. There is debate about whether Frank and Jesse were present for the Centralia Massacre, because much of the group stayed in camp that morning, but they were definitely present that afternoon when the bushwhackers wiped out a Federal pursuit force. The gleeful guerrillas scalped and mutilated some of the dead, but there are no reports that the James brothers participated in this. Anderson got killed by a Union militia the next month, and Frank went to rejoin Quantrill.

After successive defeats on the field the Southern cause seemed doomed, and Quantrill, one of the most wanted men west of the Mississippi, led his men east to Kentucky. It would not save him, however, and the Federals tracked him down and killed him. Frank went with him on that excursion, but managed to survive. Meanwhile Jesse raided around Missouri with another guerrilla group under the command of one of Anderson's former lieutenants.

As the war ended, the authorities in Missouri offered amnesty to bushwhackers who would surrender and take an oath of loyalty. Jesse spoke against surrender, but the other members of the band outvoted him. Deciding all was lost, he, too, rode toward Lexington to turn himself in, but before they made it to town they got ambushed by Federal troops. It's unclear why this happened; perhaps the troops thought they were one of the many bushwhacker groups who weren't surrendering, or perhaps they simply wanted revenge for all the suffering the guerrillas had caused. Missouri was chaotic at the time, and no one could tell friend from foe. In any case, Jesse had his horse shot from under him and took a bullet in his lung. Lying half dead in the Virginia Hotel in Lexington, he managed to raise his right hand and take the Oath of Loyalty on May 21, 1865. This action made him a rehabilitated rebel in the eyes of the Federal government. Over in Kentucky on July 26, Frank took the oath as well.

Jesse took a long time to recover from the bullet that hit his lung and had to be nursed back to health by his cousin, who like his mother was named Zerelda.

Jesse called her "Zee." As the former guerrilla lay recovering, the two fell in love and got engaged, although the wedding wouldn't happen for another nine years.

Frank, on the other hand, had more serious business to attend to. Apparently he couldn't adjust to peacetime life and on February 13, 1866, rode into Liberty with about a dozen men. They wore Union-style blue army overcoats, and some wore wigs and false beards and mustaches. Two of them walked into the Clay County Savings Association Bank, asking the cashier for change for a $10 bill. When the man turned to address them, he found himself staring at the business end of a pistol. They pushed the cashier and clerk into the vault and cleaned out the money before closing the vault door on them.

The robbers hadn't actually locked the door, however, and the cashier ran to a window to call for help as the bandits mounted up. Just then a student of William Jewell College, which Frank's father had helped found, passed by. He took up the call, and one of the robbers shot him dead. They galloped out of town as the citizens of Liberty gathered a posse.

It was too late; the robbers were well ahead and a snowstorm soon blew in and obscured their tracks. The gang got away with more than $57,000 in cash, gold, and government bonds.

The choice of the bank hadn't been random. Frank knew the area well, and the bank's president had been a Union informant during the Civil War, causing trouble for Dr. Samuel and friends of the James family. Liberty had another bank, but Frank had a score to settle with this one.

While Jesse has been said to have joined in the robbery, he was still recovering from his gunshot wound and unlikely to have been up for the job. He seems to have lived a quiet life at the time, joining the local Baptist church. Frank may or may not have engaged in other robberies in the state, but generally seems to have kept a low profile except for the occasional bender in town.

On a rather ominous note, in September 1869 Jesse made a formal request to be taken off the rolls at his Baptist church, saying he was unworthy.

In December of that year Frank and Jesse committed what was probably their first robbery together. They and possibly one other man rode into Gallatin, hitched their horses in an alley near the Daviess County Savings Association, and walked inside. They grabbed about $700 and shot cashier John Sheets before running to their horses. One of the men, probably Jesse, had trouble mounting up and got his foot caught in the stirrup. The horse dragged him down the street before he could break free. Battered and covered in dust, the robber staggered to his feet.

"Let's get him!" someone shouted, and an angry crowd closed in on him. He pulled out a pistol, and the townspeople fled in all directions. The bandit vaulted onto the back of a companion's horse, and they rode away.

Outside of town they came upon an unsuspecting traveler and relieved him of his horse, then kidnapped a traveling preacher to guide them for part of the way. The robbers boasted to him that they had killed Maj. Samuel Cox, who had led the militia that killed "Bloody Bill" Anderson near the end of the Civil War.

They had killed the wrong man, but their desire to kill Cox implicated the James brothers in the robbery. Both had ridden with Anderson. The third robber may have been Jim Anderson, another former bushwhacker and Bloody Bill's brother. The authorities traced the horse that one of the robbers left behind to Jesse James. Furthermore, a posse that went after them lost the trail but noted they were headed in the direction of Clay County, home of the James/Samuel family.

Four men showed up at the James farm to catch them, but just as they arrived a young boy ran to the stable, opened the door, and Frank and Jesse galloped out, guns blazing. One of the posse's horses was killed, and they lost the chase.

The James brothers laid low for a while, with Jesse writing to the newspapers protesting his innocence and saying he had fled because he didn't want to get lynched. The horse found at Gallatin, he claimed, had been sold to a "man from Kansas." Otherwise they seem to have drifted from state to state. The law accused them of other robberies, but it is hard to separate fact from fiction. By this time the brothers had become famous, and any major heist usually got laid at their door. Furthermore, other bandits would claim to be them, either to enhance their reputations or direct suspicion away from themselves. So many stagecoach, train, and bank robberies happened at this time that they couldn't have all been done by them, but a few probably were, including the Bank of Columbia in Kentucky and the infamous heist at the Kansas City Exposition.

That last robbery, certainly their most daring, guaranteed their national fame. The editor of the *Kansas City Times,* an alcoholic ex-Confederate soldier named John Newman Edwards, turned the thieves into noble Robin Hoods out of some epic ballad, effusing, "These men are bad citizens but they are bad because they live out of their time. The nineteenth century with its Sybaric civilization is not the social soil for men who might have sat with Arthur at the Round Table, ridden at tourney with Sir Launcelot or won the colors of Guinevere. . . . What they did we condemn. But the way they did it we can't help admiring."

Edwards would continue in this vein throughout the James brothers' careers, and his paper often received letters from the bandits themselves. Sometimes they would sign their own names, claiming their innocence. At other times they signed themselves "Dick Turpin, Jack Shepherd, and Claude Duval," famous English highwaymen from the previous century. They even offered to pay the medical expenses of the girl they accidentally shot at the Kansas City Exposition. It's not recorded if her family ever took the robbers up on their offer.

In 1874, the gang resurfaced in Arkansas, robbing a stagecoach at Malvern before heading north to hold up a train at Gads Hill, Missouri, pulling off the state's first peacetime train robbery. This last crime got the Pinkerton detective agency on their trail. The Pinkertons had gained a reputation for success in tracking down outlaws, and the railroad hired them to get the James brothers in case they decided to repeat their trick on another train.

While the Pinkertons claimed to be crack detectives, they didn't go about collaring Frank and Jesse James in a very intelligent manner. At first only a single agent, Joseph Whicher, went off to the James farm, posing as a farmhand looking for work. He must not have been very convincing, because his body turned up in another county. Next they sent two more agents, along with a local deputy sheriff, but the Younger brothers, former bushwhackers and accomplices of Frank and Jesse, got to them first and killed the deputy and one of the agents.

All this bloodshed didn't seem to affect Frank and Jesse's personal life much. On April 24, 1874, Jesse finally married his beloved Zee, and Frank married Annie Ralston sometime later that summer. The two couples enjoyed a fine honeymoon in Texas with their stolen money.

But things started heating up for the brothers. Their daring robberies had become a political issue, with the Republicans demanding they be brought to justice, while the Democrats, mostly made up of former Confederates, pointed out that corrupt Republican politicians and railway tycoons stole far more than the James brothers could ever dream of. Reward money, offered by the railroad, various banks, and eventually the state, began to pile up.

Unlike the politicians, the Pinkertons didn't just talk. They had lost two agents and wanted revenge. On the night of January 25, 1875, a group of Pinkerton detectives snuck up to the James farm, thinking the bandits were inside. Actually, only their stepfather Dr. Samuel, their mother Zerelda, and their thirteen-year-old half-brother Archie were at home. The lawmen broke open a window and tossed in an incendiary device. It rolled into the fireplace and exploded, killing Archie and mutilating Zerelda's hand so badly that it had to be amputated.

The Pinkertons claimed they were "only" trying to burn the house down, but the senseless killing of a young boy and the maiming of an aging woman enraged the population. The Pinkertons worked for the railroad, the corrupt companies that overcharged farmers for freight and had put dozens of counties deep into debt. Edwards and other newspapermen wrote scathing editorials denouncing the Pinkertons as child killers. Sympathy for the James brothers rose to an all-time high. One of their neighbors, who apparently helped out in the raid, turned up dead.

While Frank and Jesse had become legends in their own time, law-abiding citizens began to stock up on guns and get ready in case the outlaws visited their town next. The brothers would find their heists becoming increasingly dangerous. When Frank James, Cole Younger, Tom Webb, and Tom McDaniel hit a bank in Huntington, West Virginia, netting more than $10,000 in cash, a posse got on their trail right after they left town. The robbers fled into Kentucky, where a second posse chased them halfway across the state while the telegraph wires hummed across the countryside, warning citizens to be on the lookout. They fought at least three gun battles, and McDaniel got killed before the rest made good their escape.

Worse was to come in 1876 when the James brothers once again teamed up with the Younger brothers to raid a bank in Northfield, Minnesota. Northfield citizens greeted them with a hail of gunfire, and Frank and Jesse barely got away with their lives. The Youngers got the worst of it; the bloody shoot-out is detailed in the following chapter about their exploits.

The Northfield affair badly shook the brothers and their new wives. They decided to take on aliases and settle as farmers in Tennessee. Mr. and Mrs. Woodson (Frank and Annie) and Mr. and Mrs. Howard (Jesse and Zee) did well for a time, racing horses and tending crops, but they acted too differently from their run-in-the-mill neighbors to escape notice for long. People began remarking that the men seemed a bit jumpy and that the women had a lot more jewelry than people of their station would be expected to have. In one episode, Jesse James/John Howard attended a county fair and watched a contest where men tried to blow out a candle by shooting at it with pistols. As contestant after contestant missed the mark, Jesse could stand it no longer and went up, drew his revolver, and shot out the candle on the first try. Jesse, always more showy than his quiet and reserved brother, was beginning to make people talk. This, combined with various lawsuits from creditors, made him pick up stakes and move in with Frank.

But settled life didn't sit well with Jesse, and soon he headed down to the New Mexico Territory to assemble another gang. He briefly tried to get Billy the Kid to join, but Billy preferred cattle rustling to bank robbery and turned him down. Jesse did manage to collect a group of outlaws, but of inferior quality to the old crew. They included Bill Ryan, who had no previous criminal record and spent much of his time drunk; Dick Liddil, a horse thief; Tucker Bassham, a slow-witted farmer; Ed Miller, brother of Clell Miller who had died at Northfield; and Jesse's cousin Wood Hite. Another cousin, Clarence Hite, would join later. Their first holdup was of a train at Glendale station, just south of Independence, where the express mail netted about $6,000. This heist led the United States Express Company to offer a $25,000 reward, and the Chicago and Alton Railroad offered another $15,000. With all the rewards that had accumulated over Jesse's head, anyone who grabbed him would be a rich man.

Things began to turn ugly for the new gang. Bassham got captured and sentenced to ten years for the Glendale robbery. Ed Miller died under mysterious circumstances, and everyone believed Jesse killed him so he wouldn't talk. The gang continued to rob stagecoaches, trains, and payroll shipments, but often got away with very low stakes. Soon Ryan, too, found himself behind bars, after foolishly shooting off his mouth while on a bender. Jesse's earlier successes were due in no small part to the fact that he allied himself with former bushwhackers such as the Younger brothers whose skill and daring helped them get out of almost any scrape. Now Jesse kept company with lowlifes and amateurs. It would cost him.

Meanwhile, political pressure had been growing to do something about the new James gang. Missouri Governor Thomas Crittenden got the railroads to offer another $50,000 reward. State law prohibited Crittenden from offering a large reward himself, but he'd be a key player in stopping the gang's crime spree.

But by this time there wasn't much of a gang left to chase. Liddil got into an argument with Jesse's cousin Wood Hite and gunned him down for allegedly taking more than his share in a robbery. Two new gang members, Bob and Charlie Ford, were there too. Bob got into the gunplay and his bullet might have actually killed Jesse's cousin. The three men dreaded what Jesse might do if he found out.

The Fords decided to stay close and watch Jesse's every move. Hiding out first in Saint Joseph and then at the James farm near Kearney, the bandit leader planned more robberies, but Bob Ford had secretly met with Governor Crittenden, who promised him a rich reward for Jesse's capture. Bob claimed it was to bring in the bandit "dead or alive," something the governor would vigorously deny.

Soon Liddil surrendered to police, and this made Jesse nervous. While he was still ignorant of Liddil's part in his cousin's murder, he didn't trust him and worried he might talk. Jesse discussed killing Liddil and acted more and more suspicious of those around him. Bob and Charlie Ford realized they needed to get him soon.

They got their chance on April 3, 1882, as the Fords and Jesse sat in the living room in Jesse's home in Saint Joseph. Jesse complained about the heat and took off his coat and threw open the windows. Worried someone outside might see his gun belt, he took that off too. Then he stepped onto a chair to dust a picture on the wall. Bob gave Charlie a wink and they both drew their pistols. Jesse heard them cock their revolvers and began to turn just as a single shot from Bob's gun took Jesse in the back of the head. He fell to the floor, dead in an instant. Zee raced into the room and Charlie claimed that a pistol had accidentally gone off.

"Yes," she snapped, "I guess it went off on purpose."

The Fords beat a hasty retreat and turned themselves in to the law. Within hours of the news being made public, a stream of visitors came to the James farm to view the body of America's most famous outlaw. The Fords were initially charged with murder but gained a pardon from Governor Crittenden.

The press, of course, took sides. The Democratic papers, led by John Newman Edwards, railed against Crittenden, calling him an assassin. The Republican press was just as eager with their praises for the termination of the state's worst outlaw.

Frank, meanwhile, was still living the quiet life in Virginia. He hadn't participated in a robbery in several years, and hoped this clean living would help him get pardoned. He sent out feelers to Governor Crittenden via Edwards, and the newspaperman reassured him that if he gave up, he would be given a fair trial and not be extradited to other states to face charges there.

Frank decided to take a chance and turned himself in to the governor, handing over his pistols and telling him he would fight no more. People thronged to see the famous outlaw, and when he went to trial, he was found innocent of all charges. His case was helped by the fact that so many fellow gang members, the only ones who could truly say what he had done and when, were dead or on the run. The cases may have also been helped along by the governor himself, who felt convinced that Frank had turned over a new leaf and simply wanted the whole affair to be over. Frank walked out of jail a free man.

While the legend of Frank and Jesse James had been made in their lifetime, with cheap novels about their exploits being published while they were still out robbing banks, it would continue to grow to the present day, helped in no small part by those involved. Frank eventually joined Cole Younger in a Wild West show, and Jesse's son, Jesse James Jr., would make a silent Western movie in which he played his father. This would be followed by dozens of others, few having anything to do with the real story. Charlie and Bob Ford even toured with a theater troupe, playing themselves in a production called *The Killing of Jesse James.* In one performance they were booed offstage to the shouts of "murderers!" and "robbers!" Frank and Jesse's mother, still living on the James farm, buried Jesse in the yard and erected a fine monument over his grave. She sold tickets to tour the farm, regaling visitors with tales of Jesse and Frank's nobility and the evils of the Pinkertons. One stop on the tour was Jesse's grave, where she offered pebbles from the grave at a quarter apiece. When the supply got low, she'd go to a nearby creek and gather more.

A distinctly American bandit has been remembered in a distinctly American fashion, through tourism, mass media, and show business.

SAM BROWN

Just Dispensation of an All-Wise Providence

About midnight on February 28, 1860, Sam Brown and Hempton Bilbo argued over a billiard game they were playing in the Gem Saloon in Carson City. Both had been drinking, and when the argument heated up, Brown challenged Bilbo to step outside and settle it. Brown wasn't known at the time on the Comstock Lode.

Bilbo, unarmed, stepped through the door first with Brown right behind. Brown whipped out his pistol and shot Bilbo in the back of his thigh. Then he disappeared, laughing as he ran away. Bilbo bled to death, and Brown added another notch to a gun, well notched already in Texas and California.

Brown was nearly 6 feet tall and weighed 200 pounds. Strong and agile as a cat, he was dirty and quarrelsome, a human brute in appearance and a reptile in personality. He was slouchy, thick-witted, and slow to move until he made one of his lethal attacks. He reminded tough miners of a large lizard lying in wait for prey. He looked loathsome and repulsive; his hair was coarse, and he kept his long, red whiskers knotted under his chin. His beady eyes looked out sadistically at a hostile world.

Brown's long Spanish spurs rattled at his heels, and he carried a bowie knife and huge revolver in his belt. When people heard his booming voice, they hurried to get out of his way. Killing was to him an art form, a profession; his appetite for blood, insatiable. He intended to be the chief of all the bad men on the Comstock.

Brown had showed up in the southern Sierra mines of California in the early 1850s with a reputation of having killed several men in gun and knife fights in his native Texas. In 1853 he killed a man named Lyons in Mariposa, California. The next year he killed three more—Chilean miners from South America—near Fiddletown, for which he served two years in San Quentin. When he was turned loose, he returned to the California goldfields, and, in late 1859, crossed the mountains to the Comstock Lode. There, Mark Twain, writing for the Virginia City *Territorial Enterprise,* said the town's first twenty-six graves contained murdered men, and Sam Brown was the worst killer of all.

Timid men ducked into stores or crossed the street when they saw the pathological killer approaching. When Brown entered a saloon, the saloon keeper dropped whatever he was doing—even if it was waiting on the richest man in camp—to see what Brown wanted. To challenge Sam Brown was to court death.

In January 1860, Brown knifed Homer Woodruff, a helpless drunk, to death in Virginia City. That May, he joined the Carson City Rangers who, with other volunteers under Major William Ormsby, rode out to punish Paiutes near Pyramid Lake for alleged depredations against whites.

The watchword and recruiting slogan of the punitive expedition was: "An Indian for breakfast and a pony to ride." Brown loved that slogan and was often heard to say, with a sneer on his lips, that he hadn't yet had his man for breakfast. Ormsby's expedition was ambushed and nearly wiped out. The major was killed, and Brown barely escaped by jumping to the back of a mule that was carrying its wounded rider away from the charging Paiutes. Brown flung the wounded man to the ground, dug his spurs into the mule, and galloped away.

In August 1860 Brown killed a man named McKenzie in a Virginia City saloon. McKenzie, a pale-faced barroom lounger, had bumped against Brown with a remark Brown thought offensive. Without a word Brown wrapped his long, gorilla-like arm around McKenzie's neck, drawing the pale face close to his own. Then, holding the man like a snake constricting a bird, he drove his bowie knife twice into McKenzie's chest, twisting it "Maltese fashion" to slice out the heart. He dropped the bleeding body to the floor, wiped his knife on his pants, laid down with a billiard-table cloth wrapped around him, and calmly went to sleep as the blood congealed around his victim.

Four more murders, all of misfits and castoffs, quickly and conclusively established Brown as the self-imposed chief of the Comstock's bad men. Lawlessness flourished in the mining camps, and Sam Brown reigned supreme.

Another time, Brown was working at a roadhouse when a man entered, saying he wanted something to eat. Sam pointed to a hanging chunk of bacon. "Help yourself," he grunted.

"Could I borrow your knife to cut a slice?" the man asked.

Sam pulled out his knife and then slid it back into his belt. "I've killed five men with that knife," he said, smiling strangely. "Don't know as I want to lend it out to cut hog meat."

The man left quickly and quietly. He would eat somewhere else.

Sam Brown was a bad man and, like a lot of bad men, he was also a coward. Like the lion that singles out the weakest for its kill, he selected victims where there would be no reprisals. He picked on unarmed men who had no one nearby for protection. He never attacked a man who could put up a fight. Since his victims were friendless outsiders, no vigilance committees organized to stop his slaughter of outcasts. The king of terror and mindless destruction ruled over all!

Brown confronted two determined men in his short lifetime, and they each had his number. The first was William M. Stewart, a fearless frontier lawyer who had already been California's attorney general and would later become Nevada's first U.S. senator. Taller than Brown and just as heavy, Stewart had left Yale to follow the 1849 gold rush to California, and he moved to the Comstock in March 1860, a few months after Brown. Stewart had piercing blue eyes and ambition to match his courage and strength. Later, he would turn down President Grant's offer of appointment to the U.S. Supreme Court.

On Friday, July 6, 1861, when he met Brown, Stewart was representing some mining clients before an arbitrator in the Devil's Gate Toll House in Gold Canyon, near Virginia City. The house was divided into two rooms, a 10-foot by 14-foot bar and a 6-foot by 10-foot room behind. The hearing was being held in the small room.

Brown was in the bar when he learned about the proceedings. He decided to barge in and throw his weight around. "I'll go in there and tell 'em what's what," he announced. "Tell 'em who orter win."

Stewart knew by the voice in the bar who had demanded entrance. He wore a long overcoat with a large-bore Texas derringer in each pocket. He stepped back against the wall, pulled out the derringers, cocked them, and watched Brown stride in. At first, Brown did not notice Stewart in the small, crowded room.

"Swear me," demanded Brown.

The arbitrator looked at Stewart, who said, "Yes, please swear the witness."

Then Brown saw the two derringers pointing directly at him.

"Now what have you to say?" Stewart asked, "What do you know about the case?"

"Know about it," Brown replied. "I got me an interest in that ground."

But the intruder had little more to say with the derringers pointed at him, and his testimony soon ended.

Afterward, Brown waited in the bar for Stewart. The lawyer came out with both hands in his coat pockets, obviously still holding his derringers.

"Damn you, Stewart, I like a man like you," Brown said. "Come have a drink with me."

Stewart joined him, but kept one hand in his pocket as they drank.

"I think you and me could get justice in a mining camp," Brown said.

"You're right. We could," said the man who would later serve twenty-nine years in the U.S. Senate.

The next day Brown rode to Carson City to call on Stewart. He said he needed a lawyer in a suit over some rich mines he had discovered south of the Comstock at Aurora. Stewart said he needed a retainer, and Brown said he'd be back with one in a few days. Brown rode on toward Genoa with Alexander Henderson, one of the few men willing to ride with the braggart and killer.

"Alex, today is my thirtieth birthday," Brown said, "and I believe I must have a man for supper. I've killed eleven in Nevada, and I'll make it an even dozen before sundown."

They stopped at Webster's Hotel between Carson City and Genoa, where Brown thought he'd shoot Webster. But Webster seemed ready to defend himself, so the two rode on to Genoa. There, Brown wanted to kill Robert Lockridge, but again rode on when it became clear that Lockridge would put up a fight.

Brown and his trail partner then rode on to Van Sickle's station, 3 miles south of Genoa on the emigrant road to California. Henry Van Sickle, the second man of determination Brown would meet during those two momentous days, was a German from New Jersey. He had been an Indian fighter, had been a bullwhacker in the California gold rush, and had been in the Carson Valley for nine years. By training, he was a blacksmith. He had patiently built up his station, consisting of five barns, a dance hall, a bar, several sleeping rooms, a kitchen, a dining room, and a smithy. He had mined his own rock to build the station, which was celebrated on the emigrant trail for its hospitality and for the stability and honesty of its owner. Van Sickle, a genial man and a quiet one, enjoyed the community's respect.

Brown and Henderson rode toward the dining room as the bell rang for supper. Van Sickle and M. M. Wheeler were talking on the porch as the riders drew near.

"It must be the Pony rider from Fort Churchill," Van Sickle said. "I wonders why he's so late." Among other responsibilities, Van Sickle served as local agent for the Pony Express.

"It's Sam Brown," Wheeler said, squinting his eyes. "But who's with him? I didn't know anybody'd ride with that vulture."

Brown dismounted, thinking the friendly German would not offer any resistance and would be an easy man to kill. As Brown bent to reach for his revolver, Van Sickle thought he was untying his leggings to stop for supper.

Van Sickle called out, *"Guten Abend, Herren.* You want me your horses to put up?"

"I'm not stopping with you," Brown growled. "I come to kill you, you sonofabitch. Your time is up."

Brown drew his revolver, but the surprised Van Sickle ran into the dining room before he could fire. Brown followed, but the two dozen supper guests, already seated, instinctively jumped up and milled around, thus shielding their host.

Brown shouted, "You better run, you sonofabitch." Then he returned to his horse, and rode on down the emigrant road to the south.

Several guests expressed their sympathy for their host.

"I wonder why he's mad at you," one said.

"He'll be back to get you, Henry," another said. "He won't give up."

"I'm glad I'm not your insurance company."

"Get on a horse and go shoot him. There's nothing else you can do."

Others agreed that Van Sickle's life was now in mortal danger. They told him that he should arm himself and pursue Brown until he could kill him. One even offered his horse, saying he would go himself but his hand was injured and he could not shoot.

Van Sickle got his double-barreled fowling piece and decided to settle the affair at once, determined he would not live in fear of future attacks. His gun had been loaded with birdshot. Not bothering to reload the weapon in his haste, he just poured some buckshot down the barrels, and stuck two shells in his pocket. Then, he saddled and mounted a fast horse and set out in pursuit. He could hear voices of guests shouting encouragement behind him as he rode away.

Robert Fisher and a lady visiting from Placerville were riding north toward Genoa when they met Brown and Henderson about 250 yards south of Van Sickle's. Fisher heard Brown say, "I woulda killed him as quick as I would a snake if them others had stayed outa it."

After a mile of fast riding, Van Sickle had closed within range of Brown and Henderson. He shouted to Henderson to get out of the way, which Henderson did very promptly. Van Sickle jumped down, drew careful aim, and fired both barrels. He knocked Brown's hat off, although the man was not seriously wounded. Brown recovered his hat and fired two shots from his revolver as he remounted and sped away, leaving Henderson at the side of the road. Van Sickle, unhurt, jumped back on his horse, galloped after Brown, reloading his gun with the two shells he had brought with him.

Brown took refuge in the house of Bill Crosser as riders from Van Sickle's station, carrying a supply of ammunition, caught up with Van Sickle. The grim German, known for his usual cheerful manner, thanked his friends and stuffed the shells in his pocket. About this time, Henderson, riding back north, met the pursuers and said he should have shot Brown himself. "He's been raving all day about getting a man for supper on his birthday," he said.

Brown came out of Crosser's house, jumped back on his horse, and made another attempt to get away from a man who seemed determined and capable of killing him. Dusk was turning to darkness in the valley, and fear was turning to terror in Sam Brown. He rode on toward Luther Olds's station with Van Sickle still in pursuit. Van Sickle caught up with Brown at Mottsville and fired both barrels while mounted; he missed again. Brown, also mounted, returned fire three times without effect and then sped away to Israel Mott's house where he again sought refuge. By this time, the pursuit had continued for about 3 more miles, and it was quite dark. Van Sickle, catching up, dismounted and watched the house. He did not want to walk toward it in the darkness.

Finally, Van Sickle asked Levi Miles, who had come out of the house, if Brown was still inside. Advised that Brown had gone out the back door, Van

Sickle thought he might have gone on to the Olds's station. He rode there to check, but Brown wasn't there, either. While Van Sickle pondered what to do he heard spurs jingle, and he recognized them as the big Spanish spurs that Brown wore. He waited in the darkness until Brown stopped his horse and dismounted.

As Brown walked toward the station, Van Sickle called out, "Sam, now I kills you."

Mortal terror seized Brown. Abject, unutterable fear sealed his lips as Van Sickle fired both barrels point blank into Brown's chest.

Then Brown yelled like an inhuman monster. His spasmodic scream of despair filled the nighttime Nevada sky, echoing back from the mountains in the west. Seven balls of buckshot were the birthday present for the most savage killer ever to terrorize the Comstock.

Other men rode up and cursed, and several of them shot into Brown's body. "Don't shoot any more," Van Sickle said. "He's dead already."

Henry Van Sickle buried Brown at his own expense. As he said later in a statement, "I saw him well buried, thus showing that which everybody knew who was in any way familiar with the circumstances. It was a necessity I would have been only glad to have avoided."

Wheeler, Fisher, Miles, and seven others testified at the coroner's inquest two days after the killing. Interestingly, Miles had witnessed Brown's trial in Mokelumne Hill, California, when he was sentenced to San Quentin for killing the Chilenos.

Miles testified that he saw Brown standing at the back door of Israel Mott's house. When the men who had been shooting at the front of the house left, Brown came out and said that Van Sickle was shooting at him and he didn't know what it was for. "He then said that another man had come up to Van Sickle's with him and asked him to go in and drink there, but he had told the man that he would not drink in any such G_d d____d man's house; also, that if Van Sickle had said anything to him he had intended to shoot him. Sometimes he would state that he did not know what Van Sickle was after him for—and then at other times he would say that Van Sickle, about a year ago, had given a man a pistol in order to shoot him."

The coroners' jury reported that Sam Brown had met his death through the just dispensation of an all-wise providence.

People came from as far away as San Francisco to thank Van Sickle for killing Brown. The community rewarded the peaceful, friendly, but determined man who had hunted down and killed his prey, and then paid for the burial. They made Van Sickle the first sheriff of Douglas County. However, in later years he often said, "No matter how justified a man may be in killing another, he never gets over it."

JOHN MORIARTY

A Young Irishman in the Mines

John Moriarty, born in Caharciveen, Kerry County, Ireland, about 1844, showed up at a dance in the Niagara Dance Hall on B Street in Virginia City, Nevada, in November 1868. Between dances he walked to the adjoining saloon and ordered a glass of wine. The bartender poured whiskey instead.

"I asked for wine," Moriarty objected.

The bartender curled his lip and sneered, "Whiskey is good enough for the likes of you."

The Irishman squared off as though to punch the bartender when John O'Toole grabbed his arm, saying, "Watch it, my lad, or you'll be feeling the might of Irish knuckles."

Moriarty, as Irish as O'Toole, whipped out his revolver, turned to put his back to the wall, and covered O'Toole as well as the rest of the men crowding into the room. The room hushed as he backed slowly out a side door, his revolver held steady against the threatening crowd. Then the short-tempered man made his big mistake.

Moriarty walked around to the front door of the saloon, the upper half of which was glass. He saw O'Toole standing at the bar, his back toward the door. Taking careful aim, he shot and killed O'Toole. Later he would claim that O'Toole had thrown a glass at him, as though that would excuse the cold-blooded killing. Moriarty left town in a hurry, changed his name to Morgan Courtney, and showed up two years later at Pioche, the center of mining in southeastern Nevada.

He said he had come from Salt Lake City, although he may have spent some time in Montana after fleeing from Nevada. He gave the appearance of a quiet, reserved man, but he had only three items of luggage when he got off the stage in Pioche—a Henry rifle, a six-shooter, and a small satchel.

Many considered Pioche the toughest mining town in the West. Historians count forty killings between 1870 and 1875, with only two men punished. The official report of the Nevada commissioner of mining in 1872 said that two classes of people struck it rich in Pioche: lawyers hired to maintain titles of mining claims and scoundrels hired to maintain their possession.

The geography and geology of Pioche contributed to its violence. All the early, rich strikes were made in claims located in a small area on Treasure Hill, a low but sometimes steep mountain. The claims overlapped, and the county had not established a legal system for unraveling ownership entanglements, leaving the problem to the miners themselves.

In fact the language in the Federal Mining Law of 1872, still effective today, which defines the right to follow mineral veins through claims staked by others, resulted directly from the Pioche problem. That law was largely written by Nevada's first U.S. senator, William Stewart, and he knew the facts of the problem. But the owners at the time the problem arose learned quickly to hire gunmen to keep other gunmen from jumping their claims. When Courtney learned that legitimate miners hired outlaws to protect their claims from others, he knew he had found a home.

Brothers Tom and Frank Newland had a claim on the steep hillside above the Washington & Creole, the richest mine in town. They got permission to tunnel through the Washington & Creole to reach a deeply buried vein on their claim. While they were tunneling, they struck a rich vein in the Washington & Creole, and got permission from the owners to mine that ore for thirty days.

The thirty days expired and the Newland Brothers resumed their tunneling, but the temptation to take out more ore from the fabulous discovery was too much, even for them. Under cover of darkness they built a log fort at the entrance to their tunnel, hired gunmen to jump the Washington & Creole, and stocked the fort with ammunition and supplies for a siege. They continued mining the Washington & Creole, keeping the rightful owners away at gunpoint.

At this stage Morgan Courtney entered the melodrama. He hired three young gunmen, Michael Casey, Barney Flood, and William Bethards, and contracted with the Washington & Creole to drive the Newland crowd off, receiving permission to mine the newly discovered vein themselves for thirty days after they had chased off the Newland men.

Courtney studied the fort carefully and decided against a direct assault. He would rely on two prominent vices well known in the mines—dishonesty and intemperance.

The Newland gunmen must have thought that the shipment of whiskey delivered to their fort came by mistake. The brothers and their henchmen wondered how those strangers delivering the goods could believe that the address they sought was up on the side of the mountain. But they winked, nudged each other, and accepted delivery. Besides, the night wind on November 8, 1870, was cold, and the men, tired of their long vigil, gleefully opened the bottles to celebrate their victory over the rightful owners of the vein. At about three in the morning, when even the night watch had had its fill, Courtney's gang charged down the mountain, battle cries on their lips and smoking revolvers in their hands.

One would call it a humane attack by Pioche standards; only one defender was killed and the rest ran away from their arms and ammunition. Courtney and his three men took over as kings of the hill—or at least of the fort that controlled access to the treasure.

Courtney and one of the Newlands were wounded, neither seriously. But a Newland man, W. G. Snell, lay dead. The county indicted Courtney, alone, for Snell's murder. Nothing came of it. Lincoln County's incomplete court records show no trial, and the newspapers that would have covered it have been lost.

In the meantime the four men took about $60,000 worth of ore out of the Washington & Creole during their thirty-day "lease," selling the ore to its rightful owner. Michael Casey received nothing good from his share of the money. On the day it was delivered, he went to the bank to make his deposit and got in an argument with a Thomas Gorson about interest Casey owed him on a loan. They drew their guns, and Casey won the argument by better shooting. But three months later, when witness James Levy said Casey had fired first, Casey got the help of David Nagle and then unwisely threatened to make Levy eat his words. Although outnumbered two to one, Levy killed Casey.

William Bethards killed a man three years later and went to prison, where another inmate killed him.

This left Morgan Courtney and Barney Flood of the four who had attacked the fort. They were arrested the next February for the knife murder of Thomas Coleman in Pioche. Both men were fond of knives, but both were released for lack of evidence. Flood left Pioche after stabbing another man who did not die.

Courtney, the only one of the four gunmen left in Pioche, had become a hero in all the saloons. For once, he had won a fight on the side of perceived justice, if not on the side of law. Probably for the first time in his life, he had plenty of money to spend. And he spent it freely, mostly in gambling.

Courtney also developed a taste for fancy clothes. He prided himself on ordering suits of the finest black broadcloth and shirts of the purest white linen, all decorated with the most expensive-looking jewelry. He also had his fingernails manicured, certainly unusual behavior in Pioche. A stranger in town might have thought Courtney owned the Washington & Creole. In fact its true owners were a strange pair. W. H. Raymond, with his hunched back, stood 5 feet tall. His partner John H. Ely was 6 feet, 3 inches tall. They both excelled in courage and cared little about their appearance. Their mine would eventually pay $13 million in dividends.

On June 8, 1872, in Caucey's Saloon on Pioche's steep main street, Courtney and John Sullivan had words about whether or not Sullivan had invited Courtney to drink with him. Courtney, disgusted with the trivial argument, left the saloon, but Sullivan followed. Courtney would claim at his trial that Sullivan tried to sell him some mining stock. When Courtney said no, Sullivan drew his knife and said, "You damned son of a bitch, I'll kill you yet."

Courtney drew his revolver and backed out of range of Sullivan's knife, saying, "Take that back or I'll kill you."

Sullivan didn't and Courtney did. He shot Sullivan from 30 feet away.

Courtney spent the rest of the summer in the Lincoln County jail. The prosecution took nine days for its case, and the district attorney took five hours for his summation to the jury in the crowded courtroom, so they must have really wanted Courtney off the street. But juries didn't take kindly to the language Sullivan had used, sometimes deciding that it gave the other combatant the right to shoot. The saloon crowd pulled for Courtney, and at about one o'clock on Sunday morning the jury returned a verdict of acquittal.

Courtney's joy was dampened when the Lincoln County sheriff, with an old warrant from Storey County for the killing of O'Toole four years before, promptly rearrested him. Fearing vigilante action when the community learned of the acquittal, the sheriff had his prisoner on a stage for Virginia City before the day was over.

But Courtney's luck was still with him. Although the Virginia City killing had occurred in a crowded saloon, only one witness was known to be still alive, and he could not be brought to court. The charge was dismissed and Courtney returned to Pioche, where Sullivan's friends had already forgotten their anger at the verdict. For the first time in four years, Courtney did not feel a noose hanging over his head. He even got respectable, staking out a mining claim, which he called The Faro Bank.

In January 1873 Courtney and several partners—including the man who had killed Courtney's partner, Mike Casey, less than two years before—made arrangements to develop a mine. As the Irishman's business prospects improved, so did his love life. By then he was superintendent of the Kentucky Mine, and he had met and got involved with Georgianne "Georgie" Scyphers. Georgie worked in a brothel, but she knew how to hold her own with men. Once, when a man assaulted her in the brothel, she shot him with her pistol. Later, she killed a man for defaming her sister. She was just the woman for hair-triggered Morgan Courtney.

Apart from paying customers, the only other man in Georgie's life was James McKinney. There was bad blood between McKinney and Courtney from the start. McKinney claimed that a few years before, his best friend was killed in Montana and he thought Courtney was the killer.

On a pleasant summer's evening in 1873, Courtney demanded that McKinney tell him the whereabouts of Georgie.

"I'm not keeping track of her," McKinney snorted.

But Georgie had claimed to others that she was the center of a love triangle, involving McKinney and Courtney. In fact, when she failed to meet McKinney in his room, as she had promised, McKinney said it was because she was afraid of Courtney.

"I'll wring your heart worse than you've ever wrung mine, before you'll ever lay with me again," McKinney told Georgie.

Georgie also swore that McKinney had often said he hated Courtney. "He said he hated him because other men feared him," she said.

On Friday, August 1, 1873, the night Georgie stood McKinney up, he armed himself and went looking for Courtney. He carried a double-action revolver—unusual at that time—that could be fired as fast as one could pull the trigger. The large weapon would not fit into McKinney's pocket. He thrust the barrel into the pocket and kept his right hand on the butt and his left curled over the cylinder to keep the gun from falling out. He searched up and down the narrow, steep streets for his rival, carefully looking both ways before crossing a side street.

He found Courtney coming out of the Mint Saloon walking, as he usually did, with his right hand in his coat pocket holding his own pistol. McKinney later claimed that Courtney was moving purposely toward him, when McKinney drew his weapon and said, "Courtney, I am here to fight." Then, according to McKinney, Courtney made a move to draw his gun, and McKinney started pulling the trigger.

An eyewitness said that when McKinney fired the first shot, Courtney seemed to freeze as though unsure what to do. Then Courtney turned and ran, stooping forward as he dodged from side to side. Other witnesses agreed that Courtney froze at the first shot, as though surprised at someone standing up to him and uncertain how to handle it. As Courtney turned and ran, he seemed to be trying to draw his own revolver but was unable to get it out of his pocket.

McKinney followed, blasting away from a distance of 3 to 4 feet. In desperation Courtney ducked into a saloon and out again on a side street. Then Deputy Sheriff J. R. Hoge arrived. He grabbed McKinney and disarmed him. But McKinney had already emptied his fast-shooting revolver.

When the shooting stopped, Courtney staggered out of the steep side street with his revolver dangling from his left hand. By then Hoge was dragging McKinney to jail, followed by a threatening crowd. Some of the onlookers carried Courtney into a drugstore and laid him carefully on the floor, where a doctor examined him. Five of McKinney's six shots had hit him, one from the front and four from the back. His immaculate linen coat, now smeared with spreading bloodstains, had even caught fire from the close-range shooting.

J. P. Kirby, a witness to the gun battle, said that one or two nights before the shooting he had overheard a conversation between Courtney and McKinney.

"You son of a bitch," Courtney said, "I thought I told you to leave this town, and you had better do it or I will kill you."

"Courtney, why do you follow me up?" McKinney had replied.

Kirby said he moved on and heard no more. Others corroborated that Courtney had complained about McKinney not leaving town.

While the crowd speculated about the reason behind the one-sided fight, the doctor told Courtney he could not live, and if he had anything to say, he should say it quickly. Between heavily drawn gasps of breath and pausing now and then to gather his strength, Courtney slowly dictated a dying statement, which was written down by a newspaper reporter.

He said, "I think I am going to die. I was walking down the street and McKinney shot me in the back. I started to run in order to get in a place to defend myself but he shot so fast that I could not do anything but run. I did not shoot at McKenney at all. I did not get my pistol out until he fired six shots. Georgie Scyphers told me that Frank Cleveland gave McKinney a pistol yesterday."

Courtney's dying statement was interrupted once when a Catholic priest gave him the last rites. The torn piece of wrapping paper upon which the dying statement was written and witnessed remains in the present courthouse at Pioche. The man who had terrorized the town had nothing to say about the cold-blooded killings of Sullivan and O'Toole, nothing about the many unsolved murders where he was suspected, no regrets, no advice to friends about learning from his mistakes. There was not even a word for Georgie, just a recital of how he had been cut down in cold blood, as he had done others. Morgan Courtney died that night, aged twenty-nine.

The Pioche *Record* said, "Morgan Courtney, feared by some, detested by others, and respected by a few, was a desperate character. He had killed his man in Pioche some fourteen months ago, a murderer in the broadest acceptance of the term. We only refer to his tragic death as a verification of the prophecy that those who slay by the sword shall by the sword be slain."

The publisher of the newspaper ordered the volunteer fire company he commanded to turn out in full uniform for the funeral of their fallen comrade, Morgan Courtney.

The funeral procession, led by a Catholic priest and by Courtney's cousin, William J. Kelly, both in a buggy, followed by a brass band, the volunteer fire company, and over 300 citizens, moved to Boot Hill to bury Courtney.

The law handled McKinney's case. In this he was lucky, as plans had been made to storm the jail and accomplish justice with a rope. The trial started September 10 and lasted ten days. It took the jury three minutes to acquit him.

The Pioche *Record* on August 8 reported that within the previous thirty days, ten pistol shots and thirteen knife wounds had been inflicted by three Pioche citizens on their victims. The grisly accounting of violent bodily punctures included, besides McKinney's five shots into Courtney, one Huntington who inflicted five gunshot wounds on four men, one mortally, and a Ferguson who had stabbed his victim thirteen times, also mortally. Altogether, Pioche saw five homicides in the four months leading up to the McKinney trial.

Although his funeral procession to Boot Hill was impressive, Irishman John Moriarty is buried in an unmarked grave. The Boot Hill part of the Pioche Cemetery lies along its south border. Some of the thirty-seven mounds have old boots lying on them, one has an old hat, and some have nothing. None of them is identified. No one knows which one contains the bones of John Moriarty.

MILTON SHARP

Hunting Gold in Dalzell Canyon

Milton Sharp considered stage robbery a craft to be mastered. No one did it better than he. Drury Wells, editor of the Virginia City *Territorial Enterprise,* interviewed Sharp after one of his arrests and called him the most industrious highwayman in all of Nevada. "He robbed stages whenever he wanted to," Wells wrote, "and with great thoroughness, never making a mistake and never finding an empty treasure box."

Missouri born, part Cherokee and part French, Sharp was a veteran of the Confederate Army with five bullet and bayonet scars. He stood 5 feet, 5 inches tall, had brown eyes, brown hair, and a neat mustache and goatee. His dark good looks, cultured speech, and charming manners impressed all. A man of good habits, he never gambled, he shunned tobacco, and only took a drink when a friend offered and then only if he didn't have to accept a second one. His one bad habit was robbing stages, particularly in Nevada's Dalzell Canyon north of the Aurora, Nevada, and Bodie, California, mines. He usually worked alone.

Sharp had been a miner for twelve years when, at thirty-four, he turned to robbing stages for a living. Before that, he had tried to improve himself by studying bookkeeping in night school. His criminal career coincided with years of heavy production from the Aurora, Bodie, and Candelaria mines. Wells Fargo stages hauled practically all that production 90 miles north to the U.S. mint in Carson.

Wells Fargo did not expect its drivers to resist robbers. They had their hands full driving four-horse and six-horse teams. Shotgun-carrying messengers, some on top of the coach, some inside, protected stages carrying bullion. Somehow Sharp knew which stages those were, and he left them alone. He preferred stages going to the mines with less treasure and less protection. Occasionally, he encountered a stage with a messenger, either protecting a mine payroll or returning to the mines for another assignment. But he only shot one messenger, and that man would ride with him when Sharp finally was delivered to prison. Apparently, he considered shooting, except in self-defense, below his dignity.

Sharp preferred working alone, but broke that rule in Dalzell Canyon on June 8, 1880, when he and a helper, Frank Dow, met the southbound stage as it climbed up the canyon approaching Aurora and Bodie. Sharp stepped out from the cottonwoods and willows along the East Walker River and stopped the stage. In a well-modulated, polite voice, he told the passengers—they included one messenger—to step out and line up in a straight line.

"Keep your backs to me and the stage," he said. With Dow watching the driver, Sharp continued, "Just drop your cash, watches, and jewelry on the ground and take three steps forward. Keep your eyes straight ahead. The first one to turn around will be shot so dead, he'll be ready for skinning."

After selecting several watches and about $100 from the passengers, he took the gold watch of driver Tom Chamberlain and the express box containing $3,000 in coin. Then he excused himself, and he and Dow disappeared into the sagebrush. The passengers agreed that Sharp had been very businesslike. He was always gallant to lady passengers, who said he acted like a high-toned gentlemen.

A posse of law officers, Wells Fargo detectives and messengers, and Paiute Indians tracked Sharp and Dow all the way to Walker Lake, before the trail grew cold.

Exactly a week after that robbery, and back in Dalzell Canyon again, Sharp and Dow robbed another stage driven by Chamberlain and bound for Aurora and Bodie. This time they took only the express box, leaving the passengers alone. They told Chamberlain where he could find the box, without its contents, on his return trip.

"We don't want to put you to any inconvenience, having to search for it," Sharp told Chamberlain. "And as soon as we find it convenient, we'll return your fine watch and also the watches that we took from your passengers last week. We don't really need them."

History does not tell us if the watches were returned.

An hour later Chamberlain met the northbound stage. It carried a consignment of bullion, protected by three shotgun-carrying messengers. Hearing Chamberlain's report, they checked their weapons as their stage started down Dalzell Canyon, but they passed through without incident. Sharp cared more for high volume and low risk. He wasn't interested in stages carrying bullion and shotgun-armed messengers.

Two and one half months later, on the night of August 30, passengers were whooping it up on the southbound stage as it dropped down toward the stage station in Coal Valley, where it would start ascending Dalzell Canyon. Above the noise, driver George Finney heard a rifle shot and a bullet whizzing overhead. He reported the incident to the station. Men sent out to investigate found tracks where a man wearing a size six boot had waited for some time for the stage to approach.

Just five days later, the southbound stage, again driven by twice-robbed Chamberlain, was stopped in Dalzell Canyon by Sharp and Dow, wearing masks. They told the passengers to sit on the ground as they rifled the express box.

"We didn't get much," Dow said. "Shall we go through the passengers?"

Three hours later, when Chamberlain met the northbound stage, he told its two Wells Fargo messengers, Mike Tovey and Tom Woodruff, about being robbed. When that stage reached the scene of the earlier robbery, Tovey found tracks going north along the stage road. His stage continued, stopping now and then for Tovey to check the tracks in the moonlight. When they reached a fork in the road, he stepped down to search the ground carefully. Then Tovey heard a voice call out, "You son of a bitch. You thought you'd sneak up on us, didn't you?"

A shot rang out and a bullet whizzed over Tovey's head to kill one of the stage's horses. "If you fellows fire, we'll kill every one of you," Sharp called out.

"Nobody is firing any guns," Tovey said. "If you want something, come on down."

Dow stepped out of the brush, and Tovey fired, killing him instantly. Sharp, still hidden, shot Tovey through the arm. Woodruff returned the fire and thought he hit his man.

Tovey bled freely, and Woodruff and a passenger helped him down the road toward a house on Desert Creek. Driver Billy Hodge got the harness off the dead horse and tied its mate to the rear of the stage. With the two messengers gone and the driver occupied, Sharp, who had not been hit after all, stepped out of the brush. He walked past his dead partner, and calmly ordered Hodge to hand over the express box. When Sharp had it, he disappeared into the darkness.

For a week, detectives, Wells Fargo messengers, and Indian trackers combed the hills. They found two men who were soon released, but no one else. Then Jim Hume, Wells Fargo's greatest detective and one of the best in the West, took over. He dug up the buried Dow. The man had small feet and he wore size six boots, but Hume did not recognize him. He said he found no papers, only a black, glazed oilcloth mask with places cut out for nose, eyes, and mouth.

On Saturday, September 11, just one week after Dow was killed, Hume and two San Francisco detectives went to a boardinghouse in San Francisco and asked the proprietor to show them to the room of her tenant who had small, dainty feet. They found stolen articles and evidence that the room was rented by Frank Dow, who used several aliases. They kept the room under surveillance, hoping the other robber would appear. At eleven o'clock that very night, Milton Sharp walked in. The detectives found two guns on him, one that had been stolen from a Wells Fargo express box. He also had $2,500 in gold coin in a money belt, certificates of deposit, and 150 shares of mining stock. He said the gun had been given to him by Dow, and he denied any involvement in stage robberies.

Sharp was returned to Aurora to stand trial. Although Hume thought the evidence was solid, Wells Fargo took no chances. They hired famed lawyer Pat Reddy to assist the prosecution. The trial started Thursday, October 28. The case went to the jury the next day. They found Sharp guilty on Saturday. Sentencing was set for November 10 to allow time for a second trial of assault to commit murder for the shooting of messenger Mike Tovey. Sharp returned to jail.

He didn't stay long. Thoroughly depressed about hooking up with a partner who was so naive that he stepped out in the open on the assurance that he wouldn't be shot, Sharp pondered his future. He expected a heavy sentence from the conviction he already had, and he still faced another trial. What could he do with his hands and feet shackled and a heavy ball chained to the foot shackles? He borrowed a penknife from the jailer and began carving toys for the jailer's children. Then he started digging into the 3-inch brick wall of his cell. On November 2—the very day the *Bodie Daily Free Press* mentioned that "the heavy sentence that probably awaits him has given him such a fit of blues that even the jailer scarcely knows him"—his cell was found empty. He had dug a hole through the brick wall and escaped.

All Aurora felt shock. Not because Sharp had dug through the wall; other inmates had done that. But Milton Sharp, with a fifteen-pound ball chained to his shackled ankles, had escaped on the national Election Day when thousands of people came to the courthouse to vote. How Sharp escaped through those crowds is still a mystery.

Sharp had a half-hour head start by the time the jailer learned he was missing. It took another hour to organize a posse. Sharp hobbled to the southeast over Middle Hill, toward Adobe Meadows. He stopped at Five Mile Springs, about 5 miles from Aurora. There, he pounded on his leg irons with rocks gripped in his handcuffed hands until the rivets fell out. Freed from the leg shackles, he kept moving south and east, and on Sunday, five days after his escape, he reached Candelaria, a mining town 45 miles from Aurora.

Sharp couldn't travel in a straight line because the country swarmed with men seeking the large award offered for his capture. The November nights were cold, and Sharp had nothing to eat for the five days. He could have broken into miner's cabins for food, but burglary was beneath his dignity. He continued working his way south and east.

When he reached Candelaria, Sharp stumbled to the rear of McKisseck's Saloon. He looked up at the dim light shining from the window of Dobe Willoughby's faro bank in the saloon's back room. Willoughby had been in the Aurora jail for a short time while Sharp was there, and Sharp considered him a friend. Cold to the bones from five days of exposure and weakened from the exertion of pounding off the ball and shackle and surviving five days with no food and little sleep, he huddled in the darkness. What chance did he have? He had always fought fairly. He had never shot a Wells Fargo man until that day he shot at the man who had gunned his partner down in treachery. Throughout the five days, he had been constantly surrounded by armed men, combing the hills in their search. Would he ever see his family again? These questions filled what was left of his numbed mind. Finally, he reached down, clawed a few pebbles from the frozen ground, and, using his last strength, tossed them at the window.

Tossing pebbles at a window was recognized in the West as a signal of desperation. Someone outside needed help from a friend. One of the faro players said, "Maybe that's Sharp needing help."

Men from five counties had joined the search. The state's leading newspaper had its editor there. Wells Fargo had offered a big reward. The sheriff, the governor, and the county commissioners offered additional rewards. The fifteen-pound ball and shackle had been found, and the area swarmed with searching men, but Willoughby kept on dealing faro.

Deputy Sheriff Alex McLean heard about the pebble signal, and he said it was probably Sharp. But he made no move to go out in the darkness and face the lone fugitive. Other men mocked McLean's lack of courage, but they showed no desire, themselves, to go see who threw the pebbles.

Finally, a miner entered another saloon and said there was a man outside who said he wanted to talk to an officer. Word got to McLean, and he mustered up enough courage to meet the mysterious visitor. Approaching with his drawn pistol, he first asked if Sharp was armed. Sharp had no weapon.

Sharp still wore the handcuffs. After McLean adjusted them to stop the hurting, Sharp asked for something to eat. McLean took him to Billy Coalter's chop-stand, where he devoured a huge meal. Then, McLean took his prisoner to the Wells Fargo office for safe keeping until he could make arrangements to return him to Aurora. There, Drury Wells, editor of the *Territorial Enterprise,* interviewed him.

Sharp told Wells that he would never have surrendered without a fight if he'd only had a gun. He said he had worn the shackle for three days. All that time, he was surrounded by armed men hunting for him.

"It seemed to me," he said, "that I could not get out of their sight. The shackle hurt my ankle and made me very lame. I am not well acquainted in this part of the country. I don't know exactly where I went in my travels. I had to change my course every few miles to avoid the men who were tracking me. I concluded to come here and try to find a friend that I thought would help me. But I didn't find him, and I didn't like to ask for him."

Wells thought Sharp a "mild-mannered, pleasant-spoken fellow, but with a flash now and then beneath the surface which showed him alert and keen as a steel trap." He was not inclined to be communicative at first. When Wells asked how he got the shackle off his leg, he only said, "Well, I got it off, and I was glad of it."

Sharp went back to Aurora to be locked securely in an iron cell. Three days later, the judge sentenced him to twenty years in the state prison. The other indictments were dismissed. Hume and the two Wells Fargo messengers, Tovey and Woodruff, delivered Sharp to the Nevada State Prison in Carson. (Three years later Jim Hume would capture Black Bart, an even more famous stage robber.) When their stage arrived, other passengers described Sharp as "a perfect gentleman in manners and conversation."

Sharp was not a good prisoner for his first year. In May 1881, he had a ball and chain applied for making tools in an attempt to escape. In August he went to the dungeon for stealing a file and concealing it on his person. On November 24, six months after the ball and chain were applied, the ball was removed. One month later, on Christmas Eve, the chain was removed.

Then, Sharp behaved himself. In 1887, after seven years in prison, his request for pardon was denied. A year later, it was denied again. Sharp had become a trusty, with special privileges. He felt he had no hope for release, so he abused his privileges and escaped in August 1889.

We don't know what he did for the next four years, but on October 3, 1893, Sharp drove into a livery stable in Red Bluff, California, with a farmer for whom he worked. He came face to face with a former convict he had known in prison. They both recognized each other. Neither spoke, and Sharp did not think it necessary to ask the other man to not betray him. A few minutes later, while trying on a new pair of boots, Sharp looked up to see the sheriff. He had again been deceived, this time by a man he thought a friend.

Back in prison, Sharp wrote a long and detailed letter to Wells Fargo's Jim Hume. He listed names and addresses of those for whom he had worked during his four years of liberty. Hume interviewed those persons and decided that Sharp had made every effort to rehabilitate himself. Apparently, he had avoided contact with all his old associates, for the prison had received a note from a former friend that Sharp had drowned in a California flood.

Hume wrote to Nevada authorities, reporting his findings, and urging that Sharp's next application for pardon be granted. Sharp filed a new petition in May 1894, and Governor Roswell Colcord pardoned him the following July.

We don't know where Milton Sharp went or what he did, but apparently he resumed his good habits and continued to shun his one bad one—stage robbery. Betrayed by two men, one of them a friend, he was finally rescued by his old nemesis, Wells Fargo's greatest detective.

WILLIAM FREDERICK JAHNS

A Mind for Murder

On October 27, 1909, William Frederick Jahns prepared for a trip to Chicago. He and his housekeeper, Agnes Jansen, planned to leave his farm at Cedonia, Washington, and drive to Blue Creek, where they would catch a connecting train to Spokane. At least, that's what Jahns told all his friends. He actually had something else in mind.

Jahns's two hired hands, George Hilton and Tennessee Jack Tisth, helped pack the wagon for the trip. Jansen prepared some food for the two to eat while they were on the road. At midnight, Jahns drove the wagon down the road. But instead of heading northeast toward Blue Creek, he actually turned southeast. Jansen, not being familiar with the area, didn't notice that Jahns wasn't traveling in the right direction. Occasionally the two talked about their future plans. Jahns and Jansen were both German immigrants, and Jahns had told people he and Agnes were going to Chicago to recruit other Germans to settle a colony near Cedonia. He had bought land for the purpose.

At three in the morning, Jahns arrived at the Hergesheimer property and suggested that they stop for the night since he wasn't sure where he was. He surmised that in daylight he could get them back on the right track. Jansen agreed. Since the house was unoccupied, no one would object to them trespassing on the property. Jahns jumped down from the wagon to open the gate and directed Jansen to drive the team through. As she did so, Jahns pulled out a gun. Before she could react, he shot and killed her. He jumped up on the wagon and drove it over to some logs that he had piled up earlier. He placed her body on the heap and lit it on fire. Several hours later, there was nothing left of Agnes Jansen.

What could have possessed Jahns to commit such a horrible crime? A study of Jahns's past reveals that he may have been motivated by greed. Or perhaps he was just insane. He was born in Germany in 1848, but he left there at the age of nineteen to avoid being drafted into the German army. He first settled in Pennsylvania, where he adopted the name Romandorf to keep the army from finding him. He worked for a railroad before moving to Rio de Janeiro. He traveled around the world to South Africa, Hong Kong, Australia, and Asia Minor, apparently thinking that the German army was coming after him. He eventually came back to the United States and settled in Nebraska, where he worked as a farmer. Somewhere along the line he got married. From Nebraska, he moved on to Wyoming, where he lived only a short time.

Sometime in the winter of 1903 or 1904, Jahns, then known as Frank Romandorf, showed up in Maple Falls, near Bellingham, Washington. He bought some property next to James Logan. Both properties were on the Nooksack River. Jahns's son Ed and Ed's family joined him a few months later. Ed worked for a while as a butcher, then later bought the butcher shop.

Then people started disappearing. Frank Romandorf hired Fred Helms in 1905, and one day, Helms left and never came back. The following summer, Romandorf hired Jack Green. Threatening legal action, Green told the sheriff that he intended to file charges of attempted murder against Ed Romandorf for pushing him against a saw. Green went to talk to Frank Romandorf about the incident and was never seen again.

Then one fall night in 1906, both Frank Romandorf and James Logan disappeared after a severe storm. Logan had last been seen leaving a store with some purchases bundled up in a sack. At first neighbors thought the two missing men might have been killed during the storm. But a few days later, a neighbor was looking around Logan's property and found Logan's horse dead from a gunshot. The neighbors began to suspect foul play.

Sheriff Andrew Williams of Bellingham investigated the crime. Soon after the disappearance, he heard from G. M. Strickfadden, postmaster of Maple Falls. On November 15, Strickfadden had received a letter from Logan that was postmarked in Seattle. The letter instructed the postmaster to forward Logan's mail to Hoboken, New Jersey. Strickfadden doubted that the handwriting was Logan's, but he couldn't prove that it wasn't. A short while later, Logan's property was sold to a man named Frank Rankins. The title transfer was filed in Whatcom County, and Rankins paid five thousand dollars cash for the farm. Evidence seemed to support that Logan was alive, but what about Romandorf?

Three months after Romandorf disappeared, his son Ed got in trouble for selling a mortgaged horse. The charge was settled out of court, but Ed left Maple Falls soon after and joined his father in the small town of Cedonia, Washington, a few miles from the Columbia River in Stevens County. Earlier in the year, Romandorf (really William Frederick Jahns) had purchased property in Cedonia and changed his name to James Logan, the name of the man he had killed in Maple Falls. He hired his son and another man to help work the farm. Over the next year and a half, Logan bought more land around his property and organized the Cascade Land and Cattle Company.

During that time he met D. R. Shively, a landowner in Addy, about 15 miles away. After several discussions, Jahns, posing as Logan, told Shively he could get him a good deal on his land. In February 1908, he made the arrangements to sell Shively's land.

On March 1, Shively drove to Spokane to meet Jahns and close the land deal. In a quiet hotel room, Jahns slipped deadly drugs into Shively's drink. After Shively died, Jahns put his body in a trunk and shipped the trunk to his ranch at Cedonia. He instructed one of his hands to bury the trunk, without telling him its contents. As instructed, the hired man buried the trunk on Logan's property behind the house. He never looked inside it. On March 6, the land transaction was complete. Shively's property was sold to a George A. Herman of Chicago for six thousand dollars. Three or four months later Herman sold the property to a James Monaghan of Spokane. Both names were fictitious, made up by Jahns so that he could later transfer the money to himself without detection.

In August 1909, Jahns went to Spokane to hire a housekeeper. There he met Agnes Jansen, a widow who had immigrated to the United States a few months before. Jahns seemed like an upstanding citizen, so Jansen accepted his offer of work. She had been working at the Jahns farm for three months when Jahns went on another trip to Spokane and stopped at the house of Margaret Aherns, where Jansen had been living before she came to Cedonia. Mrs. Aherns gave him a letter that had arrived for Jansen. He promised to pass it on. They had grown quite fond of each other, he told Mrs. Aherns, and intended to get married.

However, his next action seems to contradict his supposed good intentions. While in Spokane, he asked a German mail clerk to translate the contents of the letter. Though he claimed to be able to speak German, he said he could not read it. He was greatly pleased with what he learned. It seemed that Jansen was about to receive a considerable amount of money. About $3,500 in American money had been deposited in a Berlin bank for her and would soon be forwarded to her in America.

The news apparently changed Jahns's romantic ideas to thoughts of murder. He decided to kill Jansen for her money. She suspected nothing when the two rode out in the wagon on the night of October 27. Just a few hours later, she was dead from two gunshots to the head.

Jahns thought he had come up with a foolproof plan to get away with her murder, but it started to unravel right away. Unbeknownst to Jahns, a man named Al Stayt had seen him pull up to the Hergesheimer ranch about three o'clock in the morning. He recognized Jahns, though he couldn't see who was with him. Then a man named Swede Johnson came up, noticing the fire in which Jahns burned Jansen's body. Jahns casually talked to him about a mule trade, telling Johnson about how one of his animals had become ill, so he had to send Jansen on to Blue Creek with a passing stranger. He hoped that Johnson wouldn't realize what was going on just a few feet away.

About six in the morning, M. D. Taylor, who owned property nearby, noticed the fire and went to investigate. Taylor saw the huge pile of burning logs, a pyre about 6 feet high and 6 feet wide. Some of the logs were so large, he knew they had to have been hauled into place by a horse. Taylor figured the fire had been burning for several hours. Jahns lay sound asleep in his wagon nearby, but Taylor woke him up and asked what he was doing there. Again Jahns told his story of taking his housekeeper to the railway station at Blue Creek when one of the horses became sick. He met someone going the same way and sent her on with him so she didn't miss her train. The story satisfied Taylor for the moment.

When the fire was nearly burned out and was in no danger of spreading, Jahns left the scene. He continued down the road to Summit Valley, 8 miles west of Blue Creek. He met F. F. Dorm and J. W. Morrison on the way, and Jahns told them he was going to Chewelah to catch a train. They drove with each other for a while before splitting up. After spending the night at the Cline residence in Summit Valley, Jahns hired one of the Cline sons to drive him to Blue Creek, where he checked his luggage to Spokane. He paid Mr. Cline to drive his rig back to Cedonia, then he rode the train as far as Hillyard, just outside Spokane. From there he bought a ticket to Davenport, 30 miles west. He walked into the Bank of Davenport to withdraw money from Jansen's account, pretending to be her husband and saying that he had her power of attorney. He showed the cashier, M. W. Anderson, the deed to his property as collateral. When Anderson called the bank's branch in Hunters, he learned that this James Logan (Jahns) was wanted for a serious crime. He did not give Jahns the money he requested, so Jahns left in a huff and checked into a nearby hotel.

Meanwhile, curiosity got the better of Elmer and Ira Gifford and their uncle Charles Gifford, who had seen Jahns's bonfire while hunting. They returned to the site of the fire. Jahns was gone by then, but he left some terrible evidence behind. As they picked through the ashes of the fire, Elmer found the remains of a human hand. As soon as the Giffords saw the gruesome remnant, they rode to the nearest farm and called Sheriff W. H. Graham at Colville. A few hours later, Sheriff Graham arrived with the coroner and the prosecutor. After inspecting the area, Graham found a box of .32 shells, a hat pin, wires from a woman's hat, belt buckles, corset stays, and a piece of dental bridgework. He also noticed wagon tracks leading away from the scene and a bloodstain by the gate. Rain earlier in the day had created muddy tracks that were easy to follow. The lawman followed the tracks back to Jahns's farm.

Jahns had not arrived back at home yet, but while the sheriff talked with hired hands Tisth and Hilton, Johnny Cline drove up with Jahns's wagon. Cline told Graham that he had driven Jahns's team back from Blue Creek while Jahns went on to Spokane. From there, he reported, Jahns was going to visit Davenport before coming back to Cedonia.

Instinct and experience told Sheriff Graham that Jahns had killed a woman and then burned her to get rid of the evidence. He didn't yet know who the woman was, but he figured that she must have had something the murderer wanted. He called Sheriff Gardiner in Davenport and asked him to keep his eyes open for the suspect.

Gardiner didn't take long to track down Jahns. His officers found him drinking in a Davenport saloon, probably trying to decide how to get Jansen's money. Gardiner's men approached him and asked him his name. When he said it was James Logan, they told him he was under arrest. When he asked why, they told him he was wanted for the murder of a woman in Stevens County. At first he seemed surprised, but then he sighed and walked away with them. Gardiner led him to the local jail while other officers seized Jahns's possessions from his hotel.

Jahns possessed a cornucopia of incriminating evidence. There was a deed to the Baslington ranch in Cedonia, transferring it from a George Hilton to James Logan, notarized by E. B. Bernhardt of Republic, Washington. There was a notary seal, made not by Talcott Bros. Jewelers in Olympia, like most notary seals were, but by Spokane Stamp Works. There were two rubber stamps used to stamp the name of a payee on a check. There was a stamp used by railroad employees to date tickets and a canceling perforator. There was an advertising flyer for inks and a box that contained papers from a safety deposit box in Chicago. There were checks written by D. R. Shively a few days before he disappeared and a letter from James Heatherington addressed to Shively dated February 24, 1908. Jahns's valise contained a letter addressed to Agnes in care of Mrs. Margaret Ahrens in Spokane.

The unfolding details of the case were getting interesting for Sheriff Graham. He started to suspect that he might clear up more than one case with this arrest. Deputy Frank Coontz of Daisy picked up George Hilton and brought him to the Colville jail for questioning. Hilton admitted that he was Jahns's nephew. He said he came to Stevens County from Nebraska in the spring of 1908 after not seeing his uncle for twenty years. He acted surprised when the sheriff showed him the deed transferring Hilton's property to James Logan. He said he had not sold any of his land to Uncle Frank.

Frank? So James Logan wasn't his real name. He sent pictures of both Jahns and Hilton to police departments around the northwest to see if anyone recognized them. The pictures reached Sheriff DeHaven in Bellingham, who recognized both pictures. He told Graham that he knew the older man as Frank Romandorf and the younger man as his son Ed. Graham asked DeHaven to come to Davenport to identify the suspect.

Sheriff DeHaven and a Sheriff Williams positively identified Jahns as the man they knew as Frank Romandorf. DeHaven had once questioned him about some stolen cattle. Williams accused him of murdering the real James Logan and assuming his identity. Jahns denied it, but then stupidly he remarked, "I suppose when you start trailing me back and find out I was once in South Africa, you will accuse me of doing things like that down there, too." Unfortunately for Jahns, this statement merely heightened the suspicion surrounding him.

So Graham started asking around. Jahns's neighbors in Cedonia told Graham about how Jahns had bragged about the great fortune he made in South Africa but lost in Nebraska. On a whim, Graham sent Jahns's photos to the South African police, who replied that the picture was of William Frederick Jahns, a man suspected of killing eight men in diamond heists. They had traced him as far as New Orleans before losing his trail. Now Graham finally knew the real name of his suspect.

While the state was building its case against Jahns, hundreds of curiosity seekers visited the jail, hoping to catch a glimpse of the murderer. Jahns mostly kept to himself and huddled in a corner to avoid being gawked at. When the official court photographer came to take his picture, a hundred men gathered around to see what the criminal looked like. What they saw did not seem to be very threatening. Jahns was about fifty-five years old, with a sallow complexion, thin face, and broad features. He had gray eyes, gray hair and mustache, and weighed about 130 pounds. He still spoke with a strong German accent.

Graham managed to track down Jahns's family in Seattle. His wife, Margaret, and daughter, Bessie, both lived there. Margaret admitted to being married to a man named Frank Romandorf and that the man known as George Hilton was their son Ed Romandorf. She said they had been married in Pennsylvania, then moved to Nebraska and on to Washington. Evidently, she did not know her husband's real name or that he had been arrested. The last time she had seen Jahns was in August, when she and her daughter visited his Stevens County ranch.

Jahns's trial for the murder of Agnes Jansen began on January 4, 1910. The case caused quite a sensation. Every hotel room in Colville was booked with those who were attending the trial. The courtroom was packed every day, and a large number of the spectators were women. Judge Carey had to warn them frequently about keeping the "screaming babies" from making noise or they would have to leave. He also told them to remove their hats so that everyone could see. High school kids skipped school to attend the trial. Judge Carey warned them about giggling in the courtroom. Later he instructed his bailiffs to prevent any school-age children from entering the courtroom at all. Everyone was eager to get a glimpse of the infamous murderer.

A man named Kirkpatrick tried the case for the state. It took several days and 150 candidates before an impartial jury was finally selected. Because some people believed that Jansen was still alive somewhere, the prosecution first showed evidence that proved she was dead. Human bones, a brooch, a gold crucifix, and some corset stays found in the fire were introduced to show that a human being had been burned in the fire and that the evidence clearly proved it was Jansen. Graham testified to finding the bullets that were the same caliber as a revolver found in Jahns's possession. The Giffords also told about the items they had found in the fire.

Others testified to Jahns's actions during the time immediately before and after the murder. Tennessee Jack Tisth verified that Jansen was indeed living at the ranch as a housekeeper and was still there on the night of October 27. George Hilton, aka Ed Romandorf, admitted that he helped Jahns get the wagon ready for the trip to Blue Creek. He noted that Jahns and Jansen left about midnight on October 27. At the time, he said, he noticed that the wagon turned the opposite direction from that normally taken to reach Blue Creek. Swede Johnson testified to seeing Jahns at the Hergesheimer farm during the early morning hours, and M. D. Taylor said he had seen him there around seven o'clock in the morning. Al Stayt testified that he had seen Jahns both on the road in the early hours of the morning and later at the Cline place.

Coroner Cook testified to finding human remains on the Hergesheimer property. He identified human vertebrae and teeth. Several other experts were brought in to identify the bones and teeth as belonging to a human and not an animal.

Several friends of Jansen's testified regarding the jewelry that they knew she wore. Mrs. Ahrens recalled the dental work that Jansen had had and mentioned that Jahns had visited her and taken Jansen's mail. J. K. Lehman told about how he had translated the letter for a man named Logan.

With the overwhelming evidence that provided method, motive, and opportunity for Jahns to kill Agnes Jansen, his various land schemes hardly needed mentioning. All the various seals and stamps and inks used to produce fake documents found in his possession were not brought out at trial. The one exception was the notarized deed, transferring the Baslington ranch from Hilton to James Logan. Mr. Howell from Olympia came to identify the notary seal used on the deed. He stated that his office was responsible for certifying all notaries and that there was no one named E. B. Bernhardt certified in Washington. The defense objected to this testimony, saying it was irrelevant. But the prosecution argued it was necessary to show the extreme measures Jahns took to acquire something that didn't belong to him.

By the time the defense took the stand, the outcome of the trial looked bleak for Jahns. At first his lawyers had decided against an insanity defense. They believed that Jahns was completely sane and evil. But as they neared the end of the trial, they changed their minds after talking with their client. The day before the defense was to present its case, Jahns spilled the beans. He claimed that people were constantly following him and waiting for their chance to kill him. He only killed them first to protect himself. He said he had run away from Germany to avoid being conscripted into the German army. He ran to South Africa, where he killed eight men and stole eighty-five thousand dollars worth of diamonds. He later lost the money in a business deal in Nebraska. He admitted to using the name Frank Romandorf most of the time he was in America.

He went on to tell about the people he had killed since coming to America. He admitted to killing Agnes Jansen and burning her in the fire. He also told them he had killed James Logan and disposed of his body in a culvert near his house. He admitted killing D. R. Shively by poisoning his drink and murdering Fred Helms and Jack Green in Maple Falls. They each had property that he wanted, he said. He stated that he had killed many other people in many other countries from Canada to Africa.

The defense figured their case was hopeless, but they did what they could. Most of the witnesses they called were questioned about Jahns's state of mind in an attempt to show that Jahns was unstable. They wanted to establish that Jahns was "non compos mentis," meaning he was not responsible for his actions. The most convincing evidence to this fact was the way Jahns acted in the courtroom. Sometimes he would babble incoherently; other times he would shout out loud.

The state recalled three witnesses to say that they had never seen any strange behavior from Jahns. I. A. Keith, who lived in Addy and had known Jahns since he lived in Nebraska, said he had never known Jahns to exhibit unusual behavior. Sheriff Graham and Jailer Lynch agreed with Keith's assessment.

After only an hour of deliberation, the jury pronounced Jahns guilty. In that hour, the jury members had voted twice. The first vote was ten to two for conviction. The second vote was unanimous. Jahns did not seem particularly surprised or upset about the verdict. When he was returned to his jail cell, other inmates asked him how the trial had gone. He told them he had been found guilty. He was taken to the Walla Walla State Prison and hanged as scheduled on April 21, 1911.

HARRY TRACY

He Wouldn't Be Taken Alive

At seven o'clock on the morning of June 9, 1902, several dozen prisoners shuffled out of their cell block on their way to the prison foundry where they worked eight hours every day making iron stoves. As far as the prison guards could tell, this day was just another ordinary day at work. The guards lined up the prisoners to be counted, but before they could finish the task, one prisoner, Harry Tracy, suddenly grabbed a hidden gun. Tracy started shooting, killing guard Frank B. Ferrell. Tracy's partner, Dave Merrill, grabbed another hidden weapon. When inmate Frank Ingram tried to stop him from using it, Merrill shot and wounded Ingram in the stomach. The rest of the inmates ducked down to get out of the way of the two felons. Rather than risk getting shot, two other guards, Frank Girard and John Stapleton, fled the foundry.

Tracy and Merrill ran out of the foundry, carrying ammunition and a rope ladder and firing at anyone who came near them. They ran for the prison wall and threw the rope ladder up over it. Several guards in the vicinity shot at them, but none of the shots met their mark. The escapees scrambled up and over the wall, still firing their weapons. Just before he went over the wall, Tracy shot and killed guard S. R. T. Jones, one of those who patrolled the wall.

But Tracy and Merrill weren't free yet. Two guards jumped over the wall after them. Tracy, however, seemed to have anticipated this action and quickly had them under his control. He used them to shield himself and Merrill from anyone who might try to shoot at them from the prison wall. Tracy and Merrill dragged the guards as far as Mill Creek, where B. F. Tiffany was either killed by Tracy or by a stray shot from another guard, and Duncan Ross was released unharmed. Tracy and Merrill had escaped.

The Salem, Oregon, prison was a long way from Harry Tracy's hometown. He was born in about 1874 in Wood County, Wisconsin. His given name was Harry Severns. It is hard to imagine where he went wrong. He had had adequate role models in his childhood. His father was in the lumber business, and his grandfather served in the Civil War and held several government posts, including justice of the peace. His family and friends considered him good-hearted and intelligent. In fact, it was his brother Ervie who was known as the troublemaker of the family.

As a teenager, Tracy worked as a cook at a logging camp owned by his friend John Goodwin. During one of his logging jobs, he worked for a man named Mike Tracy, and it is believed that Tracy adopted his new last name from that association.

Tracy's first brush with the law was probably during a wheat harvest in Fargo, North Dakota. He was twenty years old when he and some friends stole some money from another worker to go out for a night on the town. When the man discovered the theft, he called the local sheriff. A shoot-out ensued, but Tracy escaped. He headed west, on the run from the law.

Tracy made his first appearance in Washington State in 1895. He took a job as a logger at Loon Lake, about 40 miles north of Spokane. He worked there for about a year, still hiding out from the law. For some reason, he went back to Provo, Utah. Evidently he didn't learn anything from his previous experience, for in no time at all, he was arrested for robbing a residence. He was convicted and sentenced to one year in jail. Not long after he started serving his time, a man named David Lant was also arrested and jailed for robbery. Tracy, Lant, and two others immediately starting planning an escape. On October 8, 1897, the four men were part of a ten-man chain gang digging ditches outside of Salt Lake City. Tracy led the escape by getting the drop on a guard named John Van Streeter with a carved gun covered with tinfoil.

The four men fled east, where they commandeered a horse and buggy from a man named H. A. Stearns. Tracy and Lant went on to Vernal, Utah, where they began a new career rustling horses. They soon moved north to Brown's Hole on the Wyoming-Utah-Colorado border, which was a haven for outlaws at the time.

When a posse came around scouting for rustlers, Tracy and Lant fled with a man named Pat Johnson. The posse chased them to Douglas Mountain, where they took up a defensive position. Tracy warned the posse not to come after them as Valentine Hoy, Pat Johnson's boss, cautiously approached their hideout. He might not have been interested in Tracy and Lant, but he certainly wanted to talk to his employee, who was wanted for murder in another state. Tracy decided to show the posse he meant business, so he shot and killed Hoy. In the confusion, the outlaws escaped again. But not for long.

The next day, the posse caught up with them. Johnson received a one-way ticket to Wyoming to stand trial there for murder. Tracy and Lant were locked up in the Routt County, Colorado, jail, but they overpowered the sheriff and escaped. Only a day later, the sheriff captured them and transported them to the Pitkin County jail at Aspen, a more substantial building than that in Routt County. But they managed to break out of that, too. Using an old trick, Tracy whittled a gun out of soap and covered it with tinfoil. After that David Lant disappeared, ending his association with Harry Tracy.

Tracy was on his own again. He fled back to Washington State, where he began a new crime spree in Seattle. He robbed streetcar conductors and bartenders to survive. He robbed guests of several hotels, especially those who he determined were well off. He kept just ahead of the law as he gradually worked his way south. Eventually he arrived in Portland, Oregon. While there, he met Dave Merrill, a small-time crook. The two men teamed up, pulling many daring daylight robberies in the Portland area. They stole cash and a watch from a streetcar conductor and postage stamps from a drugstore, and they robbed butchers, saloons, and a grocery store. They spent their booty freely at night, wining and dining the ladies and gambling.

Finally the police received an anonymous tip that led them to the robbers' hideout. Detective Cordano and four others staked out the house until Tracy and Merrill showed up. Merrill arrived first, and they captured him with little trouble on February 5, 1899. The lawmen laid in wait for Tracy's arrival. Detective Weiner waited inside the house, pretending to be a friend of the Merrill family.

When Tracy arrived, Weiner kept up the role, engaging Tracy in casual conversion. So that there were no accidental deaths, Weiner suggested that he and Tracy take a walk down the block. Tracy agreed but grew suspicious as they walked farther away from the house. He jumped on a nearby train and tried to force the engineer to speed away. The engineer had seen that Tracy had jumped the train, however, so he slowed the train to a stop. Tracy jumped off and tried to run, shooting all the way. Returned fire by Albert Way, whose father had been robbed by Tracy, grazed Tracy's head. The wound slowed him down enough to be captured.

At the time of his arrest, Tracy was described as 5 feet, 10 inches tall and 160 pounds, with gray eyes, light hair, and a mustache. He had a vaccine mark on his left arm and a bullet scar on his left leg. Merrill was described as 5 feet, 11 inches tall, with blue eyes, fair hair, and a mustache. He had four missing teeth and two vaccine marks on his left arm. The two went on trial without delay, and both men were convicted of assault and robbery. Merrill received a thirteen-year sentence, while Tracy received twenty years because of his earlier jailbreaks. They were sent to the Salem prison on March 22, 1899.

Since Tracy and Merrill were tried together and were partners in crime, it seems incredible that prison officials would house them in the same cell. Yet they did. Three years would pass before they could take advantage of the right set of circumstances to escape.

Someone, possibly an ex-con named Harry Wright, smuggled guns and ammunition into the prison. Supposedly, Tracy convinced Wright, who was about to be released, to acquire the weapons for him and drop them over the prison wall. From there, someone inside the wall hid the guns and ammunition in the molding room of the prison foundry.

After Tracy and Merrill escaped from the Salem prison, they fled into the surrounding countryside. They forced a farmer named J. W. Roberts to give them some clothes so they would no longer stand out in their prison stripes. A short way down the road, they stole some horses from a barn owned by Felix Lebranch, then rode all night long. The next morning they stole a horse and buggy from Dr. P. S. White and Edward Bupease of Gervais. They headed north, toward Washington.

They were nearly recaptured in the woods near Gervais. Posses and the Oregon State National Guard were on one side and dog handlers with bloodhounds from the Washington State Penitentiary were on the other. Somehow Tracy and Merrill managed to sneak through during a moment of inattention by the posses. They arrived at the home of woodcutter August King. Tracy ordered him to fix them breakfast. King reported their appearance to local authorities as soon as they left, but they were long gone by the time the sheriff could get there. They were also seen at Needy, New Era, and Oregon City, demanding food or clothing.

When they reached the Columbia River, they had to find a way to get across. They had no money, so Tracy forced three men to row them across the river. Once on the other side, the two outlaws had a brief disagreement about which way to go next. Tracy wanted to go northeast to the Yakima country. Merrill favored going northwest to the Olympic peninsula. They ended up going straight north.

The first Washington victim of their crime spree was Mrs. Jones, whom they forced to fix them a meal. They then moved on to the home of Henry Tiede, where they helped themselves to clothes and more food before tying up Tiede and leaving. Tiede got loose quickly, however, and alerted Clark County Sheriff Marsh.

Up the road near the Salmon Creek bridge, the two desperadoes engaged in a shoot-out with hunters named Bert Biesecker and Luther Davidson. The four men spotted each other about the same time and started firing. Several shots were exchanged, and then all went quiet. The two hunters couldn't see anything and wondered if they had hit the outlaws. They waited about a half-hour, then decided to return home. Just as they boarded their buggy, shots rang out again. Their horse was hit by two bullets, and Biesecker was wounded in the arm. The horse reared up and ran at full gallop all the way to Vancouver. A team of bloodhounds came out to this scene and tracked the outlaws' scent to LaCenter, where the outlaws had stolen two horses. There the country became very rough, so the posse retreated to Vancouver.

Meanwhile, the outlaws escaped north across the Lewis River and headed east of Kelso, where they found a secluded chalet. They hid out there for a week in the absence of the owner before stealing two horses and continuing.

When they reached Napavine, Tracy decided he'd had enough of Merrill. Later stories suggest that Tracy had read newspaper accounts of their exploits that gave Merrill equal credit and in fact said that Merrill was the mastermind in their exploits. Tracy felt he was really the brains behind the duo and didn't like Merrill getting any credit. He thought Merrill was a coward, always wanting to stay hidden and preferring to go hungry rather than force a meal. The two agreed to a duel, but Tracy spun around early, figuring he couldn't trust Merrill to count to ten. He was correct; Merrill was already getting ready to fire. But Tracy fired first and hit Merrill three times. Tracy dragged Merrill's body out of sight and fled.

Merrill's body wasn't found until July 14, when Mary Waggoner and her son George were out picking blackberries near the Reform School of Chehalis. Mary immediately notified Sheriff Deggeller, who conducted the investigation. He called Dan Merrill, Dave Merrill's brother, who worked at a livery stable in Chehalis, to identify the body. Though it had been some years since they had seen each other, Dan Merrill was fairly certain it was his brother.

Tracy was next seen at Bucoda, about 15 miles south of Olympia, where he forced Ed Sanford to feed him breakfast. After that, Tracy appeared at South Bay near Olympia. On July 2, he walked into the Capital City Oyster Company and demanded that the manager, Horatio Alling, fix him a meal. Then he forced Captain A. J. Clark and his son Edwin to sail him across Puget Sound to Seattle in one of the company's gas-powered launches.

While sailing across Puget Sound, Tracy told Clark and the other deckhands how he had just killed his partner Merrill. He explained how the two had agreed to fight a duel. His stories kept the deckhands subdued; they made no attempt whatsoever to capture him. In fact, after Tracy left the boat, the deckhands told a story of a polite and gentlemanly encounter with Tracy.

Though he didn't outwardly show it, Captain Clark's nervousness caused him to drive the launch so fast that the engine overheated. Twice he had to shut it down. This was just fine with Tracy because he wanted to reach Seattle after dark. Clark reached the Seattle harbor about six o'clock at night, but Tracy felt it was still too light out. He directed Clark to sail north and set anchor at Meadow Point, 2 miles north of Ballard. About half past six, he tied up the captain and his crew and forced deckhand Frank Scott to row him to shore. Just as soon as Tracy was out of sight, Clark freed himself and alerted the police.

Tracy's next victims were two deputies. Cornered by a posse of five men led by Deputy Sheriff Raymond, Tracy shot his way out of it. Near Bothell, the posse had followed footprints by some railroad tracks, leading them straight to Tracy. Tracy fired the deadly shots from behind a large stump. Raymond and Deputy John Williams lay dead. He also injured a reporter named Anderson. Tracy fled the scene, then stole a horse and buggy nearby. He forced the owner, Louis Johnson, to come with him.

Tracy held a gun on Johnson while he drove the buggy past Green Lake to the home of Mrs. R. H. Van Horn near Woodland Park. He forced Johnson inside the house and then made Mrs. Van Horn make him a meal. A neighbor named Butterfield was also in the house. While Tracy was there, a boy delivered some groceries. Mrs. Van Horn whispered to the boy that she was being held captive by an outlaw. The boy fled the house and alerted the authorities. Instead of sending a large posse after Tracy, King County Sheriff Cudihee took only two men to ambush the house. Unknown to Cudihee, Officer Frank Breece and Game Warden Neil Rawley waited for Tracy, too. A few minutes later Tracy emerged from the house with Johnson and Butterfield. Cudihee held his fire for fear of missing Tracy and hitting one of the other men. Rawley showed no such restraint. He demanded Tracy surrender. For his efforts, he and Breece were shot and killed by Tracy. Cudihee shot at Tracy as he ran, but he was wide of the mark. Once again, Tracy escaped.

Tracy next appeared at the home of August Fisher in Maple Leaf. He forced Mrs. Fisher to make him breakfast and some sandwiches to take with him. Then he took a full set of clothes and a hat and shoes. As he left he warned Mr. Fisher not to tell anyone for forty-eight hours.

Tracy headed back to Puget Sound, where he forced a Japanese fisherman to sail him to Bainbridge Island. He arrived at the home of the Johnson family and made Mrs. Johnson fix him a meal. Tracy also stole some clothes belonging to the hired man, John Anderson, as well as other items, including flour, ham, sugar, a frying pan, matches, and blankets. He tied up the family before leaving, then he forced Anderson to row him back across Puget Sound to West Seattle. Tracy dragged Anderson along with him for four days, forcing him to carry his belongings and to cook for him.

Near Renton they met May Baker, Mrs. James McKinney, and Charles Gerrells, who were out picking berries. He forced them to lead him to Gerrells's home a few yards away. He made Charles go into town to purchase two revolvers for him, warning him not to tell anyone or he would shoot his family. He forced Mrs. Gerrells to fix a meal for him, and he tied up Anderson so that he could not try to disarm him while he ate. Meanwhile, Charles Gerrells ignored Tracy's warning and went straight to the police.

A man came to the Gerrells' door and asked if Tracy was there. Miss Baker and Mrs. Gerrells both denied he was while Tracy waited in the kitchen, his gun aimed at the front door. The man seemingly gave up and left. Over the next two hours, crowds of lawmen surrounded the house. Tracy snuck out the back door and down a small slope toward the Cedar River. He crawled on his stomach through some tall weeds. Despite being surrounded by deputies, Tracy was able to sneak away without firing a shot. In the dark, the lawmen and the newsmen may have thought Tracy was one of them.

From about July 15 to July 30, Tracy's exact whereabouts were unknown. He was supposedly spotted in Kent, Auburn, Enumclaw, Ravensdale, and some other small towns. Police kept boats patrolling up and down the Sound ready for the next sighting. A new team of bloodhounds was brought in to sniff out the outlaw's trail. Somewhere near Covington, he was wounded by a posse, but he disappeared into a swamp. He was supposedly spotted near Black Diamond, Roslyn, and then Ellensburg. By then Tracy's exploits were being glamorized in Seattle theaters, where actors played Tracy, Merrill, Sheriff Cudihee, and various other people with whom the outlaws had come in contact.

On July 30, Tracy showed up in Wenatchee, arriving at the home of Sam McEldowney, a man Tracy had known in Portland. He forced Mrs. McEldowney to fix him lunch and dinner, and he made Sam steal some horses from his neighbor so that Tracy could ride on. Then he rode 12 miles south of town where he forced the Mottler brothers to take him across the Columbia River in their ferry. He followed Moses Coulee north, heading for Coulee City. From there, he rode east to Almira, where he camped in some caves along Wilson Creek. He stopped at the Stirrett Ranch and asked for directions to Davenport.

While traveling through the sagebrush desert, he ran across a young man named George Goldfinch. He held the young man at gunpoint, demanding that Goldfinch lead him to the nearest farm where he could hide out for a while. On August 3, Goldfinch led him to the ranch owned by brothers Eugene and Lucius Eddy, near Creston, Washington.

When he arrived, Tracy forced the Eddys to unsaddle and feed his horses, and he later made them reshoe his horses and cut hay for them and repair his holster. Curiously, Tracy also helped them by repairing their roof. He made one of the brothers sleep with him in the haystack. After a day or two, he released George Goldfinch, believing that he would not tell the law where he was. Goldfinch returned to the Blenz farm where he worked and telegraphed Sheriff Jerry H. Gardner of Davenport.

Lawyer Maurice Smith overheard the call. He was not about to wait until the sheriff came from Davenport. He alerted Constable C. C. Straub, who immediately formed a posse that included Smith; Dr. E. C. Lanter; J. J. Morrison, a railroad section foreman; and Frank Lillengren, a hardware store owner.

On August 5, Constable Straub led seventeen men to the Eddy ranch. When they approached the ranch, they dismounted, leaving their horses out of sight and out of range of any gunplay. Then they crept up to a bluff overlooking the ranch to see if they could spot Tracy. Down below, Lucius Eddy was in a field mowing hay. Straub approached Eddy, asking him if he had seen Tracy. Eddy nervously replied that Tracy was there but told Straub not to let on that he was the law or else Tracy would kill him. Tracy spotted Straub and went to the barn for his gun. When he ran from the barn with his rifle, revolver, and ammo, the posse opened fire.

Tracy first ran to a haystack, then to a big rock in the middle of the field. Tracy held off the posse for a while but soon realized the sun shining on his rifle was giving away his position. He saw a rock nearby that would serve as a more strategic location so he darted out of his hiding spot. In that split second while he was unprotected, a bullet found him. He was struck in the leg and began bleeding profusely. He couldn't get up, so he tried to drag himself through the tall grass to reach shelter.

While crawling, he was hit again in the thigh. His strength was fading fast. He always swore he'd never be taken alive. So he made the only choice possible for him. About 10:30 p.m., he took out his revolver, put it to his head, and shot himself.

The posse kept firing for a while, fooled by the grain blowing in the wind. They had heard the single shot from the revolver and guessed what it might have meant, but they didn't want to take any chances with Harry Tracy. They waited and watched all night. At daybreak, Smith and Dr. Lanter cautiously approached the rock where Tracy had last been seen. By then, close to three hundred people had gathered at the Eddy ranch, including Sheriff Gardner and twenty-five men from Lincoln County, Sheriff Doust and twelve men from Spokane County, and King County Sheriff Cudihee. They had arrived too late to get in on the action. Harry Tracy was dead.

Sheriff Gardner arranged for the body to be taken to Davenport. Upon the arrival of the posse and the dead outlaw, the townspeople clamored to see the body and take a relic from it. By the time they were through, the body was naked. They took all his clothes and divided them up into little pieces. They took his weapons and ammunition and even cut pieces of his hair.

Tracy's body was shipped from Davenport to Seattle, and from there it was shipped south to the Salem penitentiary. Tracy was buried on the prison grounds next to his former partner Dave Merrill. Thus ended the life of a man who led the law on one of the most drawn-out chases ever.

JOHN TORNOW

"Wild Man of the Wynoochee"

Though he was carefully butchering a steer, John Tornow was listening closely to the forest around him. Suddenly, the quiet was interrupted by some noises in the dense underbrush. A shot rang out, followed by more noise. Tornow thought someone was firing at him. He quickly stood up and looked around. He saw shadows moving in the brush and fired at them. After he fired once, the first shadow dropped. He fired again, and though he hit his mark, the second shadow still stood. He fired one more time, and the shadow fell to the ground. Feeling confident that the men were no longer a threat to him, Tornow went to have a closer look. What he saw astonished him.

The two men he had just shot were his nephews, William and John Bauer. Though he was sorry about their deaths, his self-protective instinct kicked in. He knew the incident would make him a wanted man. He used a broken limb to dig shallow trenches in the soft, pine needle–covered earth and gently laid dirt and branches over the tops of the shallow graves. Then he disappeared from sight, leaving behind the half-butchered steer. He retreated even deeper into the backwoods of the Olympic peninsula.

How did Tornow come to this desperate situation? Perhaps it all started during his childhood. Fritz and Louisa Tornow moved to Washington State and bought a homestead on the upper Satsop River in about 1870. They would eventually have six children: Edward, Frederick, Albert, William, John, and Minnie. In 1890, when John was nine or ten years old, he contracted a severe case of black measles. His condition was precarious, but he pulled through. The doctor warned his parents that the high fevers might have caused permanent brain damage. They saw no immediate evidence of it, however.

Because she almost lost him, John's mother doted on him. This caused hard feelings among the other children, especially the youngest boy, Edward. He resented all the attention his older brother received. Their father went out of his way to teach the boy how to hunt and fish. He taught him survival skills and showed him how to track and how to hide his own tracks. Fritz Tornow hoped to help his son develop self-confidence and to become more comfortable around people. Unfortunately, the scheme did not work. John showed less and less inclination to spend time around people, preferring the woods. His best friend was his dog, Cougar.

He attended school for a short while and for the most part was a good student. But he was shy and did not associate with the other children very much. The other schoolchildren thought him odd because he spent so much time in the woods. He developed a lisp. Some made fun of him and called him names, which made him withdraw even more.

By the time he was twelve, he could hunt all his own food. He claimed he could understand birdcalls. He could also imitate many bird and animal calls. He could make clothes out of animal hides and burlap and make shoes from bark. Some accounts claim that he became so unmanageable that his parents sent him to a sanitarium. Modern researchers have been unable to uncover any evidence of this, however.

As he grew older, he couldn't stand to be in a crowd. He did not like to feel closed in. He would not go inside a store or other building unless it had a very high ceiling. Even then, he would do his business as quickly as he could. He was very bashful, but cheerful. He was often afraid that people were picking on him.

Tornow's sister Minnie married a man named Henry Bauer. Their two girls, Lizzie and Mary, were only a few years younger than John Tornow. Twins John and William were born when Tornow was twelve. Though they lived a few miles away from the Tornow homestead, Minnie continued to spend time at her parent's home, helping her mother with household chores and taking care of her younger brothers. Her husband did not like her spending so much time at the homestead because he was very jealous of Fritz Tornow. Fritz had a nicer home and more money than his son-in-law. The senior Tornow had been able to pay off all his debts by selling some of the timber on his property. He also had surplus crops that he could sell for a little extra spending money. After Fritz Tornow died in 1909, the Bauers' daughter Mary moved in with the Tornows to help her mother and grandmother. Henry Bauer became even more resentful.

While Minnie was busy trying to hold her marriage together and helping her mother with the chores, John Tornow moved to the woods to stay. He had reached his full height of over 6 feet and weighed over 200 pounds. Occasionally he would visit Minnie; he doted on his two nephews, passing on to them what he knew of the woods.

In early 1911, John visited the old homestead. While there, he found out that his brother Ed had shot his old hunting dog, claiming that it was too old to hunt any more. John was enraged. In revenge, he shot Ed's dog, Rex. He warned Ed never to come after him or to send anyone after him, or he would be sorry. Ed immediately went to Sheriff Mark Payette and swore out a warrant for his brother's arrest. He wanted his brother committed. The sheriff could find no basis for the arrest. But the incident didn't help John's reputation any.

He retreated again to the woods, where he built a series of lean-tos and shacks and used them for shelters while he was out trapping. He set his traps between the Wynoochee and Satsop Rivers. He stayed in the woods for months at a time, only occasionally coming to town to visit the family homestead or his sister's house. He sometimes brought game and traded it for some flour or salt.

Then came that fateful day in 1911. On September 3, the Bauer twins were out hunting for bear. A bear had recently killed one of their cows. Stories differ on whether Tornow shot the twins by accident or on purpose. Some accounts state that the incident took place in an area that had already been logged, so it should have been clear to Tornow exactly whom he was shooting at. Others say that the undergrowth was too dense for Tornow to have seen clearly who was there, but not dense enough that he couldn't hit what he was aiming at. Whatever the case, the twins died by his hand.

When the boys did not return that night, Minnie was worried. Henry Bauer went out to look for them. The next day he rode into Matlock and asked Payette to search for the missing twins. Deputies Colin McKenzie and Carl Schwartz led a posse to the homestead. With them were Ed Maas and his bloodhounds to aid in the search. Unfortunately, rainfall the previous night had washed away most of the trail, so the dogs proved ineffectual.

The next day the deputies returned to the cabin to continue the search for the Bauer twins. The situation began to look promising when the dogs picked up the scent of a bear. Since the Bauers had gone out to hunt bear, the officers thought it a good idea to follow the trail. Perhaps the Bauer boys would be at the other end of it, too busy butchering a bear to notice the time. The bear had been wounded so it shouldn't be too far away.

Deputy McKenzie had paused for a rest when he noticed a pile of tree limbs. It looked unnatural to him. Loggers didn't leave limbs in piles; they scattered them all around. He pushed the limbs aside and started digging. Almost immediately he knew he'd found the missing boys. William had been shot once in the heart. John had been hit twice, once in the shoulder and once in the stomach. Two empty cartridges were found nearby. So was the steer that Tornow had been butchering. A short distance away was a small shelter that Tornow had probably used. McKenzie left the bodies where he found them and returned to town to get the sheriff and the coroner, R. F. Hunter.

At first the attention did not focus on John Tornow, though he was a suspect. Some thought Tornow's brother Ed might try to get him into trouble because of his intense jealousy of John. The fact that Ed had tried to have his brother committed added to the suspicion. Ed had also been in some trouble with Henry Bauer when Bauer's daughter Mary had become pregnant out of wedlock. Ed took her to Aberdeen to have the baby, hoping to keep the secret from her father. Unfortunately, she died after an attempted abortion. Henry blamed Ed for the death, and he may have been justified. If Ed resented being blamed, he could have killed the twins to get back at Henry.

Another likely suspect was Henry himself. It was possible that he suspected the twins were not his biological sons. One of the times that Minnie had visited her father's house, a man had been visiting there, and she had struck up a conversation with him. While waiting for her father to return, the two had gone into the forest to pick berries. As a result, there was always speculation about whether she had been intimate with the man. If so, perhaps Henry could no longer tolerate the sight of her infidelity.

There was also the matter of the Tornow property. Upon his father's death, John Tornow had inherited seventeen hundred dollars as well as the land. Perhaps Bauer killed the boys deliberately to throw suspicion on Tornow. Perhaps Tornow could be taken out of the picture so that Minnie somehow would end up with the property.

Not long after the death of the Bauer twins, Henry Bauer disappeared and was never seen again. That left only John Tornow to be blamed for their deaths. The sheriff assembled a posse to hunt for him.

A week passed before anyone found any sign of Tornow. Two lumbermen, Mike Scully and Carl McIntosh, were out camping when Tornow approached them. They told him that he was the chief suspect in the Bauer twins' murder. He denied it flatly, saying that he had too much love and respect for them. He told them to tell everyone what he said and that they should leave him alone.

Unfortunately, the law had by then decided that Tornow was to blame. They no longer tried to investigate anyone else. Some townspeople doubted that Tornow had killed the boys, and others felt that if he had killed them, it was surely an accident.

McKenzie continued to search along the Wynoochee for signs of Tornow's whereabouts. Deputy Schwartz searched the Deckersville area. Occasionally they found caches of food or a smoldering campfire. But by the end of the year, no one had seen Tornow or a place where he could be living. Other stories circulated regarding Tornow's whereabouts. One lead said that he had been seen on Mount Olympus. As unlikely as that seemed, some deputies climbed 7,000 feet before heavy snow turned them back. Another search party combed the west side of the Humptulips River. Yet another team searched around Quinault Lake. Four trappers on the Wishkah River claimed Tornow had burned down their shack. A hunter said a man woke him up at midnight demanding salt and pepper. Some men who worked for the Simpson Logging Company said they had seen him several times. Others claimed they saw him haunting saloons at Montesano.

But try as he might, the sheriff could not find Tornow. The sheriff finally called off the search until the weather improved. That winter was very severe, and some thought that the exposure would kill Tornow. But Tornow was used to surviving in the woods. He spent part of that winter in a schoolhouse, beneath the flooring of the schoolroom. He removed two loose boards from the floor so he could easily come and go. He also took shelter in a huge, dead cedar that fishermen called "the big tree on the Satsop." At least 10 feet in diameter, it was hollow near the ground.

But Tornow knew the law would be out after him again in the spring, so he killed a large elk and dressed it out to last him for several weeks. He built a camouflaged lean-to by two downed tree trunks up next to a hillside. The root balls blocked the view of his shelter.

In late February 1912, trappers Louis Blair and Frank Getty came across the remains of the elk Tornow had butchered near the Mason County line. The way it was carefully butchered to get the most meat off of it led them to believe that the kill belonged to Tornow. They reported what they found to Sheriff Payette.

Payette sent McKenzie and a game warden named Al Elmer to look for Tornow, telling them not to try to catch Tornow, but to just see if they could find him. All through the day, McKenzie and Elmer felt as if they were being watched. If Tornow was out there, they wished he would show himself. But after a day of searching they found nothing. They spent the night in an old trapper's cabin. The next day they followed an elk trail. At the end of the trail, they found a half-butchered elk carcass. Human footprints led away from it toward a ridge.

Elmer got excited, thinking they were on the verge of catching up with Tornow. He was ready to go back and lead the posse to that location. But McKenzie insisted on looking for further proof. He would soon wish he hadn't. A few minutes later they were crawling under a fallen log too big to crawl over. Just on the other side was Tornow's hideout. As soon as Tornow had a good shot, he fired. He killed Elmer with the first shot. McKenzie tried to dodge behind cover, but it was too late. Tornow shot him twice, killing him.

If Tornow wasn't guilty of murder before, he was definitely guilty now. He had enough of his wits about him to know he had to get rid of the evidence fast. He quickly stripped the bodies of their clothes and shoes to replace his own ragged clothing. He took their guns and ammunition and the biscuits they were carrying in their knapsack. He dragged them to a spot about 15 feet from where they fell. Then he buried the bodies in a shallow grave on the hillside. Their bodies were placed in the shape of a letter "T."

Payette became concerned when he did not hear anything from McKenzie and Elmer. He sent a posse led by Deputy A. L. Fitzgerald, Blair, and Deputy Charles Lathrop to look for the men. They found the elk carcass and the tracks that led away from it. Fitzgerald came upon Tornow's abandoned camp near the headwaters of the Wynoochee. They searched the camp and found some empty shell casings that were the same kind as those found by the Bauer boys' bodies.

They also found some smoked meat and flour and some remnants of the Bauers' clothing. A few minutes later, they stumbled across the buried bodies of McKenzie and Elmer. Both were shot through the heart.

The posse went back to town to fetch the sheriff and coroner. The officials and some others arrived the next day and transported the two bodies back to town. The county commissioners finally decided that it was worth posting a five thousand–dollar reward for the capture of Tornow. Previously they had refused to post a reward on the grounds that there was no proof he had killed the Bauer twins. But there seemed to be no doubt that he had killed the deputy and the game warden.

Immediate searches proved fruitless, but then Tornow was seen on the county road about 200 yards from his old home near Satsop. He stood there just long enough for some young men in a car to get a good look at him. As soon as Tornow saw the car, he disappeared into the brush.

Francis Gleason and four other young men said that Tornow looked haggard. His dark hair was tangled, and he wore a bushy beard. He was wearing a well-worn canvas hunting coat, possibly the one Elmer was wearing when he went after Tornow. He did not appear to be carrying a gun. When Gleason told his father about what he saw, the elder Gleason was sure it was Tornow. He used to hunt and fish with Tornow, so he knew him well.

But the sighting led to nothing but more reported sightings. People let their imaginations get the best of them as they reported Tornow sightings all over the Olympic Peninsula. His story was written up in newspapers across the country, where he was given such monikers as "wild man" and "cougar man." Sightings were reported as far away as Port Angeles. One day he was reportedly seen at Pacific Beach, the next at Olympia, the next at Elma. Someone even claimed they saw him at Clallam Bay, but someone else claimed he was in jail in Chehalis the same day. Supposedly someone broke into a building at Simpson Logging Camp No. 5 and stole boots. Soon every incident of a missing person was blamed on Tornow, without any evidence whatsoever. The newspapers even tried to pin the disappearance of two prospectors on Tornow. They had turned up missing sometime in 1910, before the death of the Bauer twins.

In actuality, Tornow had retreated deeper into the forest. He only came down from the hills occasionally to beg for food from homesteaders. Most gave it willingly because they were sympathetic.

In January 1913, Schelle Matthews was elected sheriff on the promise that he would bring in Tornow. On his first day in office Sheriff Matthews led a manhunt, hoping that footprints in the snow would lead him to Tornow. But he found nothing. It wasn't until April, when Matthews was riding the train home from Tacoma, that he got his first real break. A prospector from Hoquiam, named J. B. Lucas, told him some very interesting information. Tornow, he said, had most likely gone to live at Frog Lake. This had been one of Tornow's favorite hideouts as a kid, said Lucas.

Immediately upon his return to Matlock, Matthews sent Deputy Giles Quimby, his brother-in-law, to capture Tornow. Quimby had served in the Spanish-American War of 1898 and was known to be tough and clever. Deputy Charles Lathrop and trapper Louis Blair went with him. They took Lathrop's Airedale to help track down Tornow. Eventually the three men reached a cabin deep in the woods, and inside they found the old prospector who had said he had seen Tornow asleep. They spent the night at the cabin, hoping to catch up to Tornow the next day.

Quimby wanted to wait for the posse that Matthews was assembling back in Matlock. But Blair and Lathrop thought Tornow would get away. Against his better judgment, Quimby followed them into the woods. They hiked around a small lake, through a bog, and over a marsh full of horsetail plants. They circled the lake, keeping an eye on a lean-to on an island in the lake. They spotted some smoke coming out of it.

They thought Tornow might still be close by. And he was. What they didn't know was that Tornow had a built-in warning system on his little island. He had placed a log across the water so that he could walk across it from the island back to the mainland. Some frogs near the log normally croaked constantly. But whenever anyone came near, they stopped. Tornow had heard the sudden silence and had looked to see who caused it. As soon as he was behind cover, he began firing. He shot Blair first and killed him with the first round. Lathrop dove for cover then started firing in Tornow's direction. They exchanged a few shots before Lathrop exposed himself just a little too much. He too soon fell victim Tornow's gun. Both men had been shot in the forehead.

Quimby kept firing until he was sure he had shot Tornow. He quickly reloaded, then listened. The only sound was the chirping of birds. Perhaps he had hit Tornow, but he wasn't sticking around to find out. He crawled a hundred yards or so, staying out of sight. When he thought he was out of range, he ran for Simpson Logging Camp No. 5, about 4 miles away. Matthews was there with the gathering posse.

The next day Matthews led two dozen men back to the lake. Quimby showed them the way. After searching the small island, they found the bodies of Blair and Lathrop. Then they found the body of the outlaw. Tornow was, in fact, dead. The "Wild Man of the Wynoochee" was no more. Quimby's bullet had hit him just above the breastbone and had lodged in his right shoulder.

His body was covered with several layers of ragged clothes and the good boots he stole from one of his victims. He was wearing six shirts and five pairs of pants. The posse members also searched his campsite, where they found a few silver coins, some tools, some gunnysacks, and plenty of matches. They also found McKenzie's watch. There was no food anywhere.

The body was taken back to Montesano and put on public display. Tornow was later buried at Satsop next to his parents and his nephews. Quimby collected the reward money.

In 1987, seventy-five years later, Tornow garnered sympathy from the townspeople. A marker was made for his grave in the family cemetery, 9.5 miles north of Highway 12, off the Brady–Matlock Road. The "Ballad of John Tornow" was sung at a special ceremony. The inscription on the gray granite monument reads: "From Loner to Outcast to Fugitive, John Tornow, Sept. 4, 1880–April 16, 1913."

FRANK LEROY

A Career Robber

The small towns in Okanogan country were the last outposts of civilization in rugged eastern Washington in the early 1900s. Mineral strikes brought flocks of miners to the area. As usual, the gold camps also attracted unsavory characters. One of them was Frank Leroy.

Leroy was a desperado who had committed a number of robberies in Washington. He started in the Puget Sound area and worked his way east. By the time anybody had connected the string of robberies to this lone operator, he had made his way to Brewster, in north-central Washington.

Early on the morning of November 4, 1909, Leroy broke into the A. C. Gillespie & Son store, blew up the safe there, and stole some knives. The next night he broke into the home of William Plemmons and stole a gun and a lady's gold watch and some other items. Plemmons followed some tracks around his house but found no one. A man driving the local stage saw a suspicious fellow following the road from Okanogan to Brewster, but the stranger ducked out of sight when the stage got close. The footprints Plemmons discovered led in the direction of the stage road, so everyone guessed that the person the stage driver saw was the same person who had robbed Plemmons.

For a few days the thief eluded the law. Unfortunately for him, he didn't go any farther than Conconully, a town about 30 miles from Brewster. The two towns were in the same county, and the county sheriff was on the lookout for the robber. Leroy checked into a hotel on November 6 and stayed for dinner. For some reason his black hair and auburn mustache attracted the attention of the hotel managers. As they watched him, they noticed that he was wearing a gun. They sent someone to alert the sheriff, Fred Thorp.

The following day Leroy hung around the local saloons, secretly looking for a business to rob. One possibility was the Commercial Bank. Its location right next to his hotel would make his getaway easy. But before he could make his next move, he was accosted by the sheriff. Leroy made up a story that he was there to work on the government dam that was being built at the time. Sheriff Thorp accepted his tale, but he and his deputy, Charles McLean, decided to keep an eye on Leroy.

The matter continued to bother Thorp, so he decided to talk to Leroy again. The next day, he found him in the Lute Morris Saloon. Though it was early in the day, an animated card game was already in progress. Thorp calmly told Leroy that he would have to accompany him to the sheriff's office so he could ask him some more questions. At first Leroy seemed to comply, but then he went for his gun.

Thorp and Leroy fired at each other at the same time. Somehow they both missed their targets, and their bullets harmed no one else in the barroom. Leroy ran around the saloon, making sure someone was between him and the sheriff's bullets at all times. As he headed for the back door, he felt a bullet graze his hand. The blow shocked him for a minute, and he dropped his gun. Before Thorp could take advantage of the moment, Leroy drew another gun from his pocket and headed out the door. As Leroy fled, Thorp shot him solidly in the upper back.

Leroy was now injured twice and was bleeding. He wasn't going to get far before the loss of blood began to affect him. He headed down Salmon Creek, but lurched only a few yards before he collapsed in some brush. He must have decided that small shelter would have to be a good enough hiding spot since that was as far as he could go.

Thorp and some other men went out after him. Evidently Leroy could see Thorp before Thorp could see him. Leroy was just about to shoot when Thorp discovered his hiding spot and kicked the gun out of his hand. Leroy fell to the side and passed out from pain.

Some men laid Leroy's body on a piece of wood that used to be a barn door and carried him to the hotel. Undertaker Leonard Bragg, some deputies, and two doctors were on hand to make sure Leroy didn't try to run again. The doctors noted that one of the bullets had gone clear through his shoulder and passed out his chest. As it passed through his body, the bullet punctured his lung. While the doctors looked at him, deputies searched Leroy's hotel room. They found two more guns, a set of burglary tools, some nitroglycerin, a lantern, fuse, wax, cotton batting, and a safecracker. They also found some of the items that had been stolen from the Gillespie store and Plemmons's home.

Dr. A. M. Polk declared that Leroy would live to stand trial. The deputies hauled him to the county jail just a short way down the road. With his injuries, they didn't figure he was going anywhere, so instead of putting him in a cell, they laid him on a cot in the corridor where there was more heat. The county did not have a regular jailer, so old Ed Braman, serving a few weeks' time for drunkenness, was assigned to look after Leroy. Braman was a "trusty," assigned to do odd jobs around the jailhouse. One of his tasks was to go to the Myers Hotel, where he picked up food for the jail inmates. Braman was locked up with Leroy at night.

Not long after his capture, Leroy stole Braman's pocketknife, broke the lock on the door to the corridor, and escaped the jail. As soon as he had the door open, he looked around for his clothes but couldn't find them. He stole Braman's shoes, an old brown coat, and a blanket, then he fled on foot. For some reason Braman woke up about four in the morning, discovered that Leroy was gone, and ran to the sheriff's house to alert him. The sheriff left his home immediately and headed for the jail.

Snow had fallen overnight, so Thorp hoped he might find footprints that would lead him to the outlaw. Unfortunately, all the footprints belonged to other citizens of the town. Thorp and McLean looked all over town trying to find Leroy. Thorp posted a one hundred–dollar reward for his capture. Some thought that Leroy must have had help because he was still so weak from his injuries. Some even suspected that Braman might have been in on it. In any event, most people felt he would not be at large for long because of his wounds, the cold, and his lack of familiarity with the countryside.

In the meantime, Leroy followed the main road most of the day, keeping a couple hundred yards out of sight. That night he slept in a barn at Okanogan at least 15 miles away from Conconully. With his injuries, it seemed impossible for Leroy to have traveled that far on foot. This fact later added to the suspicion that someone had helped him escape. He continued to follow the main road, occasionally making a fire for warmth. Casper Miller owned a cabin in that area, and Leroy helped himself to its contents. He took some underclothes, pants, some canned goods, crackers, a can opener, and a butcher knife. These tools and provisions helped him continue his flight even farther south. For three days and nights, he managed to stay out of sight of the law.

Thorp picked up his trail near the Maloney homestead. He followed the path through the Okanogan Valley until he found Leroy hiding in some sagebrush near the Malott schoolhouse, another 7 or 8 miles south of Okanogan. Thorp told him to surrender. Leroy was unarmed and did as he was told.

Thorp and McLean escorted the criminal to Okanogan, where they stayed for the night. In the morning they took Leroy to Conconully and locked him in a holding cell in the jail. The sheriff had been humane before, but that kindness had only caused him a lot of trouble. For the rest of his jail stay, Leroy spent his time in an uncomfortable, cold cell.

While waiting for Leroy's trial date, Thorp and prosecutor P. D. Smith investigated their unsavory tenant. It seemed he was a habitual criminal. Thorp compared the pictures of men named Charles Ray, Andrew Morgan, and Frank Leroy and saw that they were the same man. Only the most outrageous coincidence could account for all three men having a partially deformed right hand and a tattoo of a nude woman chained to a tree on the inside of their right forearm. Under the name Andrew Morgan, Leroy had been sent to prison in September 1899 for a burglary in Coupeville. He was released on December 18, 1900. He eluded the law until May 1903, when he served time for a burglary in Skagit County. He was using the name Charles Ray at the time. His stay was longer this time, just over six years. He had been released from the Walla Walla prison less than a month before he had burglarized the store and home in Brewster.

Leroy was arraigned on December 6. A court-appointed attorney represented him. He pled not guilty, and the trial was set for January 11, 1910. On January 4, Leroy's counsel resigned, and the court had to appoint a new lawyer. This attorney tried to get a continuance, stating that they had been unable to secure witnesses. But the court denied this motion, filed on January 6. The court ruled that Leroy had had ample time to secure his two witnesses, one in Clark County and the other at Spokane. The trial commenced on January 11, 1910, as originally scheduled.

Plemmons and the stage driver testified at the trial, putting Leroy in the vicinity of the burglary at the correct time. Another man testified to seeing a man of Leroy's description in Brewster the day before the store was robbed. A. C. Gillespie described the break-in of his store and produced the key that was taken from Leroy. This key unlocked the back door of the store, Gillespie said. He also identified the knives in Leroy's possession as coming from his store.

After an hour of deliberation, the jury found Leroy guilty of second-degree burglary. Since it was his third burglary conviction, Judge Taylor sentenced him to life in prison as a habitual criminal. Leroy appealed the decision to the state supreme court. Twisp attorney E. C. Jennings handled the appeal. His contention was that the court erred in the jury selection. Jurors had been selected in November for December. Because there were no cases to be heard in December, the same jurors were held over for the January trials. These jurors were the ones who heard Leroy's case. Leroy and Jennings claimed this fact prejudiced the case. The state supreme court disagreed with that argument and upheld the decision of the lower court. Two weeks later, Leroy was on his way to Walla Walla for the last time.

Leroy stayed in prison for nearly nine years. Part of that time he was sick with "inflammatory rheumatism" and could not work. Acting governor Louis Hart granted him a conditional parole, and he was released from prison on November 15, 1919. After that Leroy left the state. No one knows exactly what happened to him after that, but the Thorp family believes he died of tuberculosis.

JACK SLADE, GUNSLINGER

He Knew Mark Twain

"There was such magic in that name, SLADE!" wrote author Mark Twain in his book *Roughing It,* an autobiographical account of his visit to the West as a young man.

While traveling toward the Rocky Mountains, Twain had been hearing about a certain man named Jack Slade. He was said to be a gunslinger, a killer who was feared by all. The conductors talked about Slade on the train, and the stories only grew more outrageous after the rails ended and Twain continued on by stagecoach.

Soon, Twain was so mesmerized by these tales that he wanted to hear about nothing else. What a land the West must be to have men like Slade roaming loose across the countryside. Twain's fertile imagination could only speculate as to what this man must be like.

Nearing Julesburg, in present-day Colorado, the stage passengers were hungry after traveling all night. They looked forward to giving their knotted muscles a rest from the bumpy and uncomfortable ride, and when the stage rattled on to the next station, they poured into the little building. Mark Twain sat down to breakfast at a table with the other passengers. Some Central Overland Company stagecoach officers, who were already there, joined the group. Twain was seated next to the superintendent, who was at the head of the table. He was a gentlemanly and mannerly fellow who was dressed better than the rest.

As they made introductions around the table, Twain realized the unfathomable. The superintendent was Jack Slade! Twain would later write, "Here, right by my side, was the actual ogre who, in fights and brawls and various ways, had taken the lives of twenty-six human beings, or all men lied about him! I suppose I was the proudest stripling that ever traveled to see strange lands and wonderful people."

Twain was both awestruck and fear-filled at the same time. He was having trouble matching this man sitting next to him with the one about whom he had heard so much during his travels. Indeed, Slade was a complex character who had killed many men. He was employed by the Central Overland Company in the late 1850s to put an end to horse stealing at the Julesburg Station, but he clearly overstepped his calling on many occasions. Killing men, whether they deserved it or not, became a way of life. His eventual death by lynching would testify to his status as an outlaw. Yet many, like Twain, saw the side of Slade that was considerate and mannerly. His relationship with his wife Virginia, for instance, was a heartfelt union marked by deep caring and an abiding, gentle love—characteristics that were in sharp contrast to Slade's ever-developing reputation for violence.

Jack Slade was born on January 22, 1831 (some say it was 1829) just 40 miles east of St. Louis, Missouri, in Carlyle, Illinois. This small city was located near other rural towns including Aviston, Germantown, St. Jacob, and Pierron, all of which had been founded by immigrants who were pushing the edge of civilization ever westward. Young Slade would grow up in this atmosphere of adventurers moving west.

Part of the enigma surrounding Slade began in his childhood. He was the fourth of five children born to his parents, Charles Jr. and Mary Slade. Joseph Alfred Slade was his given name, but he was always called "Jack."

His father had founded the town of Carlyle in 1818, become its postmaster, and by 1832 was elected to the U.S. House of Representatives. Prior to this, he had been a U.S. Marshal and a member of the Illinois legislature.

Jack's parents had power, wealth, and an esteemed reputation. But in 1834, when Jack was just a small child, his father died of cholera, leaving Jack with an unfillable void and a lack of a role model to guide his life. His mother married Elias S. Dennis just two years later, but the few early accounts of Jack's young life suggest he was an unruly child, and his mother complained of her inability to control him.

Jack was bright, educated in scholarly curriculum and mannerly decorum, and lacked for nothing material. Accounts of his boyhood say he was "capable of getting strait As in school," but there were also reports of his gradual inclination toward bullying and becoming a problem student.

When he was thirteen years old, the recklessness of his later life would be foretold in one brutal event. Historical accounts vary and inevitably mix fiction with fact, but even in general terms this event was an ominous sign of things to come.

It was summer in Carlyle when Jack and two other boys escaped their chores and met up in the shady comfort along the banks of the Kaskaskia River. Jack's buddies were from poor families with little education and unpromising futures. Most townspeople thought young Jack's choice of friends was not in keeping with his family background. They had noticed that his actions and general demeanor seemed to "reek" of defiance.

On this day, a man emerged from the bushes along the bank. He was later identified as Mr. Gottlieb. Supposedly, he confronted the boys and threatened to disclose their participation in some illicit or ill-advised activity. It may have been for recent vandalism to his property, or possibly for catching them in the act of smoking as they sat there on the bank. Whatever it was, it was a challenge to the boys, and it incited anger in young Jack Slade.

While the boys argued with Mr. Gottlieb, Jack was said to have positioned himself behind the man. He picked up a large rock and proceeded to bash Gottlieb over the head with it. Jack was apparently so enraged that he kept on hitting the man, smashing in his skull until Gottlieb was dead.

The boys all ran to their respective homes. The sheriff was supposedly called. But the story's facts are murky at best. One account says Gottlieb was a stranger in the area, and the sheriff suggested that Jack and the other boys leave town. Another account suggests that Jack decided on his own to leave home, to avoid possible arrest. Still another scenario indicates that Jack's stepfather had relatives in Texas, and he sent Jack away to live with them.

Whatever actually happened, Slade's life was undocumented for the next few years. It was not until the spring of 1847 that he showed up, back in Illinois to enlist in the army. The Mexican-American War had begun, and Slade was anxious to be a part of it.

By then, at the age of sixteen (or he may have been eighteen), he had matured physically, but was always said to be of short stature. Some said he made up for it by being strong and muscular.

Although he served in the army for a year and a half, it became apparent during this time that he loved his liquor. Also, he disliked having to take orders from his superiors and often spent time in the stockade. Nevertheless, when the war ended in 1848, Slade was honorably discharged.

It is believed that he then headed for California, but by 1849 he had already returned to the Midwest. In Kansas City Slade found a job with the Central Overland Company, a freight transportation firm, as a teamster. He was a good fit for the rigors of driving horse-drawn wagon shipments of goods across the 600-mile prairie to Denver.

Slade distinguished himself in this new role. His soon-to-be-legendary exploits of killing and gore began with warding off Indians. This was a major part of survival when crossing the Great Plains. During his first two trips, it was said that he killed "a half-dozen Indians and several horse thieves" who attacked his caravan. The story says he cut off the ears of the Indians he killed and sent them back to the Indian chief as a warning. He was also responsible for capturing and hanging two "would-be armed robbers."

Slade was hailed as a hero and was soon promoted into management positions. He stepped up the ladder of success all the way to the level of superintendent, and was responsible for overseeing 500 miles of trail from Julesburg to the far southwestern corner of present-day Wyoming. This was the most remote area in which the company operated.

However, stories also began circulating about Slade's killings, which often seemed to be unnecessary and unprovoked. He was said to have killed one of his own drivers while in a fit of drunken derangement. He apparently goaded this friend into drawing his gun. When the man did, Slade shot him dead and was then deeply remorseful.

Another rumor suggested he had killed still another man with no reason other than cavalier disregard. Slade bet some companions that he could shoot the button on the man's shirt from some distance away. When he accurately shot the button, he also killed the man.

The law of the Colorado West was erratic, and the number of lawmen available—especially in such isolated areas—was minimal or nonexistent. Slade was not arrested or prosecuted for his acts. Few witnesses were willing to testify against him. Many feared him.

When Jack Slade became superintendent, he met the stationmaster of the Julesburg Station, a man named Jules Beni (sometimes spelled Reni). The settlement that had sprung up around the station was named for Beni, and he ran the place as if he owned it, causing Slade to dislike him immediately. However, at the time, Indians were Slade's bigger concern, so nothing immediately came of this personality conflict.

Around 1857 Slade met a woman named Maria Virginia. He may have met this woman he called Virginia in a dance hall, or she could have been a local widow. Whatever the case, he fell deeply in love with her and they would stay together the rest of his life. Virginia Slade said they were married, although no marriage record has ever been found.

Later that year, the Central Overland Company was having serious trouble with robberies around Julesburg. Horses and supplies were being stolen, and the newly added California and Pikes Peak Express Company was also being targeted. The robbers seemed to know when wealthy passengers were aboard. Covert information suggested it was an inside job and the most likely suspect was Beni.

The company asked Slade to look into the situation. Beni heard rumors almost immediately about why the superintendent had come to "his" town. Slade apparently was asking questions of local citizens and indiscriminately mentioning the stationmaster in connection with the robberies. Beni did not hesitate to react, and took his shotgun with him when he went to look for Slade.

Slade was leaving a local saloon when Beni walked up in front of him. Not a word was said as Beni aimed his shotgun point-blank at Slade and fired with both barrels. Slade was stunned and then fell to the ground with wounds in his chest and stomach. Beni deliberately took his time reloading his gun while the local citizens scattered to hide. He again took aim at Slade and fired two more times, hitting him in the back. Slade did not move. Beni reloaded again and shot

Slade one more time. Convinced he'd killed his enemy, Beni spat in the dirt and said, "Bury him!"

Slade, apparently a dead man, slowly lifted his head and said in a low voice, "I shall live long enough to wear one of your ears on my watch guard. You needn't trouble yourself about my burial."

Beni was surprised that Slade was still alive, but even more surprised that the outraged citizens of "his" town pulled their guns on him and arrested him. In a quick decision, the crowd resolved to lynch Beni on the spot.

Although a correct hanging knot is designed to snap the neck of the victim as he falls from a platform, this hastily tied knot didn't work that way. Strung up and hanging, the rope tight around his neck, Beni began to suffocate. He turned blue and then almost black. Suddenly he found himself dropped to the ground as his hanging rope was released. Beni gasped and choked and lay there wheezing. An official of the freight company had just arrived on the stagecoach and fired shots in the air, demanding that the lynch mob let Beni loose.

The official was Benjamin Ficklin, General Superintendent of the Central Overland California and Pikes Peak Express Company, and he threatened Beni while the scoundrel still lay on the ground. He said Beni could live only if he promised to leave the territory and never return. Beni readily agreed. He hastily ran for his horse and rode out of town.

Slade, meanwhile, was hauled over to the station where a doctor was summoned to examine him. The doctor didn't hold out much hope for Slade but worked to remove seven pellets of the dozens in his body, which came from the numerous pellets in each shotgun blast. When Slade continued to live through the night and all the next day, Ficklin ordered that the patient be transported to Omaha for better medical attention. Slade painfully endured the bumpy journey that, for lack of capable doctors, ultimately proceeded on to Kansas City and finally to St. Louis.

Slade had traveled 800 miles, and though wounded and very weak, he hung on to life. His injuries were so severe that he would be hospitalized for a full year. When he was finally released, the "prescription" given to him by his doctors was to retire.

Nine days later Jack Slade was back at work for his former company and was headed for Julesburg. His mission was to kill Jules Beni, just as he had sworn to do a year earlier.

Beni had never left the area, despite his promise to do so, and the company believed he was still robbing them. Slade was taking no chances this time, and he sent four men ahead with a bounty to capture Beni alive. They soon found Beni and held him for Slade, who arrived shortly thereafter.

Here the story has many versions, and it is impossible to know which is true. Beni may have been tied up to a post behind a stage relay station or at his own ranch. Some stories say Slade took his time and killed Beni one bullet at a time; other accounts say it happened quickly with Slade firing two bullets into Beni's head. The certainty is that Jules Beni died that day at the hand of Jack Slade. Beni's criminal reputation was so widely known that both the military at Fort Laramie and the stage company were glad Slade had taken care of the problem.

An additional part of the story, which is consistent in all the versions, tells that Slade cut off both of Beni's ears after he killed him. This is what Slade had promised when Beni shot him and left him to die over a year earlier. Now Slade made good on that oath. Many stories abound about how Slade carried the ears in his pocket for a long time afterward. Some say he actually did use one ear for his watch guard. He liked to display them often.

Slade remained as superintendent for the company and did a good job for them. Reports say that he made sure the mail got out on time and that all his operations were always on schedule. Slade hired drivers, security men, and stationmasters.

One applicant Slade took on was a young boy named William Cody, called Billy. In 1860 Billy was only fourteen years old, but he convinced Slade that he was a capable wagon-team driver and horseback rider. Slade's company had just embarked on a new venture called the Pony Express, and he hired young Billy, who remained an employee for about two years. Many years later Billy would be called by a new and more famous name: "Buffalo Bill."

But Jack Slade couldn't keep himself out of trouble when he was drunk, and this happened more and more frequently. Stories abound about his drunken rampages, during which he freely destroyed property and often shot men without reason. Slade's wife increasingly had trouble with him too, and she tried her best to keep liquor away from him.

Sometime around 1860 is when Mark Twain traveled through Colorado and met Slade. Twain, at that point of his early life, was not well known as an author. Slade likely never knew he had met the later-famous writer. But Twain was very aware that he had met Jack Slade!

Twain wrote two chapters about Slade in his book, *Roughing It*. The rest of the story about Twain's breakfast with Slade at the stage stop is completed in his book this way:

> *The coffee ran out. At least it was reduced to one tin-cupful, and Slade was about to take it when he saw that my cup was empty. He politely offered to fill it, but although I wanted it, I politely declined. I was afraid he had not killed anybody that morning, and might be needing diversion. But still with firm politeness he insisted on filling my cup, and said I had traveled all night and better deserved it than he—and while he talked he placidly*

poured the fluid, to the last drop. I thanked him and drank it, but it gave me no comfort, for I could not feel sure that he would not be sorry, presently, that he had given it away, and proceed to kill me to distract his thoughts from the loss. But nothing of the kind occurred. We left him with only twenty-six dead people to account for, and I felt a tranquil satisfaction in the thought that in so judiciously taking care of No. 1 at that breakfast-table I had pleasantly escaped being No. 27. Slade came out to the coach and saw us off, first ordering certain rearrangements of the mail-bags for our comfort, and then we took leave of him, satisfied that we should hear of him again, some day, and wondering in what connection.

Indeed, Mark Twain would hear about Jack Slade again.

The Central Overland California and Pikes Peak Express Company finally decided to transfer Slade to a new station along a new run, and Slade picked out the site himself. It was a beautiful valley northwest of present-day Ft. Collins, Colorado. Still endeared to his loyal wife, he decided to name the station for her. He called it Virginia Dale.

Slade's problem with drinking didn't improve in the new location. Reports from all around the region revealed Slade's continued drunken bouts and questionable gun battles, brawls, and killings that seemed to have no provocation. By now, U.S. Marshals from Denver were threatening the Central Overland California and Pikes Peak Express Company with criminal responsibility for their employee's actions.

The company fired Slade in 1862. He and his wife Virginia left the Virginia Dale Station peacefully and moved to Virginia City, in present-day Montana, where Slade started up a freight company. The venture was short lived, and, it turned out, so was Slade. In 1864, on another of his drunken rampages through the town, a local vigilante group captured and lynched him. Mark Twain heard of Jack Slade's demise, and devoted the second of the two "Slade chapters" in the book *Roughing It* to reporting the details of this lynching.

Jack Slade died with a legacy of having been a good man to some and a bad man to others. Buffalo Bill Cody would later write: "Slade, although rough at times and always a dangerous character—having killed many a man—was always kind to me. During the two years that I worked for him as pony express-rider and stage-driver, he never spoke an angry word to me."

JAMES GORDON, MURDERER

He Should Have Been a Gentleman

James Gordon feared for his life as the mob outside his jail cell shouted, "Hang him! Hang him!" The mayor stood on the balcony above pleading with the crowd to desist and allow the law to take its course. He could see that his words were useless in quelling the masses. They would not be denied. Gordon was alive for the moment, but wouldn't be for much longer.

Young James Gordon was only twenty-three years old when he arrived on the banks of Cherry Creek in Denver in 1860. Denver was such a small "spot in the road" that it was hardly recognized as a town. Like neighboring Auraria it was little more than a collection of shacks and tents. Yet both towns were already vying for status as "the best city," despite the fact that there was not one glass window to be seen in either place. The population numbered in the low thousands. Rugged flat streets of hard natural clay weren't very forgiving to the legs of horses or stiff wagon wheels. The Platte River and Cherry Creek ran so low most of the time that early explorers had called this land "uninhabitable" for its lack of water. When the waterways weren't running low, they were flooding after a ten-minute cloudburst. It was one extreme or the other.

The spectacularly beautiful panorama of the Rocky Mountains provided the backdrop for these struggling cities on the plains. Jagged 14,000-foot peaks ran from Longs Peak on the north to Pikes Peak on the south, and were arrayed with snow and glaciers year-round. Looking up into this vista from the tawdry downtown streets only served to remind the plainsmen that life here was always lived at the extremes.

The new attraction to this rough place was gold in the nearby hills. Silver was also found in plentiful amounts. The California Gold Rush of 1849 had passed right by Denver but was now moving in reverse. Within ten years, the miners who had played out their stakes in California came back to Colorado to take advantage of its new ore discoveries. New immigrants also came from the Midwest and the East. They were all called '59ers. More extremes came in the form of "boom or bust" depending on how well the mines produced.

James Gordon should have been a gentleman. He was considered pleasant and likable, and he made friends easily. He stood 6 feet tall and was physically well built. His hair was light and wavy, his eyes were blue, his complexion was clear, and he had a charming smile. These endowments alone made the man a rarity in the raw West, but he possessed yet another amazing feature for the time; he was well educated, as an engineer. He'd also had a decent upbringing by his father, a farmer.

However, even before James and his father had settled on a new farm a few miles north of Denver, young Gordon already had a tarnished reputation. It was said that he had knifed a man in Iowa, and that the root of his problem was his hellacious nature when drunk. He drank hard and became mean and reckless.

His father's farm held no interest for James. He liked excitement, and lawless Denver held every kind of corrupting adventure that might interest and entertain a young man. There were plenty of drinking establishments, gambling dens, and bordellos. It didn't take long for James Gordon to gravitate to the lowest level of scalawags and scoundrels. It was easy to slip into a wild and ruthless lifestyle in such a place.

Every western town eventually had to wage the fight that pitted decency against crime. Now it was Denver's turn to take up the battle, and so far it hadn't been winning. James Gordon was about to challenge almost everyone in Denver. Even some of the town's worst would be shocked by his actions.

It began on Wednesday, July 18, 1860. Young James started drinking in a saloon on Arapahoe Street. The more he drank, the meaner he became. He was soon drawing his pistol and waving it in the air. His behavior was understandably making patrons uncomfortable, and the bartender, Frank O'Neill, protested. Gordon aimed his gun at O'Neill and, without warning, shot the man down.

The next day, Gordon felt remorse. He went to visit the recovering victim, who had somehow managed to survive. He apologized and seemed to have truly regretted his actions, even offering to pay the man's expenses.

On Friday, though, the "other side" of Gordon showed up once again. This time he was with a couple of companions, wandering from saloon to saloon, drinking at each and getting drunk. He visited a bar called Denver Hall and then dropped in the Elephant Corral, where he met "Big Phil" and they got into a quarrel. Gordon drew his gun and shot at the man twice. He missed both times and Big Phil was smart enough to run out the back door.

Gordon moved on to the Louisiana Saloon on Blake Street, shooting at a dog along the way. Angered when the bartender brought him whiskey, but no water, he threw the bottle against the wall behind the bar, where it destroyed several more bottles. Many alarmed patrons headed for the door, but Gordon stood in the way of one German man named Jacob Gantz, who had come to Denver from Leavenworth in the Kansas Territory.

Gordon lost his senses completely when Gantz refused his offer of some whiskey. The German ran out the door with Gordon in hot pursuit. When Gordon caught up with him, he threatened Gantz by holding him down and pointing his gun at the terrified man's head. Gordon then cocked his gun and pulled the trigger, but no bullet fired. Again and again, the gun was cocked and the trigger was pulled, without result. Gantz begged for his life each time. At the last pull, a bullet finally discharged. Gantz was dead instantly, and Gordon stood up to celebrate.

Those who had watched the tragedy unfold ran for their own safety. This gave Gordon a chance to stumble off down a side street, where he passed out in some bushes and slept through the entire night. When he woke up, he was surprised to learn from another drunk that a mob was searching for him, ready to lynch him on the spot.

Gordon fled on a horse toward Fort Lupton, north of Denver. He was pursued by the mob-turned-vigilantes, who soon had him surrounded. But Gordon was able to elude them and sneaked off into the brush along the Platte River. His pursuers returned to Denver empty-handed. In the meantime, Gordon procured a mule and, avoiding the main roads, traveled more than 200 miles south across the eastern plains to Bent's Fort.

Back in Denver, a bounty had been raised to capture Gordon. A man named W. H. Middaugh was appointed to go after him. He hunted along the Platte River for ten days without success and believed that Gordon's trail had gone dry. As it turned out, Gordon himself would lead Middaugh in the right direction.

Gordon decided to write a letter to one of his friends in Denver. He entrusted it to a man headed north from Bent's Fort, who planned to pass through the city. The man promised to deliver it. Meanwhile, Middaugh and a deputy were tracking south of Denver trying to pick up some sign of Gordon. Purely by accident, they came across the man carrying Gordon's letter. When Middaugh described what Gordon looked like, the man said he had just seen him at Bent's Fort. He turned the letter over to Middaugh and told him that Gordon was leaving the fort for Texas on a forty-team wagon convoy.

By the time the Middaugh team reached the convoy, they discovered that Gordon had already left the wagon train and was headed first for Fort Gibson and then south through Indian Territory through present-day Oklahoma. James had joined with four other men to assure safe passage through Indian country. Middaugh forged ahead and continued in dogged pursuit.

At a small town along the route, Middaugh learned that Gordon was just a day ahead. The sheriff of Coffey County, Kansas Territory joined Middaugh and his deputy. They picked up fresh horses and kept up a fast pace. Within a day, they came across a farmer who thought he'd seen the man they were seeking at a nearby village. When they reached this place, local inhabitants said Gordon had left only half an hour earlier.

Gordon felt sure that he had eluded his pursuers long ago. He had no reason to suspect anyone was looking for him now. Confidently and casually, he stopped along the road and let his mule graze in a small meadow. He was totally unnerved when Middaugh and his group rode up and drew their guns on him. They disarmed him of his Colt .44-caliber revolver and his derringer, and then arrested him.

At the closest blacksmith shop, double irons were fashioned to manacle Gordon. Rather than travel through the isolated and remote plains back to Denver, Middaugh chose to take Gordon to nearby Leavenworth, in the Kansas Territory, where they could meet up with a stage line. Middaugh had not, however, figured on the reception they would receive there.

Jacob Gantz, the man murdered by Gordon, was originally from Leavenworth. He had been well known in the large German community, and when locals heard that Gantz's killer had been captured, a lynch mob formed. The courthouse was surrounded and chants of "Hang him! Hang him!" rang out from the crowd. Mayor McDowell attempted to calm the mob, but it was to no avail. Throughout the night bonfires illuminated the waiting mob, which continued to grow. Peddlers circulated through the crowd hawking food to those who had missed dinner in order to stand sentinel at the courthouse.

Legal wrangling ensued over who maintained official jurisdiction of Gordon. A disputed decision by the presiding judge ruled at first that Gordon should be set free. It was ultimately decided that Gordon needed to be protected while the legal details were being sorted out. That determination, coupled with a fear that the jailhouse might come under attack, led to an attempt to move Gordon out of the jail and into other quarters. The sheriff's posse tried to protect Gordon as they led him toward the Planters House Hotel, but the crowd soon surrounded them and placed a noose around Gordon's neck. He was pushed, battered, and bruised, and was so terrified that he begged to be shot dead right there. The posse soon regained control of Gordon with the assistance of a group of soldiers who had been ordered in to help. The rope was cut from Gordon's neck, and he was saved from certain death.

Another hearing took place, and the local authorities refused to give Gordon over to Middaugh for a trip back to Denver. The officials said they needed evidence of Gordon's guilt, but would hold him until it was provided. Middaugh could do nothing but return to Denver without his prisoner.

Citizens of Denver had been apprised of Middaugh's unrelenting attempts to bring Gordon to justice, and when Middaugh returned and stepped off the stage, he received a hero's welcome for his efforts in capturing Gordon. Enough money was raised to return three witnesses of Gantz's murder to Leavenworth. Middaugh accompanied them on the reverse run of the "Leavenworth to Pikes Peak" stage.

With the required proof, Gordon was finally released to the custody of Middaugh for his return to Denver. A chain was fastened around both their waists connecting them together for the long stagecoach ride.

Early in the morning on September 28, 1860, the stage from Leavenworth pulled into Denver. James Gordon was jailed to await his trial. Middaugh had covered 3,000 miles during the two months it had taken him to apprehend Gordon.

The trial began the next day. It was held by citizens in a "people's court" since there was no official judicial system yet established. Every effort was made to provide a fair hearing of the facts. A. C. Hunt was appointed judge; he would later become a territorial governor of Colorado. Gordon was represented by a defense attorney. A jury was appointed. Over 1,000 people attended the trial, which took place in a grove of cottonwood trees near Wazee Street.

The trial lasted four days. Although the participants had no legal training, they were all considered to be of high character. The prosecution and defense examined and cross-examined their witnesses. The defendant was said to have been irresponsible for murder due to his condition of drunkenness. The prosecution did not accept drunkenness as an excuse, and held that he was responsible for the crime.

By October 2, the trial ended. The jury pronounced James Gordon guilty of "willful murder." Judge Hunt sentenced him to be hanged on Saturday, October 6, and young Gordon responded by bowing to the crowd.

The lawless residents of the rough town of Denver were opposed to these proceedings, since they represented a new attitude meant to undermine their power. They threatened to storm the building where Gordon was being held. The decent citizens, however, provided a guard that deterred this possibility.

On Saturday, a well-guarded buggy brought Gordon to the scaffold that had been erected on the east bank of Cherry Creek. Middaugh had been placed in charge of the hanging at the request of young Gordon. While imprisoned, he had told guards that Middaugh had saved his life at Leavenworth. He said that hanging could not be "one-tenth as dreadful as what he had been through there," and that he had already "died a thousand deaths," only to be "saved and dragged back to the scaffold."

Thousands were present for the hanging. Members of the crowd removed their hats for a prayer while Gordon knelt. And then James Gordon was hanged less than a year after he had arrived.

Crime did not abruptly stop in Denver or Auraria due to the capture and "people's court" trial of James Gordon. Other criminals would be arrested and convicted by the same court until official law was eventually established. A new territorial government matured into statehood for Colorado.

Hoodlums were not free to run amuck as they once did. They had to consider their chances of being captured and imprisoned for their reckless acts. The young ones, especially, would have to think about whether they wanted to live beyond the age of twenty-three.

ALFRED PACKER, CANNIBAL

.♦.

Little to Redeem Him

On August 3, 1886, the *Rocky Mountain News* reported the ongoing testimony in the trial of Alfred Packer:

> *Packer's manner while on the stand was very excited. He detailed his trip, his act of cannibalism, his arrival at Los Pinos Agency, his arrest and subsequent escape from Saguache, his wanderings up to 1883, and his final capture at Fort Fetterman, in a wild, incoherent manner, standing in his shirtsleeves, waving his mutilated hand in the air and haranguing the jury in broken sentences.*
>
> *He frequently cursed his enemies in very plain words, and refused to be governed by his counsel. Replying once to a remonstrance on their part, he said, "You shut up. I'm on the stand now."*

The trial lasted for three days and the jury reached its verdict in just three hours.

Alfred G. Packer was born on November 21, 1842, in Allegheny County, Pennsylvania. Epilepsy was the scourge of his childhood and was a little understood malady at that time. Consequently, young Packer was often socially ostracized from his peers. He and his family—which included his parents, two sisters, and a brother—were members of the Quaker religion.

It is unclear why he left home at an early age, but his medical condition may have played a part in his desire to escape harassment. Some said his own family sent him away due to their misunderstanding of, and inability to deal with, his illness. He was able to serve a short apprenticeship with a printer while trying to hide his condition. Besides the epileptic fits that ravaged him, some side effects included a quarrelsome nature and a high-pitched, shrill voice.

In 1862, at the age of twenty, Packer decided to enlist in the army to fight in the Civil War. When he joined the 16th U.S. Infantry in Winona, Minnesota, his record indicates he was 5 feet 8½ inches tall, of light complexion, with blue eyes and light hair. His occupation was recorded as shoemaker. Although he had been christened with the first name of Alfred, he preferred "Alferd" and had this name tattooed on his right arm along with the name of his encampment, "Camp Thomas," and his battalion and infantry numbers. Just eight months later, he was discharged "as incapable of performing the duties of a soldier because of epilepsy."

Records show that Packer reenlisted in Ottumwa, Iowa, six months after his discharge. Nearly a year later he was discharged again due to his epilepsy. The army surgeon stated that Packer's epileptic seizures occurred "once in 48 hours and sometimes as often as two or three times in 48 hours."

Packer drifted from job to job. He worked as a hunter, hard rock miner, trapper, teamster, and guide. He had also begun to invent certain facts about his life and work experience, which was unsteady due to his epileptic episodes. In 1873, when Packer was thirty-one years old, he settled in Georgetown, in the Colorado Territory, where a mining accident caused the loss of parts of his index and little finger on his left hand. He then moved on to Sandy, in the Utah Territory, and worked in a smelter that processed ore from Bingham Canyon. By then the medical world had discovered that bromides could be helpful to epileptics, and Packer is said to have used them whenever possible.

Later the same year he heard news of rich ore discoveries in the mountains of the Colorado Territory. A group of gold-seeking miners was forming at Bingham to travel into the San Juan Mountains. Packer joined up with them, and although they said they had limited knowledge of the Colorado mountains, Packer claimed he was very familiar with the area.

By the fall of 1873 Packer and the group of twenty-one men headed for the Colorado border, along with horses, wagons, and provisions. Early in their journey it became apparent that they had brought insufficient provisions. Feed intended for the livestock began to be used for the men. Their travel was slow, the weather brought early snow, and game became scarce. As they reached the border, they encountered the Ute Indians, who led them to the camp of Chief Ouray, near present-day Delta, Colorado. The group was allowed to stay with Ouray, where they were provided shelter and warmth, as well as the opportunity to trade with the Indians.

Winter had settled in, and Chief Ouray warned against proceeding into the high mountains. But many of the men in Packer's group were restless. Those without wagons and teams eventually decided to forge ahead. Two groups were organized, with one group traveling ahead separately. That left six men in the second group, and they began their foray into the mountains on February 9, 1874. Besides Packer, the members of this expedition included "Old man" Swan, George Noon, James Humphrey, Frank Miller, and Shannon Wilson Bell.

Chief Ouray had provided directions to Saguache, in the Colorado Territory, in the heart of the San Juans about 100 miles southeast. He told them of a "cow camp" which was "seven suns away" where provisions could be acquired and instructed them to follow the creek from there to the Los Pinos Indian Agency. After that it was just 40 more miles to their destination.

The first group became lost immediately. They struggled for three weeks before reaching the government cattle camp and were near starvation when they arrived. With new provisions they continued on through raging and turbulent winter storms and finally arrived at Los Pinos, barely alive.

The second group of six men, Packer's group, was last seen headed southeast as they disappeared into a snowstorm.

It would be two months before Packer would emerge from the frozen wilderness and encounter a man who was out gathering firewood. It was mid-April, and Packer's matted hair and beard obviously revealed that he had suffered long exposure to severe weather.

Packer's first words are said to have been: "Is this the agency?" He was led to the mess hall, where he met other agency employees. It is documented that Packer could not eat their food at first, and that he related his story of having been separated from his group and left behind. He claimed to have had to proceed on his own after that. The other five men had not shown up at the agency.

For Packer, all might have ended happily right there. However, as he talked more to others about his experience, his story began to change. Those who questioned him were told different versions, which varied wildly. And soon, other travelers arrived who had been part of the original group that had stayed behind at Chief Ouray's camp. They recognized Packer and wondered how he had acquired the knife that belonged to Frank Miller. Packer also had money, which they knew he had not possessed when they were last with him.

With no evidence to back up any of his stories, Packer came under suspicion. But there was also no proof of what was fast becoming the generally held belief among the community: that Packer was involved in "foul play" regarding the men in his group, who had still not shown up.

Under pressure from more questioning, Packer finally revealed a new scenario. He told of the starvation and exposure which had led to the death of four of the men along the way. The fifth man, Bell, had attacked Packer, and in self-defense Packer killed Bell with a hatchet. He then revealed how he had survived by cannibalizing the bodies. Packer maintained his innocence in the deaths of his companions, even though he now admitted freely to the cannibalism.

The Indian agent, Charles Adams, thought Packer's story could be proved if the bodies could be found. He asked Packer to lead a search party back to the location where the men had last been seen. Packer agreed and took the group into the wilderness, where he became lost and said he could not remember how to reach the spot. Many in the search party were convinced of Packer's guilt.

Because of these grave suspicions, Packer was incarcerated in a makeshift jail in Saguache without any charges against him. Weeks later, the bodies of the five men were discovered together below a cliff with obvious hatchet wounds in their skulls. They each showed signs of having been cannibalized. Pieces of the bodies had been cut from legs, foreheads, and torsos. An empty bromide tin was also found at the scene.

A warrant for the arrest of Packer was finally issued. In one of several odd twists that would occur in this drama, Packer managed to escape before the warrant could be served. He would not be seen again for almost ten years.

In 1883 a man using the name of John Schwartze was seen at Fort Fetterman near Cheyenne, in the Wyoming Territory. The man was Alfred Packer, who had been living under an assumed name. He was recognized and turned in to law enforcement agents by one of his old acquaintances from the original gold-seeking band in Bingham, in the Utah Territory. Packer did not resist his arrest.

Packer then decided that he wanted to make a new statement about what had happened during that tragic winter in the San Juans. This time his story portrayed a group of hopeless men, sick and hungry from the cold and snow. Unable to find food, Packer said the men were "crying and praying." One of the men asked him to go up on a hilltop to see if he could see anything. Another man was acting crazy. When Packer returned, he found the crazy man sitting by the fire roasting something on a stick. He saw one body with its skull crushed in by the hatchet. The other three men had also been struck in the forehead with the hatchet. When the crazy man saw Packer, he came at him swinging the hatchet. Packer then shot him in the side, grabbed the hatchet, and struck him on the top of his head. Although Packer says he tried every day to get out of the camp, the snow-covered terrain and blizzard conditions made it impossible. So he stayed in the camp and ate the flesh of the dead men to stay alive. Eventually the weather allowed passage out so he could hike to the Los Pinos Indian Agency.

Packer also provided limited information about how he escaped from the Saguache jail and what he did for the ten years until his recapture. He says he was passed a key made of a knife blade, which unlocked the irons that shackled him. He fled to Pueblo, where he worked on a nearby ranch and later rented the ranch and grew a crop of corn. He moved on to the Arizona Territory and eventually traveled to the Wyoming Territory.

Packer's arrest became sensational news. He was tried for murder in April of 1883 at the Hinsdale County Courthouse in Lake City, Colorado. Packer decided to represent himself without benefit of a defense lawyer.

The prosecution held that Packer's motivation for the murder of his companions had been sheer greed. He had shown up at the Indian agency with considerable amounts of money and the wallet of one of the victims. The act of cannibalism was not given much attention in the trial. It was apparently thought that this occurred only as an afterthought for the purpose of survival and Packer's real interest was the money these men had carried with them.

One witness who was called to testify was Otto Mears, known as the "Pathfinder of the San Juan" because he built roadways and railroads through the area's precipitous mountains. He owned real estate all along the road he had built between Saguache and Lake City, and also ran a supply store in Saguache. He said he sold a horse, bridle, and saddle to Packer after he had left the Indian Agency. Packer had seemed to be throwing his money around indiscriminately and paid about $100 cash for the livery items. Otto recollected seeing the additional wallet, which he called a "pocketbook." He also saw other items enclosed in it, including a Wells Fargo bank draft. The possession of this draft was considered key to Packer's guilt.

Packer was outraged by Mears's testimony and maintained he did not have the draft. "Otto Mears swears that he saw a Wells Fargo Bank Draft," Packer said, "and before I get through I will prove that Mears told a lie." He lost his temper at this point and rose from his chair, threatening to kill Mears at his first opportunity. It took considerable effort to restrain Packer and calm him down before the trial could proceed.

The jury was not persuaded by Packer's defense of himself. He had often rambled and his demands were largely ignored. It took only three hours of deliberation before the jury returned its verdict. Packer was convicted of murder.

However, another bizarre twist occurred when it was discovered that the state of Colorado had no law regarding murder. The legislature had repealed the original 1870 murder statute without providing a new one in its place. Packer's crime had taken place after the repeal of the murder statute.

He was transferred to the town of Gunnison to await a ruling, since it was feared a lynching party might overpower the Lake City law enforcement officials. Packer sat imprisoned in the Gunnison County jail for three years before the judgment was finally made. The Colorado Supreme Court remanded the case for a new trial, stating that Packer could not be tried for murder since there had been no established punishment at the time for this crime. He could be tried, however, for the crime of manslaughter. A new defense on Packer's behalf argued that his rights had been violated by his lengthy confinement during the delay for the ruling. This was overruled.

In 1886 a new trial was set. Much of the same information was covered again, only this time Mears was said to be unavailable. The record of his original testimony was read to the court instead. Some felt that Mears was afraid of Packer's earlier threat to kill him, and so he stayed away from the second trial.

This time Packer was convicted of manslaughter and sentenced to forty years of hard labor at the state penitentiary in Cañon City. It became the most severe sentence ever handed down for manslaughter in American history. Many felt the sentence was overly harsh considering the lack of provable evidence.

This might finally have been the end of it, except that Packer's second conviction was appealed several times between 1886 and 1898. Each time, the Colorado Supreme Court rejected the appeal, and each time Packer gained more support from the public. In 1899, the *Denver Post* appointed their most heralded reporter, Mrs. Leonel Ross O'Bryan (known humorously as "Polly Pry") to take on the story as her only assignment. For the next two years she used the newspaper's influence to hound Governor Charles S. Thomas to either parole or pardon Packer.

Thomas was said to be a close friend of Otto Mears, the man who had given damaging testimony in the Packer case. Mrs. O'Bryan wrote that Mears was afraid of Packer being released, and she labeled him a "COWARD." She accused the governor of being influenced by Mears instead of doing the right thing.

Governor Thomas resisted almost to the end of his political career. In 1901, as the final act of his outgoing term and on his last day in office, Thomas pardoned Packer.

Having served fifteen years of his sentence, Packer was finally free. He moved to a ranch in Littleton, south of Denver, and lived for another six years. In April of 1907, Alfred Packer died at the age of sixty-five. His grave is located in the Littleton cemetery, where Packer was buried with full military honors. The gravestone displays his given name "Alfred Packer," and lists his infantry unit from his first enlistment.

Years after the death of Packer, former Governor Thomas wrote a letter to the newspaper at Lake City. For the first time he publicly related his thoughts about Packer, and explained his reluctance in granting the pardon. Thomas stated that the letters Packer had written during his incarceration in Lake City and Gunnison were shared with him by local officials who censored the inmate's mail. Apparently, Packer wrote to his sister and other family members in Pennsylvania, blaming them for his terrible life. The letters, which expressed his rage and anger in the most foul and profane language imaginable, astonished the governor. Also of great concern were Packer's threats toward his relatives, which he said he would carry out upon his release. Governor Thomas had been asked not to reveal this information publicly. He had decided to visit Packer while he was in jail, and said that he did so several times, during which he talked with him at length. Thomas saw no redeeming qualities in Packer's nature and felt the inmate's attitude had not improved. Only because of Packer's failing health did the governor finally agree to a pardon. But he stipulated this release upon the condition that Packer would not be allowed to leave the state of Colorado for the rest of his life. This was done to protect Packer's family members.

Packer's notoriety has continued long beyond his death. In the mid-1960s, the University of Colorado student body voted to rename the student union eatery, "The Alferd G. Packer Grill." And in the 1990s, a cookbook was published called *Alferd Packer's High Protein Cookbook.* It featured recipes using wild game meats.

On Memorial Day of 2004, the 700 residents of Lake City held the Alferd Packer Days festival, including bone-tossing competitions and mystery meat barbecues. During that summer, the still-standing Hinsdale County Court-house was regularly packed with tourists for the weekly reenactment of Packer's trial. The *Denver Post* reported one town citizen as saying, "Some people think it's gross, but there's still so much interest."

BUTCH CASSIDY

The Robin Hood Outlaw

Butch was certain no one was following him. Nevertheless, he stopped and wiped the sweat from his brow while he studied the back trail with field glasses. After a quarter of an hour, he was satisfied. Pushing on into the afternoon sun, he saw a rundown ranch. It had been a day since he'd eaten, and he was hungry. Maybe he could ride down and get a meal. When he came to the front door, an elderly couple greeted him. Following the custom of the day, they invited the dusty traveler in for supper. The gray-haired woman put coffee on to boil and wiped a few tears when she thought the stranger was not looking.

"This might be our last afternoon at the place," the rancher explained. "It's really hard on the lady."

The man who held the note on their ranch was due to arrive anytime, and he was going to evict them since they couldn't make the mortgage—cattle prices were down, and it had been a bad year with the drought. The couple had mistakenly assumed that Butch was the bank man before he rode in close. The woman started to cry more openly as her husband talked. Butch had seconds, and she filled his coffee cup. Butch asked how much they needed to clear the note.

The couple explained that they owed the banker five hundred dollars, but it might as well have been five million.

Butch smiled and wiped his mouth and thanked them for the fine meal. As he left, he laid a wad of dirty bills on the table and made the couple take it. Then he asked what the banker looked like and what direction he'd be coming from. Butch told the rancher to get a signed receipt from the man, stressing that this was very important.

The couple agreed. The woman hugged him. The stranger hadn't told the pair his name, but they knew who he was. He was the famous outlaw they'd heard so much about. Butch rode off, but then he circled back toward Hanksville. The elderly couple reminded him of his own folks, and he reflected over the hard times they'd had trying to make a home in this arid land. He missed his family, but with a price on his head, he didn't get home very often. Besides, he was a little bit ashamed of the life he had chosen.

Butch smoked a cowboy cigarette and waited in the rocks where he could keep an eye on the dirt track. A short time later, a man in a black suit and a string tie rode past and went up to the cabin. Before long, he rode back down the trail heading to town. After he'd gone a couple of miles from the ranch, Butch trotted up to the man and pointed a cocked Colt at his chest. He took back his five hundred dollars in dirty bills, plus the odd notes the man had, and rode off to his hideout. He never did like banks and the mortgage men who ran them.

Another time when Butch Cassidy was on the run, he visited a Chicago sporting establishment that employed a flock of "soiled doves." He was intimately acquainted with one of the girls. The misdirected maiden told the young, dashing outlaw her life story—about how she'd come to such a tragic circumstance and that she wanted, God willing, to leave this path of sin and go back to the West Coast and start all over. She wanted to go straight, get honest, find a nice guy, settle down, have kids, build a white picket fence about her cottage— and leave her past behind.

Butch was touched by the girl's story. He bought her a ticket to Seattle and gave her the last of his money so she could start a new life. It seemed that Butch Cassidy, king of the outlaws and master robber, had a heart of gold under that rough, windblown exterior. It seemed, too, that while he was an outlaw who held people up with a naked Colt .45 and took their money, there must have been some truth to the overly romanticized stories that followed him in his day—and are still part of the folklore now.

In many ways Cassidy was larger than life when he rode the West. He was nice to children and animals. He was generous and kind to the hard-working people he rubbed shoulders with. There are too many accounts of Cassidy giving someone his last dollar to be completely ignored. And like another mythic legend of yore, Robin Hood of Sherwood Forest, Cassidy mostly directed his crimes at the rich who tended to prey upon the working class. He never completely shook off his Mormon heritage, even though he associated with murderers and thieves.

He saw himself as a man of the people, if not a man of contradictions. He lived by the gun, but he preached against violence among his fellows. While he was very quick on the draw and apparently a dead-on shot, he claimed that he never killed anyone—nor is there any record that he did. He liked the fast life, but he also liked to lose himself in a library and read for days. He was an outlaw with a conscience, with a morality, or some semblance of morality, especially when compared to others in his profession—he seems to be the epitome of a good guy who did bad things. As a result, he has never failed to capture the public's curiosity—then as well as now. And his legend has only grown.

Butch Cassidy was born Robert LeRoy Parker on April 13, 1866, in Beaver, Utah. He was the first of twelve children in a devout Mormon family. His family called him Roy. His paternal grandfather, Robert Parker, had left Preston, England, after becoming a convert to the Church of Jesus Christ of Latter-day

Saints (Mormons). Robert eagerly made his way to the United States, where he crossed the Great Plains with his family, including Roy's father, Max. The Parkers arrived with the Handcart Company, reaching the Salt Lake Valley in the early fall. Roy's mother, Ann Gillies, crossed the plains with the ill-fated Martin-Willy Handcart Company. This wagon train unwisely left too late in the season and was caught in frigid storms in Wyoming. Many of the party perished in the elements—one of the tragedies of the great migration. Being a little too eager to get to the Promised Land, they paid a high price.

Since both Max and Ann had helped pull handcarts across the plains, they felt a deep sense of pride in their religious beliefs. They were cut from tough pioneer stock. They brought up their children on firsthand stories of the plains and expected strict devotion to the faith they'd nearly died for. (Even under ideal circumstances, pulling and pushing a crude handcart with all one's possessions over 1,000 miles of rough country from Iowa to the Great Basin was quite a feat.) They had sacrificed a great deal for their God, and they taught their children to appreciate their rich heritage.

Both parents also valued a good education, and young Roy learned his school lessons well. But in spite of their best efforts, their oldest son strayed from the true teachings of the faith, breaking his mother's heart by becoming one of the most famous, or infamous, outlaws of the American West. Nevertheless, Roy would never completely abandon his heritage or fully exorcise many of the fundamental teachings he learned at Ann's knee. He never lost his respect for the working class, and he hated injustice.

The Parkers lived in Beaver until Roy was about twelve. They fell on hard times and moved to Circleville, where they did well for a short time. Like so many settlers, though, they were nearly driven under by the harsh winter of 1879. Ann reluctantly left her young family to earn money at the nearby Marshall Ranch. She was allowed to keep some eggs and butter for her own use. To earn a bit more for the struggling family, young Roy, who had just entered his teens, worked on the ranch with his mother.

The ranch employed a rough crowd of men, and young Roy naturally idolized them. Ann tried to shelter her boy from the worldly influences of this godless crowd. Young Roy proved to be a hard worker and a first-rate cowhand. He was likable, smart, and quick. At fourteen he was able to do the work of a man without complaint. He quickly won the approval of the older hands and was accepted as a promising cowhand apprentice. A wild, young cowboy named Mike Cassidy took Roy under his wing.

At first Ann was pleased with how her Roy was fitting in as a ranch hand. The lad was accepted by the other men and was earning his way. It was nice, too, for Ann to have a member of her family with her. She got lonely being away from home for five or six days at a time. However, before long she noticed that her little man was changing too quickly. She stepped in and took him back to town to live with the rest of the family, but it was too late. Her son wanted to be a cowboy.

Roy worshipped Mike Cassidy and wanted to be like him. Not only did the likable Mike Cassidy have some rough habits that the strict Mormon Ann disapproved of, it was rumored that he did more than cowboy work at the ranch. He had too much money. His guns, his horse, his saddle, his clothes were a little too fancy for an honest ranch hand to afford. It was rumored that he rode the outlaw trail, that he rustled cattle and horses and sold them in Colorado. This was not the kind of man she wanted her boy looking up to. Ann hoped she'd taught her firstborn right from wrong, so he'd make his own choice and it would be the right one.

That Mike looked upon the young Roy with a great deal of affection—like a younger brother or a son—is obvious. Like all cowhands, Mike took great pride in his skills and passed them on. Roy's hero taught him how to ride, rope, shoot, and quick-draw. He even gave his young protégé a saddle. Mike taught the young Parker the finer points of being a cattleman and the art of judging horseflesh— skills Roy would never lose. In his heart, the future Butch Cassidy was always a rancher. He became a superb horseman and rider. He would later ride in a number of races and would be sought after as a jockey. He would also race for his life when the stakes were high.

It turned out that Ann was right: Mike Cassidy was engaged in some serious rustling—his day job was really a cover. He was the head of a successful group of thieves called the Cassidy Gang. No doubt these moonlighting skills were passed down as well—little was lost on his clever young understudy. After the lad's skills were up to par, he surely rode with Mike's men on their moonlight raids. Mike Cassidy probably wasn't taking livestock from the Marshall Ranch or any nearby ranches. In fact, most evidence suggests that some of the Marshall family and the Marshall hands, including a few local ranchers, had formed a working cooperative for dealing with livestock that had "questionable" brands. They were building up a herd to sell.

Mike Cassidy was skilled at picking up livestock that didn't belong to him, then covering up the trail. In all fairness, a number of the head he took probably weren't branded. They were free stock getting fat in the local draws and canyons. He was a fine stockman and an expert with the red-hot saddle ring, used to brand cattle in the field.

Ann and Max did what they could for Roy, but it wasn't enough. Their son left home for good in 1884.

Roy took his first drink of Old Crow—which became his favorite whiskey— his first smoke, and his first chew on the Marshall Ranch. He likely learned, too, about the fairer sex, including women of questionable virtue—albeit secondhand. Although he eventually became the most famous outlaw in Utah, and one of the most famous outlaws in the West, he retained many of his traditional values. He knew the difference between right and wrong, but he couldn't resist financial shortcuts. He vowed that he'd never be poor like his parents.

He changed his name to Butch to protect his parents' reputation. At different times of his life he went by George Cassidy, James Ryan, and Butch Cassidy. He used the name Cassidy in honor of his friend Mike Cassidy. The name Butch came a little bit later—probably when he worked as a butcher in Rock Springs, Wyoming, since a lot of butchers were called Butch.

Butch was a bold, good-looking man who made a good impression. He was just under 5 feet, 11 inches tall. His frequent smile was broad on his square face. He was reckless, but he was smart, and he knew how far to push and when to back off. He liked people, ranchers, farmers, and Indians, and they liked him— liked him a lot. They protected him as one of their own, which often made the difference between capture and escape. He tipped his hat to the ladies. He was rarely drunk or disorderly. He made friends easily.

While he strayed from the faith of his youth and the fundamental teachings of Mormonism, he had a strong work ethic. And although he was a thief, his word was good, and he was a devoted friend.

In June 1889, Butch crossed the line, entering the world of serious crime. Up until this point, his offenses had been petty by comparison. He had been involved in the rustling trade, but that was considered a minor, if not a forgivable, offense. He fell in with Tom McCarty, a regional, small-time outlaw; Bert Madden, a former bartender; and Matt Warner, a small-time rustler from Brown's Hole (in the northeastern corner of Utah). The four started off as drinking buddies and became good friends who all shared an interest in racehorses.

The group raced three horses in the Four Corners area rather successfully and were involved in petty rustling and petty theft. But they had higher ambitions. They wanted to get rich quickly. Butch was familiar with the setup of the San Miguel Valley Bank in Telluride, Colorado. He had been to Telluride many times. McCarty was the leader of the planned caper, since he had the most experience, but all were eager participants.

Above all, they wanted a big score. The McCarty Gang, as they were called, held up the bank and rode off with a cool $10,500. But they were recognized as they left town, and they became wanted men. Their lives would never be the same again.

The robbery had been well planned—they accounted for contingencies. McCarty had insisted that they use only the best horses—including fresh horses along the escape path—since their lives would depend upon them. This was a lesson the young Butch would never forget. They fled for their lives, trusting entirely in their fine mounts. Central Utah was too hot to hide out in, so they headed north where the winters were colder (and the climate healthier for men with a price on their heads).

McCarty's brother, Bill, and Bill's son, Fred, joined the gang. They weren't so lucky and were later killed in Delta, Colorado, trying to rob the Merchant's Bank. Apparently, at this point Tom McCarty learned his lesson, took his money, and escaped, dropping into semiretirement. Butch's appetite for the high life was only whetted.

He hung out in Brown's Hole, working on ranches and quietly living off his share of the Telluride loot. He actually considered going straight. It is reported that he even worked at the huge Swan Land and Cattle Company. But old habits are hard to break. He went back into business for himself—rustling cattle and horses, trying to build up a herd—but he drew some bad luck. He bought a horse ranch near the Wind River Mountains with Al Hainer (sometimes spelled Rainer). Along with Al, he was caught in 1893 with horses he hadn't paid for.

The case came to trial the following year. Al was acquitted, but Butch was found guilty and sentenced to two years in prison. He was a model prisoner. After serving eighteen months, he asked if he might be paroled since he'd served a good deal of his sentence. It seems the warden was impressed with Butch and said, "You're smart enough to make a success in almost any field. Will you give me your word that you will quit rustling?"

Butch reportedly said, "I can't do that, sir, because if I gave you my word, I'd have to break it. I'm in too deep to quit this game. But I'll promise you one thing: If you pardon me, I'll not rustle in Wyoming."

After being released from prison, Butch headed toward Wyoming's Hole-in-the-Wall, where he hooked up with Flat Nose Curry, Bub Meeks, Elza Lay, and Kid Curry. After a reunion of sorts, they headed down to Brown's Hole to plan their next job.

For the next few years, trains and banks drew their special focus. Butch would give new meaning to the term *organized crime*. Rustling would become less important. The Union Pacific was especially hard hit. Within a few years, nearly every law enforcement agency in the West was homing in on Butch's gang. The Pinkertons would become especially problematic—they would not give up. By the early part of 1900, Butch Cassidy had been a professional outlaw for nearly twelve years, and it was wearing him down. The heyday of outlawing in the West was about over. During his career, he had spent two years in prison, he had thrown some wild parties, and had played hard, but he had almost nothing to show for it. The constant pressure put on him and the Wild Bunch by law enforcement was too much. There were too many close calls, too many days on the trail freezing and roasting, eating only half-cooked beans, if that. His former strongholds, Brown's Hole, Robber's Roost, Hole-in-the-Wall, had all been compromised.

In this frame of mind, Butch made a bold move. He considered going straight and wanted to make a deal. Butch's so-called Train Robbers Syndicate was posing serious problems to banks and railroads—especially the Union Pacific. The famous outlaw contacted Judge O. W. Powers and explained his desire to start over. The judge was convinced that Butch wanted to change his life, so convinced, in fact, that he personally contacted Utah governor Herbert Wells. Governor Wells finally met with Butch, who asked for amnesty from his offenses. After all, he had never killed a man during the commission of his crimes. After a frank discussion, Wells was willing to pardon Butch. His agreeable personality and pleasant manner won the Utah official to his side.

While Wells was willing to consider amnesty, it would only apply in the state of Utah. Butch was wanted in a number of western states, but Governor Wells had an idea. If they could convince the Union Pacific that Cassidy was going straight, the railroad might be willing to drop all pending charges against him, including those in other states. Furthermore, Butch was willing to go to work for the railroads as a sort of roving troubleshooter—protecting the lines from robbery.

A man named Douglas Preston, working in conjunction with the governor, contacted the Union Pacific. The railway was willing to make a deal—and it was more than willing to hire Butch, at an inflated rate, to police the rail lines. While he was waiting for the final meeting, Butch stayed straight as a token of good faith. He was nervous, though, suspicious that this was a ruse for a carefully planned capture. He requested that the meeting take place near the Green Mountains of Wyoming.

As fate would have it, the train bringing the officials for the meeting was delayed. Butch waited and waited, but Preston and the railroad officials didn't show up at the appointed time. Growing more and more nervous about a double-cross, and more bitter, Butch decided to leave. He had waited nearly a day longer than planned. He left a note: "Damn You! You double-crossed me. I waited all day and you didn't show up. Tell the U.P. to go to hell."

Butch felt he'd gone too far. No one was going to let him go straight. He had tried to become honest, and they wouldn't let him. It was probably at this point that he started to seriously consider going to South America. Unsurprisingly, his next job was against the Union Pacific. Butch supposedly told the Wild Bunch, "I understand that the Union Pacific is looking for trouble. Let's give it to them."

Butch wanted to get revenge and vent his anger against the railroad. It didn't take long to plan the next job. There was a coal station outside of Rawlins, Wyoming, at a place called Tipton where the trains stopped. It was a desolate location, and there were a number of good escape routes. Perhaps the best one was to the Green River region of Utah. Butch presented his plan to his associates, and they agreed it was sound. It was similar to the plan the outlaws had used successfully in the 1899 Wilcox train robbery.

The Wild Bunch rode several hundred miles to get into position. Along the way, they left extra horses at key locations and fine-tuned their getaway plans. On the last day, the outlaws walked their horses to the coal station to save their strength. They fed and watered the mounts against the hard ride to follow. It was August 29, 1900.

When the train arrived at about two in the morning, Butch and Kid Curry jumped on board. At gunpoint they made the express man uncouple the train. They blew up and looted the safe, and got away with around fifty thousand dollars. This was an expensive bit of revenge.

Butch was on a roll. The Pinkertons, not to mention every lawman in the West, were on high alert, looking for Cassidy and his gang. But he knew he'd need a little more money before he could slip out of the country, so he planned to hit the bank in Winnemucca, Nevada, right on the heels of this job. This was going to be his last haul.

On September 19, 1900, Butch Cassidy and the Wild Bunch robbed the Nevada bank. An outlaw named Will Carver had slipped into the lobby first, dressed like a hobo with a shabby bedroll. No one suspected that concealed in the bedding was a new Winchester—cocked and loaded. The holdup went off as planned, and the gang rode off with a cool thirty-two thousand dollars. The outlaws made their way to Texas for one last big Wild Bunch party at their favorite house of ill repute, Hell's Half Acre, before going their separate ways.

After a short stay in New York, Butch Cassidy, the Sundance Kid, and a woman named Etta Place sailed for South America. There they tried ranching, were guards at a mine, and did a number of outlaw jobs—wearing out their welcome quite quickly. By 1908, word got out that they'd been killed in Bolivia. The outlaws were probably glad to have this rumor spread—indeed, they probably started it.

Most historians now agree that Butch and Sundance came back to the United States sometime between 1910 and 1913 and led separate lives. There are numerous accounts of both Butch and Sundance visiting acquaintances in the United States after this time. Such stories are cloaked in secrecy, since friends and family didn't want their loved ones apprehended. There was still a price on Butch's head, so he had to be careful. But Matt Warner, Elza Lay, and others claimed that Butch visited them during this time.

Butch worked in a number of places, and most likely lived in Spokane, Washington, part of the time. It's thought he took a new name—William Phillips. It is also rumored that he worked at ranching and mining—even as a mercenary. Most agree he spent the later part of his life as a businessman in the Pacific Northwest.

LeRoy Parker, aka Butch Cassidy, is reported to have died in 1937.

THE SUNDANCE KID

The Gunfighter's Reputation

The Sundance Kid often called Utah home. He liked the land, and he liked the people. At least for a while, it was a haven from posses and lawmen. He came to escape, relax, and hide. Other than some rustling, he committed few crimes in the Beehive State's boundaries.

The Kid's real name was Harry Alonzo Longabaugh. He was born around April 1868. There was a fire in the courthouse in Mont Clare, Pennsylvania, so there are no official records. His birthday might be a year or two off either way. Young Harry was the last of five children brought up in a strict, God-fearing home. His father, a farmer, was a Civil War veteran who had served with the Union army. In the Longabaugh home, God was a northerner, and strict rules were needed to keep one on the straight and narrow.

Like all farm boys in his day, Harry could handle a rifle and a shotgun. Marksmanship came easy for him. He enjoyed hunting and shooting and being out in the woods. Young Longabaugh also liked school and was a better-than-average student. He loved to read and enjoyed the study of history. He even joined a literary group in 1882. He had a keen interest in Shakespeare, and his attitudes were somewhat more liberal than his folks appreciated. He read the classics, but he also had a passion for dime novels and could be considered a romantic. He was especially fond of stories that dealt with the West. More than anything else, the young lad dreamed of going to the territories and becoming a cowboy. He also wanted to be a gunfighter, an Indian fighter, and an explorer.

As a schoolboy, Harry seemed to get in his fair share of fights. Besides the black eyes and bruised knuckles, this activity always brought a scolding from his mother. Harry had a short fuse, so his mother encouraged him to work on his temper. Once he was pushed to a certain point, he flew off the handle and was unmanageable. While he had a small, close circle of friends, he didn't mind being alone, and some considered him a bit of a loner. Like his famous partner-to-be, he was a loyal man—to his friends and family, especially his older sister.

The siren call of the West, however, was too much. When he was fourteen years old, he left Pennsylvania for Colorado and adventures in the real West. In 1882 he hugged his beloved sister, Samana, wished his family a farewell, and went to live out his dream. He traveled by train and later by covered wagon to reach his cousin's ranch near Cortez, Colorado. The aspiring young westerner helped around the ranch for a while, but he had a wandering heart, and he didn't want to stay in one place when there was so much to see. He wanted to experience this exciting new world he'd inherited, so he moved around from ranch to ranch. This was not uncommon, as much of the available ranch work was seasonal.

He embraced the West and the cowboy trade. He learned his craft quickly and soon mastered it. He became a top hand in anyone's book. He took to ranch work and livestock as if he had been born to it. The future Sundance Kid drifted down to New Mexico. By now he could call himself a cowboy. He had a way with stock, especially horses, and was soon working as a horseman, a highly competitive position. He was indeed living out his dream and was eager to see the vast land called the American West before it was roped and tamed.

After a while, he rode north to Utah. He might have been tired of the range war he found himself in near Springer, New Mexico. He took work at the Lacy Cattle Company south of Monticello, Utah. The LC was one of Utah's very large spreads, with nearly fifteen thousand head on its ranges in various canyons. He worked as a horseman, breaking stock, and did some cowboy work during the slack time. Like all hands on the LC, he did his share of chasing rustlers. His ranch foreman at that time was a capable man named Bill Ball. Ball was shot to death by cattle thieves while young Harry was working for him. Not long after Ball's murder, Harry drifted up to the La Sal Mountains near Moab and worked for the Pittsburgh Land and Cattle Company, another large Utah ranch. Utah was developing into an important range at this time, although most of the ranches were considerably smaller than the two he had worked for. In the early part of the 1880s, there were 150,000 head of cattle in the Utah Territory. Within five years, the number of cattle had doubled to nearly 300,000 head. There was always a job for a good cowboy.

Ranch life was hard work, but when the day was done, the hands would hang about the bunkhouse, drink coffee, talk, or shoot their guns. There was a lot of target shooting going on, since many cowboys were vain about their marksmanship. By the time he was in his mid-teens, legend has it that the young lad could outshoot most any cowboy on the ranches he worked on. He was good with a rifle, but it was while he was a ranch hand in New Mexico and Utah that he learned and mastered the finer points of a Colt Peacemaker. He was also a quick study on the elements of the fast draw. Ironically, he couldn't afford his own handgun at this time.

A new Colt .45 cost one to two months' salary for a cowhand. For a lad who had grown up on the dime novels of his day, reading about Wild Bill and Buffalo Bill and the other gunslinging heroes of the pulp novel, this was living. No doubt he was saving up for his first pistol and gun belt with every paycheck. At any rate, he was very accurate on the fast draw (it's rather difficult to hit a target with any accuracy when one quick-draws, so this skill was noteworthy). And he was reported to be very fast. Shooting this way came second nature to him.

He drifted back to the Cortez area again, to visit his cousin and family. At this time he might have become acquainted directly or indirectly with Butch Cassidy, Matt Warner, and Tom McCarty through horse racing. Harry was a good trainer and a skilled jockey himself. Horse circles in the intermountain West were not that large. Butch, Matt, and Tom were working a four- or five-county circuit with their racehorses, so it's likely that he at least knew who they were (and they him).

After a while, racing got old and times got tough. Harry took a job pushing a herd from Texas to Montana.

In the mid-1880s, the restless young hand headed north. He worked on a ranch near Culbertson, Montana. He left and drifted down to Wyoming. He was between riding jobs and was hungry. Things were getting desperate. He lived off what he had saved. Then he started to sell off his possessions one at a time for eating money, waiting for something to come up the following spring. On February 27, 1887, broke, hungry, and cold, he became truly desperate.

The drought of 1886 had been severe, so ranches weren't hiring. Following the drought came the Great Blizzard of 1886–87—one of the worst winters on record in Montana and Wyoming. In early November the first storm hit. The temperature was below zero, and soon 6 to 8 inches of snow covered the ground. This snow was followed by storm after storm. At one time in January, it snowed more than an inch per hour. During another blizzard that January, it snowed for three straight days and nights without letup. Some snowbanks in gullies were said to be 70 feet deep. Houses, cabins, and barns were sometimes completely covered. The herds weren't in good shape to begin with because of the tough summer. The range and the necessary feed were limited. Cattle were dying, their frozen bodies littering the range like the leftovers of a buffalo shoot.

The situation was desperate. There were few jobs. Harry became a thief—possibly to survive. Until this time we have no evidence to suggest that he was anything but an honest cowpoke and horseman.

He took a six-gun from James Widner. From Alonzo Craven he took a horse, a bridle, and a saddle. Both were cowhands at the VVV Ranch near Crook County, Wyoming. Sheriff Jim Ryand was on Harry's trail immediately. For the first time in his life—and certainly not the last—he was on the run. He dodged Sheriff Ryand for four months. He was captured once but escaped. He was finally caught near Miles City, Montana. While he was running from the law, similar robberies occurred that were subsequently blamed on him.

For a wanted man, the future Sundance Kid had a lot to learn about being careful. He was new at this sort of thing. He should have left northeastern

Wyoming, but he didn't. Sheriff Ryand caught up with him for the first time on April 12 and took him aboard a train. Ryand wasn't a trusting man, but he had only three locks on his prisoner. The good sheriff felt the call of nature and left, thinking his captured thief couldn't get away, chained up as he was. Before the sheriff returned, Harry had picked the three locks and jumped from the train. This was the first of several miraculous escapes from the law. He said he felt like the train was going 100 miles per hour when he leaped to freedom.

This close call should have convinced Harry to leave Wyoming, but he continued to hang about the area. Finally Ryand caught up with him again. It was personal for the sheriff this time. He'd looked quite silly when his prisoner got away while he was in the head with his pants down. The sheriff took the thief to Sundance, Wyoming, for his trial. His prisoner was locked up and guarded very carefully this time, Ryand fearing he would escape again.

Harry was upset by the way the newspapers were treating him before his trial. He had admitted to the crime he committed against the two cowhands at the VVV but denied the others he was accused of. In jail awaiting trial, hoping to set the record straight, he wrote the following letter to the editor of the *Daily Yellowstone Journal* on June 9, 1887:

> *In your issue of June 7th, I read a very sensational and partly untrue article, which places me before the public not even second to the notorious Jesse James. Admitting that I have done wrong and expecting to be dealt with according to law and not by false reports from parties who should blush with shame to make them, I ask a little space to set my case before the public in a true light. In the first place, I have always worked for an honest living; was employed last summer by one of the best outfits in Montana and don't think they can say aught against me, but having got discharged last winter, went to the Black Hills to seek employment—which I could not get. . . .*
>
> *After this my course of outlawry commenced, and I suffered terribly for the want of food in the hope of getting back south without being detected. . . . Contrary to the statement in the* Journal, *I deny having stolen any horses. . . .*

The young man went to trial with a public defender. At first he entered a not guilty plea, but he later changed it to guilty when the saddle, bridle, and pistol thefts were dropped in a plea bargain. He decided to skip the jury trial and have the judge pass sentence. He was charged and convicted of horse theft. On August 5, 1887, he was sentenced to two years of hard labor. Since the Laramie prison was full, he got lucky. The state of Wyoming contracted with the Sundance jail to keep the prisoner (it was paid $4.20 a week to keep him; an additional fee of $2.00 was paid for clothing). Other governmental sources kicked in more funding.

In February 1889, Territorial Governor Thomas Moonlight pardoned him, so he was fully vested in his civil rights. The governor's pardon read: "He's still under 21 years of age and his behavior has been good since confinement, showing an earnest desire to reform and . . . the sheriff, clerk, court . . . and others have this day made application to me to grant unto the said Harry Longabaugh a pardon of said crime of which he stands convicted."

He walked out of the jail a free man. For the next few years he drifted. He headed down to Cortez, Colorado, for a visit with his cousin. From this point on, his sobriquet was the Sundance Kid—in satirical honor of the town where he'd been tried and done time. Some have suggested that Sundance might have been the extra man in the 1889 Telluride, Colorado, bank robbery. Telluride is only 80 miles from Cortez, where he stayed with kin. They conclude that as a horseman and horse racer in that area, Sundance obviously knew Tom McCarty, Matt Warner, and Butch Cassidy, who might have invited him to be in on the heist. They suggest that Sundance was identified by name as the bandits fled (even if he wasn't on the official Wanted poster). Additionally, in Longabaugh family lore, the escaping outlaws took shelter at George Longabaugh's ranch in Cortez. George Longabaugh's wife, Mary, supposedly fed the outlaws a number of times.

It is possible that Sundance helped rob the Telluride bank. He had just spent nearly two years in jail, and his worldview had changed. However, the evidence of his involvement is only circumstantial. Maybe more information will come to light at a later date. As suggested, he likely knew the soon-to-be-famous members of the McCarty Gang, but at this time in his life, this kind of criminal participation seems out of character. He was a minor rustler in those days, not a bank robber. Matt Warner, in his biography, doesn't mention Sundance being involved.

After leaving Cortez, Sundance rode the grub line in the Powder River country, working here and there. He also rode with a few different rustling outfits, stealing cattle and horses as the occasion arose. He drifted through Colorado, Utah, Wyoming, and Montana. He had a few scrapes but nothing too serious. Nevertheless, the crowd he started to hang with was a little bit rougher and more questionable than those he'd previously been seen with.

He started to hone his shooting skills. He was already an excellent shot, but he worked on his draw speed. He'd been out of practice for two years. Those who knew him at the time said he stayed away from trouble, but he already had a reputation as someone to avoid. He was a bad man to tangle with in a fight—especially a gunfight.

Throughout his career, he was known as a serious gunfighter, but he surely didn't have a killer's instinct. While he was in jail awaiting trial, a newspaper reporter said he was a young Jesse James. Sundance was not flattered by the comparison. In fact, he was offended. He had developed a quiet confidence about his skill with Samuel Colt's equalizer. But he wasn't eager to have a reputation as a killer.

Ironically, while considered a gunfighter, he very likely never killed anyone in the Old West—at least there is no record that he did. Apparently, he was so good that no one wanted to cross him, or he finally learned how to control his temper.

He spent time in Alberta, Canada, working at the Bar U Ranch near Calgary. He is recorded on the Canadian Dominion census. Further accounts confirm that he attended the wedding (and was best man) of a good friend who was the ranch foreman. During the winter of 1892, he went into business at the Grand Central Hotel Saloon in Calgary. The partnership soon dissolved, and he moved on.

Until November 29, 1892, Sundance's crimes never went beyond livestock rustling. However, he was about to change his professional status. Harry A. Longabaugh, drifter, cowhand, horseman, would become the Sundance Kid, a wanted criminal. There would be no going back.

With Bill Madden, an out-of-work puncher he had known back in 1884 near Cortez, and another jobless cowhand named Harry Bass, he held up the Great Northern train just outside Malta, Montana. The desperadoes climbed onto the first car, often referred to as the blind baggage car. They pulled the robbery in the wee hours of the night when it was dark (the train was on its way from St. Paul to Butte). The robbery had a number of comic elements about it. This was their first job, and they weren't very good at this crime business. It was an amateur effort. It wasn't well planned or thought through.

While they were holding up the train and shoving their Colts on the rail agent, their bandannas kept falling down. The agent got a good look at all three of the outlaws. (He was able to give such detailed descriptions that Bass and Madden were quickly captured.) Two outlaws took the agent to the express car while the third kept watch. There were several safes. They had the fellow open up two small safes—they got a whopping nineteen dollars plus change from one and six dollars from the other. When they told the agent to open the large safe, he said he couldn't. He said only a few officials along the route had the combination. Whether or not this was true, and it probably was, they seemed quite discouraged and went back to collect their partner with a staggering twenty-five bucks (some accounts say it was closer to seventy).

More experienced bandits might have threatened the agent with bodily harm to see if he was bluffing. Or more likely they would have planned for this contingency and had a few sticks of TNT handy. To make the job pay, most bandits would have at least robbed the agent and possibly some of the passengers, too.

This robbery was pulled off with little forethought. The disappointed trio rode away into the dark with pocket change. Madden and Bass enjoyed a few days of freedom. On December 1 at ten in the evening, because of the clear description given by the railway agent, the two were taken into custody while drinking in the local saloon. Sundance had the good sense at least to get out of town. Madden, thinking it would help him, confessed to their crimes almost at once and fingered all of his partners. Because of the description and since the law knew his name, Sundance was now a wanted man. He learned about the five-hundred-dollar reward on his head and took off, eventually heading south. There's a good chance that he might have been scared straight after this fiasco if he hadn't been fingered by his partner.

Shortly after their arrest, Madden and Bass were taken to Great Falls, Montana, for trial and were sentenced to ten years in prison. Both were released a few years later for good behavior. One dropped out of western history, and the other was killed in a gunfight in 1895.

Since Sundance was now a wanted criminal, he figured he ought to start acting like one. He headed for the safety of Brown's Hole. He'd been there before, but now as a wanted man he appreciated the "don't ask, don't tell" philosophy of the basin. He was well liked and made a number of close friends among the ranchers and settlers, as well as the outlaw contingent. Before long, he became a trusted member of a semi-organized group of outlaws. He liked Utah and the region and was glad to be back among friends. Sundance did a share of rustling at this time to keep the financial wolves away. He hung with all the regulars, including Kid Curry and Butch Cassidy. In 1897, after the famous meeting at Cassidy Point, he took off with Kid Curry to hold up the Butte County Bank in Belle Fourche, South Dakota. This bank was less than 30 miles from Sundance, Wyoming. This area was his old stomping grounds, and he knew the territory well.

Like his first robbery, the Belle Fourche job turned into a disaster—this time far more serious and potentially more deadly. It was better planned than the train robbery—but not much better. He and his crew were still pretty inexperienced at this sort of thing. Some of the men were at best flaky. The outlaws planned to rob the bank on June 27. They thought the vault would be stuffed with money because the town would be holding a big celebration for Civil War veterans. There would be a lot of drinking and merrymaking, and the outlaws hoped the town collectively would have its guard down as a result.

The bandits included Kid Curry, Sundance, Flat Nose Curry, Walt Punteney, and Tom O'Day. They camped out of town on June 26. O'Day was assigned to go into town to look over the place. He couldn't resist the watering holes and the party going on. He forgot about the job at hand and spent that day and the following night getting liquored up with the locals. He finally staggered back to camp with a hangover—it was now too late to pull the job that day. Worse, O'Day had forgotten to collect the information they needed. He did report that the jail had burned down.

They planned to hit the bank the next day.

O'Day again went ahead of the group to look things over, but he never got past the first bar. Rumor has it he tucked two whiskey bottles into his saddlebags and drank them before the others rode in.

The bank job was a disaster, and the take was very disappointing. They bungled the holdup, but they managed to escape, barely.

Sundance, the Currys, and Punteney were taken prisoner following a shoot-out in Montana. They were brought back to Deadwood and jailed (since the jail in Belle Fourche had burned down). O'Day was jailed too. Not being able to pass up a whiskey bottle, he had been captured rather quickly. The bail for the outlaws was ten thousand dollars.

John Mansfield was the jailer at the time. He was feeding the prisoners about eight o'clock one evening when Sundance jumped up and knocked the wind out of the surprised jailer with a few well-timed punches to the gut. Kid Curry and Sundance let out O'Day and Punteney. They escaped into the night.

Saddle horses were waiting for the men. Legend has it that Butch Cassidy and a few friends were there to help. It would be the kind of thing Butch would have done for a pal, but there is no evidence to prove this theory. Certainly someone had left the horses there, but perhaps it was just a lucky break. O'Day and Punteney were captured within the week. Kid Curry, Flat Nose, and Sundance made tracks. The object was to get as far from Deadwood as they could. Sundance headed south to meet up with Butch and Elza Lay. He wanted to be a long way from this part of the world—it held bad memories.

Likely at this time he began to realize that he wasn't a rocket scientist when it came to planning a job—and neither was Kid Curry. He did pull another job with Curry, but that was a few years later in Elko, Nevada. On one of his long vacations, Sundance went to Elko to gamble, a favorite pastime. The cards weren't turning well after a week or two, so before he left, he decided to even things up. In the wee hours, Sundance, Kid Curry, and Flat Nose Curry entered the Club Saloon and forced the proprietor to open the safe at gunpoint. The robbers got between five hundred and three thousand dollars, probably not enough to break even, but enough for them to get back to Utah.

Within a few weeks, they were back in Brown's Hole. They knew that Butch was planning some big jobs, and they wanted to be a part of the action.

It was after Elza Lay went to prison in 1899 that Butch and Sundance became close friends. Sundance became a trusted second in command. He was obviously a quick study and tried not to make the same mistakes twice. It is generally understood that it was on the Wild Bunch's Tipton train robbery in 1900 that he first took Elza's place.

It's important to note that like Butch and many of the other Wild Bunch riders, the Sundance Kid was a criminal. He threatened deadly force to get money—stealing from people was his occupation. He could have been a fine rancher, but he was too busy taking shortcuts. He liked to drink, although he was rarely drunk. He liked to gamble, and he probably gambled too much. He enjoyed women of the evening. Nevertheless, he wasn't a mean-spirited man, and he had a number of good qualities. He was faithful to his friends, and he was charitable.

As with his partner in crime, Butch Cassidy, the evidence is conclusive that the Sundance Kid was not killed in San Vicente, Bolivia. (DNA tests on the bodies in question proved negative in 1995.) Their reported Bolivian death was surely a smoke screen to cover their tracks on both hemispheres, so they could slide into obscurity.

A number of people visited with Sundance after his return to the United States, including Matt Warner, the Bassett sisters, Butch, and Elza Lay. Calling himself Caleb Landreth, Sundance helped Elza look for the lost Caleb Rhoades Mines on Ute Indian land. Like Butch, the Sundance Kid likely lived to a ripe old age.

DART ISOM

The Black Rustler from Brown's Hole

Dart Isom, sometimes known as Black Isom, was one of the original settlers in Brown's Hole—probably arriving in the mid- to late 1870s.

A respected man and a top cowhand in anyone's book, he had a way with horses. His gentle-trained, hand-raised cow ponies were among the best in the Rocky Mountains. Dart was a patient man, a man beloved by local ranch children. It was not unusual for him to get down on his hands and knees and play with the kids for hours while the adults talked. He was a friendly sort, helpful at branding time or during roundups, a good fighter, an expert with a lariat.

Dart was a skilled rustler (which also made him a respected man in the Hole). He could slip in and "take cattle out from under your nose." But that wasn't all. He was a noted artisan at doctoring brands with a hot iron or a saddle ring. He had a nice herd built up, thanks in part to Hoy and Two Bar cattle. Branding questionable stock was his specialty. At one time he was indicted in the Sweetwater country, but his case wasn't brought to trial.

Born in 1855, Dart was a former slave and a cowman from Texas. With his saddle partner, Matt Rash, Dart had helped push a herd to the northern prairies. When the cattle were sold, the two drifted south and found a niche in Brown's Hole. In that part of the West, Dart discovered, a man was judged more on his ability and less by the color of his skin.

Dart was a flashy dresser, wearing a floppy sombrero with a wide rattlesnake band. He sported a silk bandanna about his neck, and a large topaz ring graced his finger. He played a mouth organ and the fiddle and was often featured at the local dances, along with Rash, who played the Mexican guitar.

As a loyal friend of the Bassett family, especially Elizabeth Bassett (matriarch of the Bassett clan), he was a member of the Bassett Gang—following Elizabeth on highly successful raids against the Two Bar and Hoy Ranches (neighbors she was feuding with). He was Elizabeth's right-hand man.

His daring rustling exploits, especially against the Two Bar in Colorado, were the toast of the local ranchers. After a while, Dart's midnight "cattle round-ups" brought him to the attention of the baron ranchers whose herds he (along with Rash) had lightened considerably. He'd rustled a few cattle too many. The big ranches put pressure on the Rock Springs sheriff to do something about "that damned nest of outlaws living in the Hole"—the worst being Black Isom. The sheriff was a sensible man who knew there was no way he'd ride into and out of Brown's Hole alive—let alone find Dart Isom. No lawman had ever ridden into those parts and ridden out alive. The good sheriff liked to drink whiskey, listen to the piano at the dance hall, and hunt antelope—things he couldn't do if he was pushing up sagebrush. It was a fool's errand, anyway.

To keep the big ranchers off his back, he talked an outlaw named Joe (in some accounts his name is listed as Jim) Philbrick into bringing the rustler Isom to trial. Never mind that Joe was wanted in three states and suspected of rustling in Wyoming. The sheriff kept the new appointment quiet so the news wouldn't spread, pinned the deputy badge on Philbrick, gave him some traveling money, and wished him luck as he headed for the biggest nest of rustlers in the United States. He doubted that this temporary deputy would return alive. Chalk another one up to Brown's Hole, since Deputy Joe Philbrick, one-time outlaw, would never see Rock Springs again.

But sometimes it takes an outlaw to catch an outlaw.

No one is sure how Deputy Joe got the drop on the wily Dart Isom, but he did. It was likely Dart was on his own turf and had his guard down. No lawman had dared come into the Hole before. Joe had the drop, so the rustler went without a fuss. You don't argue with a cocked Colt six-gun. Joe tied Dart up and put him in his buckboard—which was a curious way to travel. Nearly everyone at that time rode on horseback because the roads were less than desirable for wheeled transport.

A day out of Rock Springs, on a steep section of rough road, the wagon slid off the track and tumbled down a gully. Dart managed to jump free as the buckboard flipped. The deputy wasn't so lucky. Joe was seriously hurt in the accident and pinned under the wagon. Dart loosened his tied hands and pried the wagon off the injured man with a pole. He dragged Joe free, stopped his bleeding, and tended to the man's injuries to the best of his abilities. When his patient was stable, he righted the wagon, gathered up the spooked stock, repaired the broken tack, and started off to Rock Springs as fast as he could. He knew that Joe had internal injuries and needed serious medical help. Nearly killing the poor horses, he got Joe to a doctor. He stopped, had a stiff drink, and turned himself in to the Rock Springs sheriff.

He was promptly thanked for his heroics and jailed.

When Deputy Joe started to mend, he vowed he would do all he could to get Dart out of jail. Dart could have freed himself, but he had put his life in jeopardy to help the man who was bringing him in to trial—and that meant something to a westerner. Joe said that he'd shoot the sheriff or break Dart out of jail himself if he had to. Most of the townsfolk felt the same way. Dart had showed moral character, and that certainly overshadowed any crimes he may or may not have committed.

Dart Isom came to trial in Rock Springs a couple of weeks later.

Deputy Joe testified in his favor. It didn't take the jury long to find the man not guilty. Few of the townspeople, including the sheriff, cared much for the big cattle bosses anyway. At that time in the West, it was rare for a local jury, usually composed of workingmen—most of whom had taken a few cows when no one was looking—to convict a fellow of "borrowing cattle" from a man who could afford to miss them (and who probably stole them "legally," himself).

Dart had some drinks with the locals and headed back a free man to his ranch and his growing herd in Brown's Hole. The large ranchers in southwestern Wyoming and northwestern Colorado were quickly losing faith in the criminal justice system. They could bring a cattle thief to trial, but it was difficult to get him convicted by an unsympathetic jury.

Two could play this deadly game of frontier chess. If the courts wouldn't help the large ranches clean up the range, they'd be forced to take the law into their own hands. Yes, the large cattle barons were often ruthless and immoral in their practices. Yes, they frequently rode roughshod over smaller ranching concerns who couldn't stand up to their political clout or their hired gunslinging cowboys. Yes, they yielded little local sympathy and too often administered their own brand of justice. Men like Tom Horn, so-called range detectives, charged up to six hundred dollars a body. There were no juries to contend with, and a bullet had a finality of its own. Of Horn it was said, "He had a method that never failed." If the law wouldn't do its job, the big cattlemen could find someone who would.

Dart didn't know it, but when he saw two men riding off Cold Spring Mountain near the draw where he was hiding, it was the beginning of the end. He knew the two men: Matt Rash and his new summer hand, a man named Hicks. They were coming off the summer range. Dart noted that Hicks was tall and weathered, and he rode a horse like a man born in the saddle. Dart liked him.

Hicks was good with stock. It appeared that Matt had hired himself a good hand. When Dart and Matt had played at the schoolhouse dance the previous Saturday, Hicks had joined in with his mouth organ. Later, he stood his two new friends at least four stiff drinks. You had to like a man who wasn't tight with his whiskey. The next day, Dart showed Hicks where Matt's line cabin was in the high country.

As Dart was leaving the mountain, Hicks offered to buy the sorrel gelding he was riding. The pony might have been the best cow horse in the basin. Matt, too, had tried to buy the horse a number of times—even though he knew it wasn't for sale. Dart had raised the pony from a bottle, and he'd have sooner lost an arm than part with it. Hicks didn't miss much with those deep eyes of his— he knew a good horse.

As the two men rode up the trail, Dart pointed his Winchester and half-heartedly said, "I'll shoot ya if ya comin' up fath'r."

Matt knew Dart wouldn't shoot, so he nosed his horse up the draw and saw what Dart was trying to hide. A dead animal was lying in the gully. It was a roan shorthorn, Sam Spicer's prize breeding bull. Old Man Spicer, a crusty sort, had spread a bunch of rumors about Dart. There'd been bad blood between them for a long time. No doubt, shooting the animal was Dart's way of getting back.

Dart cocked his Winchester in a threatening manner—something he shouldn't have done when facing his friend. Like lightning, Matt drew his six-shooter and shot a hole in the stock of the weapon, not appreciating Dart's gesture. Hicks and Dart were a little stunned at how fast he'd pulled his pistol and fired.

"You got one chance," Matt grinned, looking at his smoking Colt. "Go tell Sam about your shooting his bull and pay him 'fore he hunts you down with that buffalo gun. If ya want me to keep mum and take yore chances—I won't tell. But I'll be wanting that sorrel horse of yours as payment for my silence."

Dart wasn't going to tell Spicer about the bull and Matt knew it. Nor was he going to give Matt his best horse to keep quiet. Later, Matt would take the prized cow pony when Dart wasn't looking. He'd tell the Hole folks he'd bought it. Dart couldn't press the issue since Matt would tell about him shooting the bull. Dart wasn't happy about how things turned out, but he'd wait and let the bull issue die down, then he'd steal back his horse when Matt had his back turned.

During these few weeks, Hicks had seen and heard enough to convict both Dart and Matt. Hicks's real name was Tom Horn, and he was undercover to get the goods on the worst rustlers in the Hole. Specifically, he had been sent to collect evidence on Matt Rash and Dart Isom. He'd first worked for Sam Spicer, owner of the bull. He despised Spicer and didn't care about the shorthorn—the old man deserved it for bad-mouthing. But he now had hard evidence on Dart and Matt for rustling.

The jury was in. Both men were guilty, and Tom knew what to do—Matt first, then Dart.

It happened during a chilly autumn. It had been four months since Dart had plugged Spicer's bull in the draw at the bottom of Cold Spring Mountain. Tom had since executed Matt Rash. Now the leaves were turning, and there was a heavy frost each morning. The elk bulged. Winter wasn't far off. At first Dart had been blamed for Matt's murder, the way Tom had planned it. Dart's name had been circulated in the Brown's Hole rumor mill, but after the initial investigation, few considered him a suspect in Matt's death.

The locals had come to realize that Hicks was really the killer Tom Horn. After shooting Matt, Tom had walked out to the corral and put a bullet in the horse he'd tried to buy earlier. Folks knew Dart had raised and trained that pony and loved it. Dart surely wasn't the killer since he'd never shoot a fine pony.

On October 4, partway up Cold Spring Mountain, Dart's good friends, including the Bassett brothers and Billy Rash, were visiting. Everyone was still a little jumpy since Matt's murder. They hadn't seen Tom for months, so they hoped he'd left the country. It was chilly that morning as Dart walked out to the woodpile to get fuel for their breakfast fire. The Bassett brothers were coming out the door for some extra armloads. They were laughing and telling stories. In the still, frosty air, two shots rang out so fast that at first they sounded like one. The first slug took Dart in the face, killing him instantly. As he was falling, a second bullet ripped a hole in his chest. The Bassett brothers were frightened and ran for the safety of the cabin, where they spent the rest of the day. They slipped out the next evening by sawing a hole in the back of the shack.

Later, two .30-30 cases were found next to a ponderosa pine a little over a hundred yards from the cabin. It was obvious who'd killed Dart. The .30-30 Winchester was Tom's calling card.

Tenderly, the murdered man was wrapped in a blanket and buried near his cabin. The funeral words were spoken by the fiery Ann Bassett. She prayed for God to strike Tom Horn dead for this poor man's murder and for the murder of her betrothed, Matt Rash.

After Dart Isom was laid to rest, the Two Bar and other ranches noticed a significant decrease in their cattle losses.

BLACK BART

A Famously Friendly Stagecoach Bandit

Before the railroads came in, people and valuables were usually transported throughout the West by stagecoach. Clattering along networks of primitive roads in remote country, they were extremely vulnerable and tempting targets for thieves. Robbers who specialized in stagecoach heists were often referred to as "road agents." A novice highwayman might think the obvious strategy would be to lift the personal valuables from the stage's passengers. The savvy road agent knew the juicy targets were the stages that traveled gold country, usually carrying lots of cash, gold coins, gold dust, and registered mail for the taking. In the mid- and late 1800s southwest Oregon offered plenty of juicy targets.

In 1848 gold was discovered in California, and the rush was on. Men, mostly in their twenties and thirties, journeyed to the Golden State not only from places throughout America, but from England, Europe, and other parts of the world as well, hoping to strike it rich. As the horde of gold seekers fanned out across northern California, they made their way into southern Oregon as well, lusting for that glitter of yellow in its streams and rivers.

In 1850 and 1851 the search paid off, with gold strikes on Oregon's Josephine Creek, the Illinois River, and a number of streams in the Jacksonville area. This sparked a second rush of gold seekers from both northern California and Oregon's Willamette Valley, who staked claims along the Rogue, Applegate, and Pistol Rivers, among others. Rowdy mining camps sprang up, and from the prosperity brought by the gold economy, Jacksonville grew into a real community—the first in Jackson County.

By the early 1860s regular stagecoach service had been established between Sacramento and Portland. Run by the California Stage Company, the route was more than 700 miles long, and stages ran daily, with one headed south and the other north.

On those stagecoaches, in addition to passengers, rode a variety of items of interest to road agents: cash, gold coins, registered letters filled with gold dust, and other valuables on their way from the goldfields and local businesses to big city banks. A gold shipment carried by stagecoach might commonly be worth as much as $10,000.

But it wasn't just the fact that southern Oregon was gold country that made the area enticing to stagecoach robbers, but the nature of the country as well and the Siskiyou Mountains in particular.

The wild and remote Siskiyou Mountains straddle the Oregon-California border and lie within Jackson County to the north and Siskiyou County on the south. Their lonely trails seldom saw lawmen, and their rugged terrain worked in favor of outlaws on the run. The Siskiyous were the perfect place to rob a stagecoach.

Road agents figured that out pretty quickly, and several gangs formed during southern Oregon's gold rush days specifically to prey on stagecoaches. Holdups along the Siskiyou Mountains stagecoach roads were a fairly regular occurrence—sometimes as often as one per week.

Planning a stage robbery didn't take a great deal of deep thinking, and the strategy was generally the same. The stage was most vulnerable as it was lumbering uphill with the horses pulling at a slow walk. The road agents would suddenly step from behind a tree or bush, brandishing rifles, shotguns, or pistols, and order the stage driver to halt and throw down the Wells Fargo "express box" that held the loot. Taking an ax to the box, they would remove the goods and vanish into the silent mountains, leaving behind a frustrated driver to continue on his way, his load considerably lightened. But by no means did all road agents get away with the goods.

In May 1857 one of southern Oregon's crack stagecoach drivers, Jack Montgomery—who was always in demand—was hired by the Jacksonville office of the Oregon and California Stage Coach Line to haul a Wells, Fargo & Company gold shipment worth about a half million dollars. He was to take it to Portland where Wells Fargo would then arrange to have it shipped to company headquarters in San Francisco. The company offered Montgomery $250 for the job, and he accepted. Secrecy, for obvious reasons, was paramount, but word of big gold shipments tended to get around.

Pulling a ten-horse stage with the gold stuffed into canvas bags, Montgomery, along with a few passengers and accompanied by two armed guards, made his way north at top speed. But at Umpqua Falls an explosion rocked the trail ahead, sending the horse team into a panicked run that spun the coach out of control.

Montgomery leaped from the stage as rocks crashed down upon it, killing one of the guards. The other guard ran off screaming and then collapsed in the forest. Passengers, trapped in the stage, cried for help as the four bandits who had placed the dynamite charge grabbed as many sacks of gold as they could carry. Montgomery, although injured, tried to stop them but had to run for his life instead, making it to a nearby stage station before falling to the floor unconscious.

Montgomery recovered, but the robbers fared less well. Not long afterwards, a group of vigilantes found four men holed up in a cave in the Siskiyou Mountains with several sacks of gold. The posse hanged them on the spot.

Although southern Oregon's gold boom was just about played out by the late 1860s, it didn't cause too much hardship on the part of the road agents since northern California's goldfields were still producing. And that gold still traveled by stage through the Siskiyou Mountains between Oregon and California.

Two of those routes that regularly carried the kinds of cargo coveted by road agents were the Roseburg to Yreka and Roseburg to Redding roads. Sometime in the summer of 1880, Black Bart, who had mainly been working the California side of the Siskiyous, decided that he had not been giving the Oregon side of the mountains the attention it deserved.

Black Bart was fast becoming the most famous and successful stagecoach robber in the West. He had made his debut as a road agent on July 26, 1875, on Funk Hill along the Sonora–Milton stagecoach road in Calaveras County, California. Stagecoach robberies and highwaymen had been a dime a dozen in northern California and southern Oregon since the early 1860s, but in spite of the routine nature of these holdups—if being robbed can be considered a routine experience—Bart had managed to pull off his first heist with a certain flair and presence that had made him an immediate standout.

What stagecoach driver John Shine first noticed about the man standing in the road—besides the shotgun, which unbeknownst to all his victims over the years was always unloaded—was that the road agent said "please" when he ordered the Wells Fargo express box and mail sacks to be thrown to the ground. He wore plain homespun clothes under a duster and a flour sack over his head with eyeholes cut out. The T-shaped slashes he made in the mail sacks to gain entry became another distinctive aspect of his holdup signature.

When the outlaw had finished his work, he had $160 in gold notes and an undetermined amount of cash and other valuables. The next day, Wells, Fargo & Company offered a $250 reward for the capture of the "flour sack" bandit.

He gave himself his outlaw moniker during his fourth robbery. After relieving the stagecoach driver of about $600 in gold coins and a check, he left behind a bit of verse:

> *I've labored long for bread*
> *For honor and for riches,*
> *But on my corns too long you've tread*
> *You fine haired sons of bitches*
> *Black Bart, the Po8*

The name Black Bart came from a character in a popular novel of the time, and it had caught his fancy. But he was really Charles Boles, in his early forties, with gray hair, a mustache, and neatly trimmed chin whiskers. Standing about 5 feet 8 inches tall, he had a dignified and urbane countenance.

His family immigrated to the United States in the 1830s, settling in Jefferson County, New York. When gold fever struck California, Boles and a cousin headed west, arriving in the goldfields in 1850, hoping to strike it rich. They returned home unsuccessful the following year. He made another ill-fated mining trip to California with his cousin and brother, both of whom died shortly after arriving in San Francisco.

Boles went back to the East, married, had two daughters, and worked and farmed in the Midwest. When the Civil War broke out, he enlisted in the Union Army, mustering in as a private in Company B, 116th Illinois Volunteers on August 13, 1862.

During the war he saw a good deal of action, fighting in such battles as Vicksburg, Arkansas Post, Chickasaw Bayou, Champion Hills, and Black River Ridge. He also marched to Atlanta with General William Tecumseh Sherman. He was wounded in action, rose to the rank of first sergeant, and would likely have been offered an officer's commission if he had not left the army at the end of the war.

After military service he returned home, but over the next decade apparently tired of domestic life and living in the heartland. In the mid-1870s he moved to Montana and then, by 1878, to San Francisco where he posed as prosperous mine owner, Charles Bolton, slipping away periodically to ply his real profession. He would never see his wife and daughters again.

By the time he turned a larcenous eye to the Oregon side of the Siskiyou Mountains, he had thirteen stagecoach robberies under his belt, was a favorite subject of newspaper reporters, and was the focus of an all-out investigation by special agents of the Wells, Fargo & Company.

Conventional highwayman wisdom said that you robbed a stage coming from the goldfields when presumably there was gold aboard, not when it was going to the fields to pick it up. But Black Bart (his real identity was still unknown) was no conventional road agent, and he made his plans to rob the southbound Roseburg to Yreka stage on September 16, 1880. It was going to be a night job, a tactic that had become something of a specialty with Bart, the cover of darkness making his trademark escapes on foot more effective.

This would be Black Bart's fourteenth stage holdup, and he was becoming more than a nuisance to Wells, Fargo & Company. The gold he was stealing belonged to the company or its customers to whom company policy demanded reimbursement for losses. The company was extremely frustrated, even if the robber was a famous folk hero.

Henry Wells and William Fargo had founded Wells, Fargo & Company in 1852. Based in San Francisco, the economic center for the northern California gold rush, the company provided banking services, including buying gold and selling bank drafts backed by gold, and delivered gold and other valuables to various points throughout the West. As their success grew, they opened offices in other western cities and even in remote mining camps.

The company's stagecoach empire had its beginning in 1858 when it helped found the Overland Mail Company stage line. Eventually the company took over the western leg of the Pony Express and by 1886 assumed control of virtually all the major stage-line routes in the West, from Nebraska to the Pacific Ocean.

The centerpiece of Wells, Fargo & Company's stage operations was the famed Concord Coach. Built in Concord, New Hampshire, and costing about $1,100 each, they weighed about 2,500 pounds and were each pulled by a team of six horses. Their interiors were leather and damask cloth, and the special "thorough braces" suspension composed of leather strips provided what passed as a comfortable ride for the time period. The company also used another model stage called a Henderson, which was a little lighter than the Concord and could be pulled by four horses.

Sometimes referred to as "mud wagons," they were both designed to carry people and freight through just about any kind of terrain the West could throw at them.

The men who drove the stages or rode shotgun were as tough as they came. Striking out on the trail well before dawn and driving until late at night, they stopped at a stage station along the way to water, feed, and rest the horses— and maybe even get a little food and rest themselves—before hitching up and getting under way again in the early morning darkness. Their job was to get the stage through, no matter what the weather, how deep the mud, or how thick the bandits.

George Chase was just that kind of driver as he guided his horse team up the Oregon side of the road to the 4,466-foot-high Siskiyou Summit. It was sometime between 11:00 p.m. and midnight. Although there was a bright moon out, the carriage lanterns provided a little extra light as they rocked back and forth with every swaying movement of the stage, casting weird and erratic shadows on the road and the trees.

But then, there in the moonlit way, just half a dozen or so miles from the state line, stood a man in work clothes and a linen duster. He had a flour sack over his head and a 12-gauge shotgun pointed at Chase. He politely asked the driver to throw down the express box.

The Wells, Fargo & Company express box was what every road agent was after, although none asked for it so graciously as Black Bart. Made by San Francisco cabinetmaker Joseph William Ayer, they were wooden boxes 20 inches long, 12 inches wide, and 10 inches high, reinforced with iron straps.

This was where the gold and cash resided. The express boxes were stored in the "boot" of the stage located under the driver's feet. As robberies became more common, the boxes were bolted to the stage to make it more difficult for outlaws to get at them. Eventually, the company went to all-metal boxes.

On this night the wood and iron-strapped express box was chained to the boot at the rear of the stage. Keeping driver Chase covered—he had no shotgun rider with him this run—Bart took an ax and went to work on the box. Next, he went hunting through the mail sacks slashing them with his trademark T design.

With business completed at just about midnight, he vanished into the mountains, leaving not a trace of evidence for the lawmen who came to investigate the crime scene the following day.

In reporting the incident, the Yreka (California) *Journal* noted that the southbound stages were rarely robbed because there was usually not much of value on stages headed in that direction. But the joke was on them, for Black Bart had made off with about $1,000 in cash and a purported significant haul in the registered letters. It was, in fact, his most profitable robbery to date.

With a success story like that, how could anyone resist coming back for a replay? Certainly not Black Bart. A week later, on Thursday, September 23, he was back in Jackson County. This time he was after the northbound Yreka to Roseburg stage.

Just a few miles north of the state line, the driver (who was either George Chase or Nort Eddings) heard the familiar road agent cry of "throw down the box." There was Black Bart with his duster, flour-sack face, and unloaded shotgun. The box landed on the packed dirt with a thud. Bart fell upon it immediately, fleeing a few minutes later, $1,000 richer. As usual, he left no incriminating evidence behind.

Back in town, the *Jacksonville Democratic Times,* in noting that the driver had been previously robbed by a road agent at the exact same location, quoted the driver as saying that he was "getting tired of this sport."

On September 26, President Rutherford Hayes, the first U.S. president to visit the West Coast, accompanied by General Sherman, traveled on a stage from California to Oregon taking the Siskiyou Pass road. If Black Bart had waited a few more days to pull off robbery number fifteen, he might have really made history.

Black Bart moved back down into California after that, but continued to rob the Roseburg stage line. He finally made his fatal error on Funk Hill on November 3, 1883, the site of his very first depredation. In fleeing the scene of the holdup under a hail of bullets, he left behind a handkerchief with a laundry mark. James Hume, chief of Wells, Fargo & Company detectives, and his agents, who had been chasing Bart for eight years, found his San Francisco launderer, who identified Black Bart as upstanding citizen Charles Bolton, who was really Charles Boles.

Before long they had Boles in custody and had convinced him to plead guilty to the Funk Hill robbery rather than risk a trial for the twenty-eight or twenty-nine other stagecoach holdups he was suspected of committing. Never admitting to any other robberies but the one, he was sentenced to six years in San Quentin prison. He was released in just over four, in January 1888, for good behavior.

Black Bart promptly disappeared, although rumors of him robbing stages from Colorado to Alaska popped up for years. One persistent story told of a dignified, graying gentleman who was shot to death while trying to rob a stagecoach in Nevada and buried in a shallow grave among the sagebrush. But there were never any verified sightings of the old road agent after he left prison. If the ghost of Charles Boles, aka Black Bart, roams the earth, he must surely be somewhere waiting along the dark and fading stagecoach trails of the Siskiyou Mountains.

DAVE TUCKER

From Bank Robbery to Redemption

Dave Tucker was an upstanding citizen in the northeast Oregon ranching community of Joseph. How could the vice president of the Joseph State Bank be anything else? Before that, he was a respected businessman, rancher, and farmer. And before that, he had worked tending and shearing sheep until he earned enough money to start his own sheep and cattle business. What more respectable a background could a man raised in the wild, frontier days of Wallowa County have?

If you were to have walked into the Joseph State Bank to do business with Tucker, you would have found him honest and forthright—a pleasure to work with. But when you shook his hand to seal the deal, you probably would have noticed that his "trigger finger" was missing. That's because before Dave Tucker had gone respectable, he'd been a bank robber whose finger had been blown off during a getaway shoot-out. The bank he robbed, thirty-two years earlier in 1896, was the very one of which he had just been made vice president.

The Wallowa County of the late 1800s was very different from the one Tucker lived in now. His family came to the Wallowa Valley in 1877, and Dave was one of several boys in a large family of brothers and sisters. His father, a veteran of the Civil War, settled his brood on a homestead along Prairie Creek.

This was wild country in those days with lots of wilderness and few roads. Farming, cattle and sheep ranching, and timbering were the main occupations. The setting and the landscape were, as they are today, breathtaking, with the jagged peaks of the Wallowa Mountains towering above the immense Wallowa Valley.

Dave Tucker attended school for a short time and regularly worked with his father on the ranch. When his father could spare him, he worked for another rancher, Peter Beaudoin, herding and shearing sheep. When he sheared sheep, it was said, he carried with him a Bible that was given to him by former schoolmate and sweetheart Minnie Proebstel, whom he would later marry.

But some contemporaries have written that the Tucker boys could be trouble. Dave had a little trouble early on when he was charged with stealing a calf—a charge he vigorously denied—and sentenced to a year at the Oregon State Penitentiary. Out of prison, he was embittered and resentful of the experience, and it gave him a poor attitude. Nevertheless, when he got out of jail, he went back to work at his former occupation in the sheep camps.

Sometime in the summer of 1896, when Tucker was twenty-five years old, a couple of drifters wandered into the Wallowa Valley from Idaho. They were James Brown and Cyrus Fitzhugh, and had come to visit the wife of a Wallowa County homesteader to whom Fitzhugh was related. After visiting for a short time, the men took jobs in local sheep camps. This is probably where they met Dave Tucker.

Somewhere during the course of their long hours of labor, Fitzhugh suggested that they rob the First Bank of Joseph. Fitzhugh claimed to have experience at this sort of thing, having robbed a payroll in Montana. He also lied and said that he had been a member of the McCarty Gang that had held up the bank in Enterprise in 1891. Tucker felt he had a score to settle with society and told Fitzhugh and Brown to count him in.

In 1896 Joseph had only been an official town with a post office for sixteen years. It was a typical, remote frontier community of the day, with just a handful of buildings, including, of course, a bank and several saloons. Even in such a small ranch town, robbing a bank required some advance planning, and the three men began meeting at Martin's Saloon in Joseph to plot the details. Over the course of a couple of months, saloon owner John Martin and his bartender, Ben Ownbey, were drawn into the scheme.

It's difficult to say why the latter two men joined in. Martin was a successful and well-known businessman in town, and business was reputed to be good. Ownbey, in his mid-thirties, was a former deputy sheriff and deputy county clerk in Enterprise about 7 miles to the north. After losing his last political job in the 1890 local election, he moved to the outskirts of Joseph with his wife and three children and took a job at the saloon.

Finally, after many evenings around bottles of beer and glasses of whiskey, the plan was ready for execution—the date set for October 1, 1896. They estimated they would make off with about $6,000, assuming that the bank would be holding cash brought in by ranchers from the sale of the season's lamb crop. But as the date approached, Ownbey developed cold feet and wanted out. He got no sympathy from ringleader Fitzhugh, who told him if he tried to back out now he would "get him." Ownbey considered going to the bank and warning them about the impending heist, but figured Tucker, Fitzhugh, Brown, and Martin would just deny it and maybe murder him in retaliation. So he kept his mouth shut, but vowed to play as little a role in the robbery as possible.

Reports say that October 1, 1896, was one of those warm, gorgeous autumn days, with a clear blue sky and the aspens and cottonwoods resplendent in their gold-leaved glory. J. D. McCully, who was a cashier at the bank and a clerk at the McCully Store across the street, had been dividing his time between the two businesses all day long, locking the door of the bank when he left. Unknown to him, that afternoon Dave Tucker was casually hanging around in the street outside the bank, watching and waiting for McCully to open the doors once again.

At about 2:30 p.m. McCully unlocked the bank doors so he could attend to some customers' business. That was just what Tucker had been waiting for. He walked across the street and then back again—a predetermined signal for Fitzhugh and Brown, who were mounted on their horses and watching from a distance down the street, that the bank doors were open. (Another version has Ownbey giving the signal by walking across the street wearing a red bandanna around his neck.)

The bank was ripe for plucking. Fitzhugh and Brown rode purposefully down the dusty street, jumped off their horses, tied them to the hitching post and ran into the bank with six-shooters drawn. They wore bandanna masks and black soot rubbed on their faces to disguise their identities. One of them also carried a shotgun. Inside, along with cashier McCully, they found four bank customers—three women and one man who carried no weapon.

McCully was in the bank vault when the outlaws entered. They were so quiet that he didn't hear them and only realized the two interlopers were there when he walked out of the vault to see a couple of revolvers aimed in his direction.

"Throw up your hands," one of the masked men ordered.

As he believed it was a joke, McCully's first reaction was to laugh. But a closer inspection of those guns and the grim, disguised faces behind them made McCully realize this was no prank. It was a real bank robbery.

Outside, Tucker stood at the bank entrance with his revolver drawn, stopping anybody who passed by and keeping them there so as not to run off and sound the alarm. Ownbey stood alongside Tucker, but was not armed. John Martin appears not to have been at the scene of the robbery at all.

Before long, Tucker and Ownbey had a small crowd held hostage in front of the bank. Inside, Fitzhugh and Brown were stuffing cash and gold into a sack, while threatening McCully with death if he tried anything funny. In about ten minutes the two robbers had found all the cash and gold they could, a disappointing $2,000, and moved toward the door, using McCully as a shield. Once outside, the bandits got something they hadn't factored into their plans—a shoot-out.

Despite Tucker and Ownbey's efforts to keep a lid on the robbery in progress, the unusual situation of a crowd standing around in front of the bank was arousing suspicion among the townsfolk, many of whom were armed. One man who quickly figured out what was going on was rancher Fred Wagner. Standing behind his wagon in front of the McCully Store, Wagner picked up his .45-70 Winchester rifle and waited for the outlaws to show themselves. As they came out the door, he began firing. Another man commenced shooting from the upstairs window of a nearby building.

McCully dived to the ground as bullets whizzed by and ricocheted off the bank's front wall. Brown was hit before he got off the bank steps, falling backwards and landing in a sitting position with his head and shoulders propped against the bank wall, dead.

Bullets flew everywhere. Fitzhugh and Tucker, in a state of confusion and shock, began to fire back wildly but without fatal result. Brown had been carrying the bag of cash and gold, which now lay by his body directly in the path of withering gunfire. Fitzhugh, without hesitation, dashed for the treasure. Grabbing it while still firing his six-shooter and dodging the slugs meant for him, he ran to his horse. The town blacksmith tried to grab the horse away from the outlaw, but Fitzhugh knocked him aside. Holding onto the saddle horn, Fitzhugh hung on as his steed bucked up and down across the street. Swinging into the saddle, he reined his horse to the east and sped out of town with the sack of loot slung over his shoulder. On his way, he encountered a man walking down the street, a Southerner who had fought in the Civil War on the side of the Confederates. Fitzhugh shot at his feet to scare him, but it just made the gent, who was uncharacteristically unarmed that day, mad. Fitzhugh supposedly gave him instructions to tell the crowd at the bank "they can put their hands down now." With that, Fitzhugh rode off.

Meanwhile, back at the corner bank, things were still pretty hot. Dave Tucker had taken a bullet in his right hand, causing his revolver to go flying and hopelessly mangling his right index finger. Unarmed and bleeding, Tucker ran. Then, from out of the post office came local resident Alex Donnely with his shotgun. He fired it at Tucker as he sprinted away, and the pellets caught him in the side. Tucker staggered but kept going. With an angry crowd following him, he only got a couple of blocks.

Their first instinct was to string Tucker up on the spot. Upon further consideration, the crowd decided, since he was a local boy, to turn him over to Sheriff E. J. Forsythe instead. Tucker was lodged in the jail in Enterprise.

Ben Ownbey miraculously slipped off unscathed during the confusion of the getaway shoot-out. He and John Martin were arrested later when Tucker confessed to the crime and implicated his accomplices.

No trace of Fitzhugh could be found. It has been speculated that he stayed briefly at a friend's ranch near the upper Imnaha River and then crossed the Snake River into Idaho.

On April 21, 1897, Dave Tucker received a seven-year prison sentence at the Oregon State Penitentiary for his role in the robbery. Ben Ownbey got a slightly more lenient penalty because he was unarmed and played a less active role in the crime than Tucker. John Martin hired a Union County lawyer named

Carroll for $700 and was acquitted. James Brown's body was buried in the Hurricane Creek Cemetery. Legend has it that the young man had a sweetheart in the area who planted on his grave a rosebush that grew and bloomed for many years. Cyrus Fitzhugh and the $2,000 in cash and gold were never located. Fred Wagner received a gold watch from the First Bank of Joseph for his role in foiling the robbery.

While in prison, Tucker had ample time to mull over his mistakes. Determined to use his time as constructively as possible, he dropped the tough attitude to eventually become a model prisoner and trusty.

Released after four and a half years for good behavior, Tucker returned to his home in the Wallowa Valley to try to rebuild his life. He started working, once again, for sheep grower Peter Beaudoin. In a few years he saved up enough of a grubstake to buy a small number of lambs that he eventually parlayed into a herd of cattle and sheep and a 1,200-acre ranch. He married his childhood sweetheart, Minnie Proebstel, in 1906. His fortunes grew and his business prospered. He became known for the kindness and generosity he showed to his neighbors. It was said, "No one ever came to Dave Tucker for help that didn't get it." He hired those who needed work and gave a few bucks to those who were broke or in dire straits. He had literally transformed his life.

This full and remarkable circle was completed in 1928 when Tucker was elected vice president of the Joseph State Bank (formerly the First Bank of Joseph), the same establishment that he had robbed of $2,000 three decades before.

Years later, sitting in his bank office, Tucker must have sometimes cast his mind back to that beautiful October 1896 day and wondered how he had ever come to be standing before the bank door with revolver in hand. Perhaps he would idly wonder what became of Cyrus Fitzhugh and the $2,000. Maybe he recalled his anger and bitterness that Fitzhugh had escaped with the loot and left him missing a finger and serving time in prison. But it didn't matter anymore. All these years later, it was Dave Tucker, not Cyrus Fitzhugh, who had ended up with the real treasure.

FRANK NASHVILLE
"BUCKSKIN FRANK" LESLIE

The Lady Killer

May Leslie's knees buckled as she awaited the next volley of gunfire. The slightest movement from her might be her last, and she commanded her body to remain as rigid as a corpse as bullets whizzed about her head. Maybe one more round would satisfy the gunman. She heard the bullets click into the chamber as her husband prepared to fire again. He always took careful aim, as careful as anyone full of liquor could muster.

May watched him sway as he pointed the gun at her head. He slowly pulled the trigger and painted her portrait in bullets along the wall. As the gun clattered to the ground, so did Frank Leslie in a drunken stupor. May, known around Tombstone, Arizona, as the "Silhouette Girl" because of her husband's proclivity for shooting around her profile, fell in a trembling heap. She had survived seven years of marriage to Leslie, a man of sweet charm and deadly aim, but she figured her odds of surviving one more year were not good.

Leslie had been hanging around Tombstone since 1880, and he had earned a reputation as a hard-drinking, free-fisted, fast-shooting, storytelling lady's man. He related so many versions of his origins that even he probably didn't remember the truth. He usually claimed he was born in the early 1840s in Texas, but once told a reporter his family roots were in Virginia. He also said he served in the Confederate Army as a bugler; studied medicine in Heidelberg, Germany; served as a deputy sheriff in Kansas under Wild Bill Hickok; prospected in Colorado; had been a roughrider in Australia and a boat pilot in the Fiji Islands; owned a bar in San Francisco; and served as an army scout in the Dakotas, Oklahoma, Texas, and along Arizona's borders. Somewhere he acquired the nickname "Buckskin Frank" and dressed to suit the title in a fringed buckskin jacket.

Of course Leslie never offered any proof of his past whereabouts or his accomplishments. Texas and Virginia birth records do not exist for Frank Nashville Leslie. Neither are there records of him serving in the Confederate Army, of him attending a Heidelberg medical school, or of any lawman named Leslie riding with Hickok.

A couple of his stories have a semblance of truth, however. He probably did serve as a scout on the San Carlos Indian Reservation around 1877. And he tended bar in a couple of saloons in San Francisco until he moseyed into Tombstone.

Tombstone in 1880 was a town filled with gambling dens, saloons, and houses of pleasure. Leslie found work bartending at the Cosmopolitan Hotel, a two-story wooden building boasting a veranda, ladies' parlor, and sitting rooms. The saloon advertised a variety of wines, liquors, "and the finest brands of cigars." When not working behind the bar, Leslie could be found visiting any number of Tombstone saloons imbibing enough liquor to satisfy an entire herd of trail-dry cattle. His proclivity for liquor was only surpassed by his eye for the ladies, and he dressed to please them in his buckskin jacket, custom-made boots, and pearl-studded shirts.

May Killeen had recently separated from her husband, Mike, and taken a room at the Cosmopolitan. She and Leslie had exchanged pleasantries on more than one occasion. On the night of June 22, 1880, May asked Leslie to escort her home from a dance, and Leslie was more than happy to oblige. They headed for the hotel accompanied by Leslie's friend, George Perine. No one noticed the shadowy figure watching as they entered the hotel.

Now Mike Killeen had already warned Leslie to stay away from his wife, and Leslie had taken the precaution of borrowing a gun for the evening. It was against the law to carry weapons in Tombstone; all had to surrender firearms at the first saloon they encountered upon entering town. But those who felt the need of protection could always borrow a gun from behind the bar. Leslie had no problem obtaining a weapon for his evening stroll with May Killeen.

Mike Killeen watched the threesome enter the hotel and wasted no time following his wayward wife and Leslie. Perine headed for the bar while Leslie and May made their way to the second-floor veranda. From his place at the bar Perine spied Killeen entering the hotel. He shouted to Leslie that Killeen was on his way with murder in his eye and a gun in his hand.

The roar of gunfire sent hotel guests stumbling sleepily from their rooms only to hastily retreat behind locked doors as the two men emptied their guns. Killeen tumbled down the stairs and into the saloon with Leslie in hot pursuit. From behind the bar, Leslie grabbed a second pistol and fired another round at Killeen. When the smoke cleared, Killeen lay mortally wounded. He lingered for six days, long enough to swear Leslie started the ruckus. Leslie insisted Killeen came in shooting and he had no recourse but to return fire.

Arrested and charged with Mike Killeen's murder, Leslie relied on his own testimony and that of the not-so-grieving widow to swear Killeen came onto the veranda with gun blazing. It didn't take the coroner's jury long to acquit Leslie on the grounds of self-defense.

On August 5, just weeks after Leslie was released from jail, the same judge who officiated at Leslie's court hearing pronounced Frank Leslie and May

Killeen man and wife. The ceremony took place in the parlor of the Cosmopolitan Hotel. The *Tombstone Epitaph* congratulated the couple on their nuptials, lauding Leslie as *"un chevalier sans peur et sans reproche"* (a knight without fear and reproach).

Leslie moved down the street to the Oriental Saloon to work for owner Milt Joyce. The Earp brothers hung out at the Oriental and Leslie was welcome to drink with them, but he took no part in the infamous October 26, 1881, shoot-out at the O.K. Corral. Wyatt always said Leslie had the second-fastest draw in the territory, just behind Doc Holliday.

Over the years Leslie developed an interest in prospecting and filed several mining claims in the Dragoon and Swisshelm Mountains. But he preferred life in town where drinking, gambling, and a little "bird" watching embodied his nightly pleasures. When he had money, he spent it. When he didn't get what he wanted, he turned surly and dangerous. Those were the nights May Leslie soon learned to dread. As old-time Tombstone resident Billy King noted, "He was a likable damn fellow when he was sober . . . but when he was tanked up he turned as sour as a barrel of Dago red."

Leslie's quick draw earned him a reputation on both sides of the badge. In March 1881, a detachment of eight lawmen set out from Tombstone on the trail of bandits who had held up the stagecoach as it headed toward Benson. The posse consisted of lawmen Wyatt, Vigil, and Morgan Earp; Cochise County Sheriff Johnny Behan and Deputy Sheriff Billy Breakenridge; and sworn-in deputies Doc Holliday, Bat Masterson, and Frank Leslie. Separating as they traveled, Leslie came upon one of the outlaws and reportedly sat down to eat with him before returning alone to Tombstone claiming he had lost the trail. Rumors circulated that Sheriff Behan, supposedly a friend of the robbers, had paid Leslie to ride a cold course.

The sun had barely risen above the horizon when Leslie walked into the Oriental Saloon on November 14, 1882, but already a group of men hovered near the bar having their usual liquored breakfast. Leslie was welcomed into their discussion, which may have had political overtones, and the men finished several rounds before cocky young Billy Claiborne entered the saloon about 7:30 a.m. Claiborne was as mean as an angry snake. He had ridden with the murdering cattle rustler John Ringo and often worked both sides of the border stealing cattle and horses. Claiborne blamed Leslie for John Ringo's death; Leslie and Ringo had been seen together shortly before Ringo was found straddling a tree with a bullet in his head.

It was obvious Claiborne had downed his breakfast at a neighboring watering hole. He sidled up to the group at the bar and immediately interrupted the conversation. Leslie took him aside and asked him to leave. But Claiborne refused and again butted into the assemblage. Leslie booted Claiborne out the saloon door. Claiborne shouted he would return to get even, but Leslie just turned his back on the youngster.

When Claiborne reappeared, he was carrying his Winchester. The street emptied as he headed toward the Oriental. "I don't allow any man to spit on me," he swore.

Leslie, warned that Claiborne was looking for him, left the saloon by a side door. Rounding the corner to the main street, he saw Claiborne hiding behind a fruit stand and warned the youngster not to shoot. But Claiborne stood up and fired, the bullet landing harmlessly at Leslie's feet. Leslie floored him with one shot. "I told him I was sorry," Leslie later stated. "I might have done more, but I couldn't do less."

Leslie again faced a coroner's jury pleading self-defense. He walked out of the courtroom a free man.

Milt Joyce, proprietor of the Oriental Saloon, also owned the Magnolia Ranch in the Swisshelm Mountains east of Tombstone. Leslie had a one-quarter interest in the place, and Joyce left most of the ranching business in Leslie's hands. Since Leslie spent more time there than Joyce, the Magnolia was often mistakenly called Leslie's ranch.

In 1883 Leslie experienced a run-in with Apache raiders at the Magnolia. He lost most of the horses and about fifty head of cattle to the marauders. Two years later, in May 1885, when Geronimo and a band of Apaches escaped from the San Carlos Indian Reservation, Leslie was more than happy to hire on as a scout under Captain Wirt Davis. It took three months of hard riding before Davis and his men located Geronimo's camp. And although Geronimo escaped, the soldiers killed a handful of his men and captured a few women and children.

Davis sent Leslie to inform General George Crook of the battle. According to Leslie, he had to swim the Bavispe River eleven times in one day to deliver the report. Leslie knew how to make himself look good in the eyes of the law.

Each time Leslie returned from scouting, battling Apaches, and even one stint as an inspector along the Arizona-Sonora border looking for smugglers, he made up for lost time in the Tombstone saloons. He would then go home to May, slap her around a bit, and stand her up against the wall to practice his shooting. May knew she would soon die beneath his hands or at the end of his gun. On May 27, 1887, she filed for divorce, claiming Leslie beat and choked her along with framing her silhouette in bullets. She also accused him of infidelity. The court awarded May half of Leslie's interest in the Magnolia Ranch, which she immediately sold back to Milt Joyce. Leslie eventually sold Joyce his remaining interest, but continued to manage the place.

Leslie was soon seen dallying with Mollie Williams, also known as Mollie Bradshaw, Mollie Edwards, and Blonde Mollie, a singer at the Bird Cage Theater. She had arrived in town with a man named Mike Bradshaw. Shortly after

Leslie made Mollie's acquaintance, Bradshaw lay dead with his head bashed in. Fingers pointed at Leslie, but no evidence was found implicating him. He and Mollie headed off into the Swisshelms, to Magnolia Ranch.

Unfortunately, they didn't stay put on the ranch and often spent days frequenting drinking establishments from one end of Tombstone to the other. Mollie could hold her own with Leslie, and the two often loudly disagreed well into the night as they guzzled copious amounts of liquor.

In early July 1889, the couple headed into Tombstone to celebrate Independence Day. Their revelry continued for almost a week. Finally, hitching up their horses, they headed out of town, drunk when they left and still sotted when they arrived back at the ranch on July 10. An argument started in Tombstone continued to rage.

The next day, Leslie, still swilling a potent brew, rode over to William Reynolds's ranch where he informed his neighbor he was going to kill him. He ordered Reynolds to defend himself, but when Reynolds, who had obviously seen Leslie in this condition before, refused to pick up a rifle, Leslie left in a huff and staggered home.

James Neal worked off and on for Leslie at the Magnolia Ranch. He understood his boss's frequent fits of rage and usually stayed out of sight when trouble boiled. But on the night of July 11, he took pity on the tipsy Mollie and sat with her while Leslie was off harassing his neighbor. When Leslie returned, he suspected Neal and Mollie had been up to no good. After smacking Mollie around a few times, he determined he would "put a stop to all this." He picked up his pistol and aimed. With one shot, Mollie fell dead to the floor in a heap of skirts and petticoats.

Neal had no time to react before Leslie fired at him. "Don't be afraid, it's nothing," Leslie told him and, at first, Neal believed him. But as blood started trailing down his legs, Neal bolted through the door and into the desert. The next day, rancher Reynolds found him collapsed on his doorstep.

Leslie came looking for Neal at the Reynolds ranch and related the evening's events, claiming Neal had killed Mollie and he had shot Neal in self-defense. Reynolds denied seeing Neal, so Leslie assumed the young man lay dead somewhere in the desert and figured there would be no witnesses to dispute his story.

After Leslie left, Reynolds sent for the doctor who patched up Neal and took him into town. Neal told his story to the sheriff leaving little doubt who had perpetrated the double shooting.

Two days later, deputies found a disheveled Leslie riding along the road into town and took him to the sheriff. Distraught, Leslie confessed to killing Neal after Neal had slain his beloved Mollie. Suddenly, Neal appeared in the doorway, weak but strong enough to call Leslie a liar.

This time the jury did not agree with Leslie's self-defense argument. He was sentenced to serve the remainder of his life in the Yuma Territorial Prison for the murder of Blonde Mollie.

Leslie and ten other prisoners were escorted from the Cochise County Jail to Yuma Territorial Prison in January 1890 under the watchful eye of Sheriff John Slaughter. According to the *Tucson Citizen*, they all arrived drunk. Maybe Leslie was able to persuade the sheriff to make one last stop before sending him into the depths of Hell.

Leslie actually spent only seven years in Yuma Prison. There was talk he was part of an attempted breakout in March 1890, but no mention of the incident appears in prison records. For the most part, he was a model prisoner and spent most of his time working in the prison infirmary as a pharmacist.

In 1893 a reporter from the *San Francisco Chronicle* visited Leslie at the prison. He must have believed every word out of Leslie's mouth as the story he wrote is comprised of tall tales right from Leslie's vivid imagination. But when Belle Stowell of San Francisco read the *Chronicle* story, she began corresponding with Leslie and sending gifts of food and clothing to the imprisoned man. Eventually their friendship blossomed into love.

Leslie's exemplary behavior behind bars, plus the pleas of Belle Stowell and other friends who petitioned Arizona Territorial Governor Benjamin Franklin for his release, set him free on November 17, 1896. He ran right into the arms of Belle and the two were married in Stockton, California, on December 1.

How long the marriage lasted is uncertain, as Belle soon disappeared from Leslie's life. He went to Mexico in early 1897 to assist a geologist seeking coal deposits for the Southern Pacific Railroad. While there, he supposedly killed three men when they attempted to steal wood from the work site.

Leslie may have headed next for the Alaskan goldfields, but by 1902, he was back in San Francisco. When the *Chronicle* reported he sustained a gunshot wound as his pistol fell out of his pocket and went off, he told the reporter, "I suppose that my friends will tell me I'm not fit to carry a pistol. After forty years on the frontier to be hurt by my own gun, looks like it."

Leslie worked as a stocker for a couple of grocery stores and as a janitor in a billiard hall, but he usually lived off handouts from the barrooms he frequented. Wyatt Earp, now living in California, sometimes staked his old friend to a set of clean clothes and maybe a drink or two.

Leslie was last seen alive around 1920, sweeping floors in a San Francisco saloon. One night he disappeared, supposedly taking the bartender's gun with him. Maybe he was just borrowing it like he used to do in Tombstone. About three years later, a skeleton and rusty gun were found in the hills north of Martinez, California. The serial number on the gun was the same as the one taken from the bar that night. "If it [the story] is indeed real," said writer/historian Douglas Martin, "then Leslie was not all bad; he did one good thing before he died. He killed himself."

Leslie once admitted to killing thirteen men. "It was my fourteenth that caused all my trouble," he bemoaned. "But then, my fourteenth was a woman."

JAMES ADDISON REAVIS

The Noble Forger

Imagine walking into the state capital of Arizona and demanding ownership of more than twelve million acres of land spanning 235 miles west to east from Phoenix to the western boundaries of Silver City, New Mexico, and 75 miles north and south encompassing not only the Phoenix population but dozens of outlying agricultural and mining communities including Tempe, Mesa, Casa Grande, Florence, Safford, Globe, Miami, Superior, Clifton, Coolidge, and Morenci.

Five rivers run through this massive desert region and just as many Indian reservations occupy territory within its boundaries. The San Francisco and Mogollon Mountains jut out the eastern portion of the expanse with the Picacho, Galiuro, and Pinaleno Mountain ranges spanning the southern end.

Military enclaves fall within these boundaries and railroads run across the territory. Thousands of people occupy the land. Some claim less than an acre while others hold deeds to hundreds of acres that they farm, ranch, and mine. About 125 years ago, James Addison Reavis sought to claim all this land and everything that was on it as his own, and he almost got away with it.

Reavis was already in his thirties when he arrived in Arizona in 1880, but he had not been idle during his formative years. A Missourian by birth, he joined the Confederate Army at the age of eighteen but found military life dull and uninteresting. To keep himself occupied he practiced forging his commanding officer's signature and was soon handing out bogus leave papers and furloughs to his army buddies. When his ruse was discovered, he headed across the Mason-Dixon Line and enlisted in the Union Army. Boredom overtook him again. He asked for an official leave to marry and left the military, never to return. Neither did he marry.

Young Reavis spent a year in Brazil before settling in St. Louis around 1865 where he worked as a conductor on horse-drawn streetcars. He invested his meager earnings in land and property, never hesitating to produce a missing deed or document by falsifying the necessary papers. Soon his proclivity for fraud and forgery brought devious businessmen to his door. He gladly created counterfeit papers for those willing to pay for his talent.

In 1871 Doctor George M. Willing Jr. came looking for Reavis. Willing had abandoned his wife and children in St. Louis some years back to seek his fortune in the lucrative western goldfields. He claimed he had purchased a large tract of land in the Arizona Territory from Miguel Peralta and his father, descendants of Spanish nobility who were now living in poverty. It was rich land, ripe for farming and ranching, and, according to his calculations, a wealth of gold and silver lay beneath the rocky soil. Would Reavis be interested in entering into a partnership to develop this valuable property?

Reavis listened intently as Dr. Willing described the bounty that awaited in Arizona. Whether he believed Willing or not, he saw opportunity far beyond what the good doctor envisioned and readily entered into the partnership. Willing headed west in late 1873. Reavis tarried long enough to marry Ada Pope on May 5, 1874, but left shortly thereafter and did not see Ada again for over six years. She divorced him in 1883, claiming desertion.

Reavis's route took him through the Isthmus of Panama into California. He arrived in San Francisco only to discover Willing had died in Prescott, Arizona, in March 1874. Willing's unclaimed gunnysack of belongings, including the deeds he said he had acquired from the Peralta heirs, was stowed in the coroner's attic in Prescott.

Reavis stayed in California for several years and taught school in Downey before hiring on as a subscription agent with the *San Francisco Daily Examiner*. During this time, he formulated a convoluted plan to make the best of his deal with the deceased Willing.

Reavis took the meager information Willing had related to him and set about creating a dynasty of enormous proportions. He knew that under the terms of the Treaty of Guadalupe Hidalgo (1848) and the Gadsden Purchase (1854), the United States was obligated to recognize valid Spanish and Mexican land grants. Most of the Arizona grants were considered worthless and had been abandoned by the original owners.

By now Reavis must have doubted that Miguel Peralta and his father even existed. Or if they did, they were far from the noble inheritors Willing had proclaimed them to be. He had seen enough forged documents in his day to figure out that the papers Willing had shown him were worthless. But those official-looking certificates, now reposing in the attic of the Prescott coroner's office, would become the impetus upon which he planned to defraud the people of Arizona out of millions of acres of land, and they must be dealt with. He had to obtain clear title to continue with his devious plot.

The Peralta Grant, as he decided to call it, would become property bequeathed to the family by proclamation of the King of Spain. Now all he had to do was create the Peralta clan, falsify existing records, and deposit these fraudulent documents where they could be "discovered" as evidence of the family's legal right to the land.

The family Reavis concocted began its reign in Spain in 1708 with the birth of Don Miguel Nemecio Silva de Peralta de la Córdoba. Don Miguel entered the service of the King of Spain and was sent to Guadalajara in New Spain (now Mexico) as a city inspector. Reavis gave him the title the Baron of Arizonaca and had the king bestow upon him a grant of land.

Don Miguel, according to Reavis, visited his northern tract of land only once, declaring the area around what is now Casa Grande the Barony of Arizona. Murderous Apaches purportedly drove him out of the region back to Mexico.

Don Miguel did not marry until he was sixty-two years old, Reavis claimed, but he soon had a son, Jesus Miguel Silva de Peralta de la Córdoba y Sanches de Bonilla, born in 1781. To eliminate the need for another generation, Reavis allowed Don Miguel to live to the age of 116. When he died, all his property went to Jesus Miguel. Under Reavis' penmanship, Jesus Miguel became the father of the miner who sold the Peralta lands to Dr. Willing. The Peraltas seemed to have long lifelines.

Reavis now had to get his hands on the deeds Willing had showed him in St. Louis.

When he stepped off the stagecoach in Phoenix in 1880, Reavis passed himself off as a reporter for the *Examiner*. Dressed in a long black coat and carrying a silver-knobbed cane, the tall, imposing man with sapphire blue eyes and a startling shock of red hair set out almost immediately for Prescott to locate the gunnysack Willing had left behind. He found the bag filled with Willing's clothing and odd items. At the very bottom lay the deeds signed by father and son, Jesus and Miguel Peralta. Reavis now had only one more person to eliminate in order to claim the Peralta property as his own.

Mary Ann Willing had known Reavis in St. Louis and trusted his friendship without reservation. So when Reavis promised her thousands of dollars if she would sign over to him her late husband's interest in the Peralta documents, she did not hesitate. Now with complete control of the false Peralta Grant, Reavis set about producing the documents he believed would convince the government of Arizona that the land grant actually existed.

With his penmanship expertise, he spent weeks perfecting forged documents. He re-created inks used in the 1700s and painstakingly practiced writing with the flourish of old Spanish monks and scribes. When he was satisfied with his masterpieces, he traveled to Spain and Mexico, surreptitiously inserting these well-crafted, ancient-looking papers into church records and official depositories verifying the existence of the Peralta family. At the same time, he furtively filched documents that disproved the existence of this noble clan.

All this planning and scheming took an enormous amount of time, effort, expertise, lying, cheating, and counterfeiting before Reavis felt he had established the Peralta lineage. By 1882 he was ready to lay claim to twelve million acres of prime Arizona land.

The man with the well-manicured mustache and sweeping sideburns who appeared in Tucson in March 1882 carried a suitcase brimming with "authentic" documents. He quickly hustled down the road to the Graham County courthouse in Safford to file papers asserting his legal ownership by purchase of the Peralta Grant. When the court refused to recognize his claim, Reavis returned to California to manufacture even more documents. In March 1883 he was back in Tucson filing a raft of deeds, documents, photographs, and conveyances with the U.S. surveyor general, claiming himself the rightful landowner to the twelve-million-acre Peralta Grant.

Reavis wasted no time collecting from those he insisted were usurping his land. He sold quitclaims to nervous farmers, ranchers, and settlers who were fearful of losing property they believed they already owned. They worried that if Reavis was the rightful owner, they would never obtain clear titles to their homes and properties unless they gave in to his demands. He requested little money from these landowners and often, for the price of a meal, he would give away a quitclaim or two. His purpose was to show that by signing the deeds, the good citizens of Arizona recognized his legal right to the land. Many were skeptical and refused to sign, but Reavis persevered in his quest for his "rightful" and "legal" property.

After it was reported the Southern Pacific Railroad had capitulated to his demands and agreed to pay $50,000 to continue building track across his property, Reavis felt he had the territory of Arizona up against a wall. But the papers he had filed with the surveyor general were under careful scrutiny.

In 1885 the court determined Reavis's claim was invalid. Tempers mounted against the stately gentleman. He fled to San Francisco with the *Weekly Phoenix Herald* proclaiming him the ". . . Earl of the Iron Jaw, Count of Confidence Land, Lord of the Limber Tongue and Great Mogul of the Territory. . . . Cheek thy name is Reavis!" He did not return for two years.

Reavis determined he needed a direct Peralta descendant to convince the courts the grant existed. He found his "angel" on the streets of California and transformed her into the Baroness of Arizona.

Sophia Treadway was born about 1864 to John and Kate Treadway, but they were long gone from her life when she ran into the devious Reavis. He sent her to a convent to become a lady and educate her in the refinements of royalty. In 1887 he introduced her to Tucson society as Doña Sophia Micaela Maso Reavis y Peralta de la Córdoba, his wife.

Reavis had to concoct the story of his wife's pedigree and place her within the Peralta dynasty. His fictional narrative proclaimed she was the great-granddaughter of the first Baron of Arizona. She had been born a twin but her brother died at birth and her mother shortly after. She was raised in Mendocino County, California, by her grandmother. Reavis said he first laid eyes on Doña Sophia

while on a train and he immediately recognized her ancestral features as belonging to the Peralta clan.

When he was satisfied he had established Doña Sophia's royal birth, Reavis
got out his ink pen to create the documents perfecting her lineage.

He set off once again on his well-traveled route to Spain and Mexico, leaving
his newly crafted papers in the same depositories he had previously visited. When
he returned to the states, he revealed documents "miraculously" found proving
his wife's heritage, including the old will of Jesus Miguel bequeathing all his hold-
ings, and particularly the Peralta land, to his granddaughter Doña Sophia.

In September 1887 Reavis, now calling himself James Addison Peraltareavis,
filed the previously missing will with the Tucson office of the surveyor general. The
Arizona Daily Citizen lamented, "It seems as if the woes of Arizona were never to
end. First come the Apaches and then the blackmailers and land grabbers."

"Everything that I have done has been in the interest of my wife and not for
any claim preferred by me," he told the *San Francisco Daily Examiner*. "I have
nothing to do with it except in my character as her [Doña Sophia's] husband.
It is my duty to see that her rights are given her, and you can rest assured that I
intend doing it."

While Reavis was busily counterfeiting, filching, and inserting the documents necessary to establish his argument that the Peralta Grant existed, Royal
Johnson, the surveyor general, was working diligently to disprove the validity of
the reams of papers filed by Reavis. In 1889 he reported his findings noting that
many of Reavis's documents were written with a steel pen, an instrument not
used until after 1800. He accurately pointed out the differences in penmanship
between authenticated documents written in the 1700s and those filed by Reavis
purportedly written at the same time. Paper watermarks appeared that were not
available until the mid-1800s. There were misspellings of Spanish words in some
of the fraudulent documents. Johnson ordered a search of Spanish archives for
papers pertaining to the Peralta claim and found no evidence of the family. His
report concluded with a recommendation that Reavis's claim be denied, "it being
in my mind without the slightest foundation in fact and utterly void."

Reavis filed suit against the government, seeking damages in the amount of
$10 million. He said the monies already paid to him proved the validity of his
claim. Along with the Southern Pacific Railroad's $50,000, the Silver King Min-
ing Company had handed over $25,000. In all, Reavis had already collected over
$145,000 from landowners for the rights to use Peralta land, a sum equivalent to
over $3 million today. Reavis brought his claim before the newly formed Court
of Private Land Claims (established in 1891) in Santa Fe, New Mexico.

When court convened on June 3, 1895, Reavis was nowhere to be found, nor
did he appear the next day, but the trial went forth without him. On June 5 the
court received a telegram from Reavis asking the trial be continued until June 10.

Finally appearing and placed on the stand, Reavis proclaimed his sole desire in obtaining the Peralta Grant was "to develop Arizona. As a fact, I never cared that much for the grant, except the honor of having done something in it. I am not a lover of money, but I am a lover of development and building up a country. Therefore my whole life has been in the interest of building up Arizona. . . ."

For two and a half days, he rambled on about the Peralta family. Then he wheeled a large trunk into the courtroom that he claimed contained absolute proof of his wife's heritage. He began pulling copious amounts of documents out of the trunk. Next came dozens of portraits, pictures of his wife's ancestors, he said. He argued this was all the proof the court should require to award his wife her rightful property. This is most likely the evidence he was creating when he was absent from court.

The court did not believe a word he said. His claim was deemed "wholly fictitious and fraudulent," and he was immediately arrested and charged with conspiracy to defraud the government.

Unable to provide bail, Reavis languished in jail for more than a year. His criminal trial commenced on June 27, 1896, and lasted just a few short days. Much of the same testimony presented at the first trial was again introduced. Witnesses who had initially backed Reavis's story now admitted they had lied. He was found "guilty as charged in the indictment to default the United States Government out of parts of its public lands in connection with the effort to establish the fictitious and fraudulent Peralta Grant."

Reavis's sentence was pretty mild considering he had hoped to acquire a good portion of the Arizona Territory with his fraudulent scheme. He was sentenced to serve two years in the Santa Fe Penitentiary and pay a fine of $5,000. He promised he would appeal his conviction but never did. On April 18, 1898, he walked out of prison proclaiming he would once again "return to the world of business."

His wife, now using the name Sophia Treadway Reavis, and no longer asserting her noble status, settled in Denver with the couple's twin boys, Miguel and Carlos, born in 1893, and their adopted son, Fenton. In 1902 she filed for divorce, citing desertion and nonsupport. Reavis languished in California, never again experiencing the opulent lifestyle he enjoyed as an Arizona aristocrat. Penniless, he took up residency in the Los Angeles County Poor Farm but moved to Denver in 1914. He died on November 20, 1914.

No other criminal came close to robbing Arizona of the vast sums of money and millions of acres of land that James Addison Reavis tried to swindle. He was a brilliant and talented man who lived a life of fraud and fantasy. His scheme to be acknowledged as a nobleman earned him only one thing, the dubious title of the Baron of Arizona.

THE APACHE KID

Army Scout, Apache Rebel

On May 3, 1887, the earth trembled across southwestern U.S. territory and northern Mexico. The earthquake, estimated at about 7.2 magnitude, lasted a full minute with massive rocks careening down mountains and huge fissures dashing jaggedly across the desert terrain, sending adobe homes crashing to the ground. Newspapers reported "deep rumblings" in the desert near the town of Superior, Arizona, where ". . . large pieces of rock were detached on all sides of Picket Post Mountain . . . raising a cloud of dust, and for several minutes it ascended about the mountain giving it the appearance of a live volcano."

About 20 miles east of Superior, Apache Indians, forced to live on the San Carlos Indian Reservation, believed that earthquakes foretold the onset of doom and disaster. To alleviate their fears, they gathered to brew *tizwin*, a potent, fermented mixture combining the heart of the maguey or mescal plant with fruits and vegetables. The ensuing tizwin party altered the lives of many Apaches that day, but the life of Has-kay-bay-nay-ntayl, known to the whites as the Apache Kid, or Kid for short, was changed beyond redemption.

A trusted Indian scout with the white man's army on the San Carlos Indian Reservation, the Apache Kid knew his people were forbidden to brew the intoxicating tizwin, but as he was mourning the slaying of his father, Toga-de-Chuz, he joined the illegal gathering. Toga-de-Chuz's murderer, Gon-zizzie, had been killed by Toga-de-Chuz's friends, but as the eldest son, Kid was expected to avenge his father's death in his own way.

Kid drank his share of the liquor and was soon plotting to kill Rip, the brother of Gon-zizzie. He enlisted his half brother, As-ki-say-la-ha, who was also an Indian scout, and the two rode off to roust three more scouts before setting out to find Rip.

Rip stood no chance against Kid's precise aim—he was dead before he hit the ground. Their mission a success, Kid and the four scouts returned to the reservation. They had been gone without permission for five days. Al Sieber, chief of the Indian scouts, had been looking for his wayward men.

For the most part, Sieber managed his troop of Indian scouts with an iron hand and a compassionate heart, but trouble spewed across his face when the scraggly group appeared before him. Sieber demanded their weapons, and Kid was the first to obey. A crowd gathered as Sieber ordered the men arrested and locked in the guardhouse—a smelly, bug-infested hole furnished with only a handful of straw and a bucket.

Suddenly shots rang out from the crowd, and Sieber, unarmed, fell to the ground with a bullet embedded in his ankle. Seizing the opportunity, Kid grabbed a horse and fled the ensuing melee. He did not intend to lose his freedom for avenging his father's death, something he was compelled to do according to Apache law. As he turned his back on the white man's rules and laws, his days as a trusted Indian scout were over.

Has-kay-bay-nay-ntayl was born around 1860 near the Aravaipa Canyon in eastern Arizona. A loose translation of his name, "brave and tall and will come to a mysterious end," seemed to predict his calamitous future.

Has-kay-bay-nay-ntayl was forced onto the San Carlos Indian Reservation, as were many Indians, through the actions of President Ulysses S. Grant, who established San Carlos in 1872. The government determined that the only way to control warring Apaches was to confine them to reservations where they were expected to raise crops instead of raiding nearby ranches. Has-kay-bay-nay-ntayl's father was a member of Capitán Chiquito's band of White Mountain Apaches, who in 1875 were herded onto the dry, desolate reservation aptly called "Hell's Forty Acres."

As a teenager, Has-kay-bay-nay-ntayl seemed to adapt to reservation living. He learned to speak English and shunned the traditional dress of his father, opting to wear suit jackets, felt hats, and leather boots—white man's clothing. On the reservation he was in charge of shooting cattle as they came into the pens for slaughter and he became an expert marksman by running along fence lines surrounding the cattle pens while taking dead aim on the doomed creatures. He also herded cattle for ranchers in the nearby town of Globe. When white men found his name too hard to pronounce, they dubbed him Kid.

Around 1879 Al Sieber made this cocky nineteen-year-old his orderly and cook. With Sieber's encouragement Kid enlisted as an Indian scout in 1881 and reenlisted seven times until 1887. He often took time off between reenlistments, and during one of these respites, he married and had a child.

The military quickly promoted Kid to first sergeant, a rank he held during most of his enlistment, when they discovered how accurately he could spot distant riders and decipher whether they were whites or Indians. He was considered better than any military posse at tracking down runaway Indians, and Sieber often relied on him to help train new Indian scouts. In 1882 he fought in the Battle of Big Dry Wash on the Tonto Rim near the town of Payson, and he accompanied Sieber into Mexico during the 1885 Geronimo campaign.

He did not always toe the military line, however. In Mexico in late 1885, he almost got himself killed when he and two other scouts were accused of molesting a Mexican woman. As the scouts fled, shots rang out—one dead, one wounded, and Kid arrested. Mexican authorities feared an international incident if they tried the scout, so they released him back to the States after charging him a $25 fine.

When Sieber departed San Carlos for Fort Apache on an inspection trip just before that fateful day in May 1887, he left Kid in charge of the Indian scouts. Tizwin and trouble soon merged into the incident that found the Apache Kid a renegade outlaw hunted by the very scouts he had trained.

About a dozen rebels fled the reservation along with Kid, and his band increased in numbers as days turned into weeks. When two ranchers were found dead near Benson, their cattle butchered and horses long gone, word spread that the runaway Indians were the culprits.

As the posse closed in, the Indians surrendered. On June 25, 1887, Kid and the four Indian scouts who had ridden with him to avenge his father's death were tried for mutiny and desertion in a general court-martial. Kid wasted no time admitting his guilt:

> I am 1st Sergeant Kid, San Carlos, Arizona Territory. God sent bad spirit in my heart, I think. You all know all the people can't get along very well in the world. There are some good people and some bad people amongst them all. I am not afraid to tell all these things because I have not done very much harm. I killed one man whose name is Rip because he killed my father. I am not educated like you and therefore can't say very much. If I had made any arrangement before I came in, I would not have given up my arms at Mr. Sieber's tent. That is all I have to say.

At the end of the day, all five scouts were found guilty and sentenced to death by shooting. When military commander General Nelson A. Miles reviewed the case, he requested leniency for the men, arguing they were "ignorant, unlettered Indians . . . ," and while their deeds were certainly serious, they were "not of that extreme gravity which would justify the death sentence." The same court that had condemned them to death reduced their sentences to life in prison at Fort Leavenworth, Kansas.

For six months the Indians languished in the fetid San Carlos jail. On January 23, 1888, orders arrived transferring them not to Leavenworth Military Prison but to Alcatraz Island, California.

Completed shortly before Kid's arrival, Alcatraz boasted 185 wooden cells with 2-inch plank flooring covered in sheet iron. The only ventilation in each cell came from a 4-inch gap above the door and a meager 2-inch space below.

Fire was always a concern, and in March 1888, while Kid was at Alcatraz, a blaze destroyed several buildings.

The five ex-scouts were freed from Alcatraz in October 1888 when Judge Advocate General G. Norman Lieber successfully argued that the white jury that had convicted them was prejudiced against the Apaches and the sentences handed down were too harsh for the crimes committed.

Sieber was so angry when the Apache Kid reappeared at San Carlos that he immediately ordered him rearrested. He charged Kid with attempted murder, claiming his once-trusted scout had fired the bullet that shattered his ankle. Sieber conveniently ignored the fact that Kid had handed over his gun before the shooting started. He also disregarded the time Kid had already served for the San Carlos incident and ordered Gila County Sheriff Glenn Reynolds to lock the former scout in the Globe jail. "That evening," according to Apache Kid biographer Phyllis de la Garza, "bells clanged in the wooden tower of the Methodist church, Globe's customary practice signifying bad Indians were in town."

Sieber swore under oath that Kid had fired the shot that left him crippled for life. On October 30, 1889, the Apache Kid was sentenced to seven years in the Yuma Territorial Prison for the attempted murder of his mentor. Two days later he was on his way to Yuma.

Threatening rain clouds hovered overhead that All Saints Day as eight handcuffed Apache convicts shuffled out of the Globe jail and boarded the stagecoach for Yuma Prison. Stagecoach driver Eugene Middleton rubbed the dust off his brand new, heavy-duty, bright green Concord stagecoach with sunny yellow wheels as he watched the men board. Sheriff Reynolds and his deputy, William "Hunkydory" Holmes, would escort the prisoners. Kid climbed into the coach, and Reynolds secured leg irons on the man considered the most dangerous of his charges.

The stage would carry the prisoners to Casa Grande, a two-day trip from Globe. From there, they would board a train for the final trek into Yuma.

Rain started falling before the stage skidded into the Riverside station for the night. After supper the prisoners lined up on benches, their leg irons and handcuffs securely tightened. In this upright position, they tried to sleep.

The next morning the stage had to maneuver the wet and slippery Kelvin Grade, and Middleton feared the coach, laden with passengers, would not make it up the muddy incline. Reynolds ordered the prisoners out of the coach—all except the Apache Kid and another convict shackled to him. Reynolds did not want Kid footloose.

Middleton maneuvered the stage as Reynolds and Holmes escorted the prisoners on foot up Kelvin Grade. The Apaches talked among themselves but since neither Reynolds nor Holmes spoke their language, their conversations were nothing more than gibberish to the two lawmen. Too bad for them.

As the stagecoach disappeared around a bend, two prisoners attacked Reynolds while two more grabbed Holmes. Both men died instantly with bullet wounds from their own rifles.

One of the prisoners ran toward the stage and fired at Middleton, sending him tumbling from the coach with a bullet through his mouth and neck. As the prisoners freed Kid and his companion, one angry Indian stood over the paralyzed Middleton ready to smash his head with a rock. For some reason, Kid stopped the man and spared Middleton's life. The Indians disappeared on foot across the desert plain and into the hills they knew so well.

News of the murders spread rapidly. The *Silver Belt* reported bloody clothing was found a few miles from the murder scene. "A carcass of a steer was also discovered, a part of which had been taken and some of the hide stripped off and used for foot-covering, as evidenced by the peculiar tracks made by one of the fugitives after leaving the spot."

Al Sieber assumed Kid had orchestrated the deadly escape and requested military posses to capture his nemesis. Five Arizona forts responded with troops tracking the fugitives' trail of destruction.

Although the prisoners were on foot and most were unarmed, the posses were no match for the elusive Apaches. Once, Kid was spotted near the San Carlos River, but he quickly vanished into the hills. Another time, a posse found a cave where the Indians camped, but they magically disappeared as the law closed in. The fugitives raided ranches and stole horses, then headed farther into the mountains.

Territorial Governor Lewis Wolfley offered a $500 reward for the conviction of any of the outlaw Apaches. Still, no one could catch the swift-footed renegades, who were obviously making their way toward Mexico.

The Apache Kid and the men who followed him became the most feared Indians in Arizona history. Ranchers were gunned down, their cattle butchered, and horses stolen. Cowboys were found with their heads split open. In March 1890 a freight hauler was murdered near Fort Thomas. That August, three men were killed at Hachita, about 50 miles southwest of Lordsburg, New Mexico. Even western artist Frederick Remington feared crossing Kid's path. While looking for a lost mine in Sonora, Mexico, Remington noted, "The vaqueros I am riding with are not only looking for the lost mine of Tiopa, but are also primed for a fight with the Kid if we cut his trail. And if he cuts ours, we may not live long enough to regret it."

Eventually five of the original eight Apache prisoners were captured; two others, killed. By October 1890 only Kid remained free. The *Silver Belt* considered him "a legal target for those who can cock a gun and draw a bead through the sights of a Winchester."

That December, three ranch hands killed an Indian they found butchering one of their steers. From the nearby brush Kid and his men came out shooting. The cowboys took shelter behind a large boulder, and gunfire resounded across the hillside for hours until one of the ranch hands barely dodged a bullet that shattered his corncob pipe. His two buddies, amused at his startled expression, carelessly leaned out from behind their boulder refuge. One was stopped in mid-laugh by a bullet in the head, and it wasn't long before the second cowboy lay dead. The pipe-smoking gunman headed for the nearest ranch, successfully eluding Kid and his men, but chances are he never lit up a pipe again.

In 1891 an ex-army scout said he chanced upon the Apache Kid in the Santa Catalina Mountains about 20 miles north of Tucson. Neither man backed off and all day the two sat facing each other, their eyes never leaving the gaze of their adversary, knowing either could kill with one shot. Along about sundown, Kid rose from his rock and announced he was leaving. "As Kid disappeared down the trail, I lit a shuck for home!" the old scout recalled years later.

Occasionally Kid returned to the San Carlos Indian Reservation to retrieve bundles of food, clothing, and ammunition secreted in caves by his family and sympathetic friends. He often took a woman with him when he departed once again for the hills. Some of these women went willingly, while others had no choice.

By November 1892 Territorial Governor Nathan Oakes Murphy upped the reward to $6,000 for the capture or death of the Apache Kid. Several Arizona counties offered their own rewards; and since he was blamed for murders in the New Mexico Territory as well as south of the border, additional reward money resulted in an accumulated total of $15,000 on his head. Still, no one came near arresting the elusive Indian.

In 1894 Al Sieber, maybe having a change of heart after falsely accusing his trusted scout of attempted murder, tried to get word to Kid that if he would turn himself in, Sieber would help clear his name with the reward money. Sieber waited at several designated spots for Kid to appear, but he never did.

The December 1895 day was bone-chillingly cold as Horatio Merrill and his daughter Eliza steered their wagon from Pima toward the town of Clifton. About six miles from Ash Springs, they were attacked and slain. Lawmen believed at least thirty Indians, led by the Apache Kid, had set upon the pair. When they found the Indians' campsite, they discovered Eliza Merrill's purse; nestled inside, her newly acquired engagement ring lay undisturbed.

As years passed, tales of the Apache Kid's death began to sprout as often as the offenses laid at his feet. From about 1895 until the mid 1930s, just about everyone had a story to tell. He was found dead in a cave, killed in a cornfield, ambushed at a waterhole, shot off his horse, and slain by Mexican *rurales*.

Arizona pioneer Charles Genung said Kid appeared at his Wickenburg campsite in 1895 obviously dying from consumption. That same year, rancher John Slaughter supposedly followed Kid into Mexico and killed him.

In 1899 the chief of the Mexican *rurales* claimed Kid was living peacefully in the Sierra Madre Mountains.

In 1915 Kid supposedly rode with Pancho Villa, rebel general of the Mexican Revolution.

A nephew of Kid, Joe Adley, said his uncle was still alive in Mexico in 1924. And as late as about 1935, an old cattleman swore he had recently talked with Kid, who claimed he and his family were living in Mexico. After that, the stories stopped.

"Torn between bewildering laws in a white man's world and old Apache tribal traditions, [the Apache Kid] tried adapting to both, and lost," wrote de la Garza. Freedom to live his life according to Apache custom was all Has-kay-bay-nay-ntayl wanted. The price of that freedom cost him dearly.

"RATTLESNAKE DICK" BARTER

No Jail Could Hold Him

The hot wind howled through the shrieking forest like a troop of demons around the Trinity Mountains between Yreka and San Francisco. Four masked men waited in the shadows of the massive oak trees for a mule-drawn stagecoach lumbering along a rugged path. The Wells Fargo carriage was carrying more than $80,000 worth of gold shipped from the rich mining communities in Shasta County to the crowded City by the Bay. An armed convoy of six guards surrounded the shipment. Their eyes were fixed on the wooded area that lined the trail. As the mules pulled the heavy vehicle through a rocky ravine a shot rang out. One of the guards toppled off the back of his spooked horse with a bullet hole in his chest. The abrupt disturbance caused the mules to buck and squirm and the driver tried desperately to regain control of the frightened team. Another gunshot rang out and a second fatally injured guard was thrown from the saddle.

In a few quick moments the ruthless outlaws had overtaken the stage. All four men helped tie the inept sentries to tree trunks and then began the process of unloading the gold bullion from the vehicle. "Where the hell is Dick with those mules?" one of the robbers asked his cohorts in a panicked voice. "Don't know," replied another. "We'll unload as much as we can, send this buggy on its way, and bury the loot."

The outlaws worked feverishly to remove the riches from the stage and place it into the packs hanging off their horses. When the weight of the gold was nearly overwhelming in the saddles on the overly burdened animals, the bandits remounted and took off.

In the nearby town of Auburn, Dick Barter, better known by most at the time as Rattlesnake Dick, stared anxiously out the narrow window of his jail cell. The bandit in the room with him dragged his scarred knuckles nervously back and forth over the bars. "Think they'll use the jackasses already pulling the shipment to get out?" asked Dick's cellmate. "Doubtful," Dick replied. "The mules are branded. The boys would be stopped by the law as soon as they made it to Folsom."

Dick cursed and took a drag off his cigarette. His job in the robbery was to steal four mules to transport the stolen gold. He and one of his men had been arrested in their attempt to acquire the animals and were now awaiting trial.

If successfully executed, the Wells Fargo gold transport would have been the largest amount ever stolen from a stagecoach. Dick had spent six years honing his criminal skills, robbing single riders, stores, and cabins in preparation for the day he could attempt a rich heist. July 15, 1856, started out as a promising day in the life of the notorious lawbreaker, but it ended in a bungled holdup and the vigilante pursuit of his gang.

The devilishly handsome Rattlesnake Dick was born in 1833 in Quebec, Canada. His father was a British Army officer and his French-Canadian mother was a homemaker. They named their oldest son Richard and provided him and his younger sister and brother with comfortable surroundings and a quality education.

Their father's sudden death in 1850 prompted the family to seek its fortune in the United States. The siblings had read about the vast opportunities available there, particularly in the West. The plan was to join an Oregon-bound wagon train in Independence, Missouri. Once the Barters arrived and secured a homestead, they would become ranchers.

Dick made the long journey with his brother, sister, brother-in-law, and cousin. While en route, the Barter brothers and their cousin discussed the exciting news of the Gold Rush. After they made sure their sister and her husband were established in the town of Sweet Home, Oregon, they moved on to California.

Rattlesnake Bar in northern California was one of the richest locations in the West. Gold seekers had converged on the area like locusts. When twenty-year-old Dick and his teenage brother and cousin arrived at the mining district on the American River, they went right to work. Sifting through rocks in the icy water in order to find gold nuggets was not an easy task. It proved to be tough, backbreaking labor for young men who had the idea that the glittery rocks were simply lying around ready to be scooped into a bucket. Within twenty-four hours of arriving at Rattlesnake Bar, Dick's brother and cousin decided to return to Oregon. However, Dick was determined to stick it out.

Regardless of the grueling, tiresome labor, Dick was convinced he could locate a rich claim. He raved about the beauty of the scenic mining camp and boasted that Rattlesnake Bar would prove itself to be the best town in the Placers. His optimistic attitude and eager work ethic earned him the name "Rattlesnake Dick."

Dick's insistent will and natural ability earned him as many enemies as friends. Fellow prospectors felt he was "arrogant, vain, and void of that native sense of honor that distinguishes intuitively between right and wrong." Three years after arriving on the Bar, problems between the competing miners and the overly confident Barter arose.

In 1853 several head of livestock had been stolen from a corral near the camp store. A miner who disliked Dick accused him of the crime, and Dick was arrested. He was exonerated in court, but he found himself in a similar circumstance a few short months later. This time he was accused of stealing a prospector's mule. The trial that ensued did not have as positive an outcome as the first. Dick was convicted and sentenced to two years in a state prison.

While Dick was being transferred to the penitentiary, word came that another man had confessed to the crime. Barter was released, but the effects of the allegations were permanent. Residents on the Bar treated him as though he were guilty, and he felt pressure to move and start over again in another camp.

In early 1854 Barter moved to Shasta County, 150 miles away from his beloved Rattlesnake Bar. He changed his name to Dick Woods and spent every waking hour panning for gold. For two years he lived a quiet, productive life. He was able to eke out a living as a gold miner, but the big strike eluded him. At least Dick was able to escape his past, until the spring of 1856, that is. A series of petty thieves and bandits began terrorizing the mining camps and once again jealous prospectors accused Dick of being behind the crimes. To further complicate matters a resident from Rattlesnake Bar who had been passing through the area recognized Barter and informed residents there of his real name.

Dick was frustrated that his true identity had been made known and that he had to deny yet another charge. "I can stand it no longer," he shouted to the miners around him. "Hereafter my hand is against everyone and I suppose everyone's is against me."

Distraught by the barrage of slanderous accusations, Dick decided he would become the outlaw he was rumored to be. He began his illegal career by holding up a lone traveler riding through the countryside. He told his victim to tell authorities that he had been robbed by "Rattlesnake Dick, the Pirate of the Placers."

Dick's exploits as a solitary highwayman extended over three California counties and included the theft of cattle and horses as well as miner's sluice boxes. (A sluice box is a tool used by prospectors.) Rattlesnake Dick was not content to work alone, and in the summer of 1856, he organized a gang of like-minded criminals to help execute even bigger robberies. The men he assembled were ex-convicts, and together they robbed stores, homes, and isolated saloons.

The self-proclaimed Pirate of the Placers and his collection of outlaws rendezvoused at an inn near Folsom called the Mountaineer House. It was at this location that Dick laid out plans to rob a Wells Fargo gold shipment. He believed the ambitious job would not only make him rich, but it would also make him the most feared bandit in northern California. His plans unraveled quickly once he was caught stealing the pack mules to be used to carry the gold away.

Rattlesnake Dick's gang panicked at the scene of the holdup when he didn't arrive to help them. They didn't get far with the heavy bags of gold before they realized they couldn't outrun the law hauling the weight of the bullion. They decided to bury half the gold in the hills and return for it at a later date.

The outlaws headed for the spot where they were to meet after the holdup and waited for Dick to arrive. After three anxious days Dick had still not shown. A few of the bandits demanded they be given their share of the money so they could ride on. The majority of the men argued against dividing the gold and insisted on waiting for Dick. The argument became heated, and one of the outlaws was shot trying to make off with his cut.

Four of Barter's remaining men decided to return to Auburn to find out what had become of their leader. A posse attempted to apprehend the outlaws on the outskirts of the mining town. One of the bandits was killed in an exchange of gunfire with the law, two were injured, and one was unharmed. All were arrested and escorted to Folsom to stand trial. One of the men was persuaded to lead the law to the area where the gang had buried half of the stolen gold, but he was unable to find the exact location. After several days of searching for the riches, the authorities decided the treasure was lost.

Dick and the fellow gang members who had gotten caught stealing mules escaped from the Auburn jail and fled to San Francisco. He managed to pull together another band of outlaws, and they began robbing stages that were traveling between mining camps along the American River.

Placer and Nevada County sheriffs and deputies tracked Dick down and threw him in prison. Every time the bandit was apprehended he would escape. According to early historians, "No jail could hold Barter."

In June 1859, territory officials had had enough of Dick's illegal activities and hired noted lawman John C. Boggs to find the desperado and bring him in dead or alive. Boggs was relentless in his pursuit and paid informers to alert law enforcement if they saw the gangster. On July 11, 1859, a tax collector sent word to the sheriff that Dick had been spotted in the vicinity. Boggs and four of his deputies saddled their horses and rode after the bandits. The lawmen caught up with the robber and his gang a mile outside of Auburn. One of the deputies called out to Rattlesnake Dick, "I'm looking for you!" Dick turned toward the man and shouted back, "Who are you and what do you want?" At that moment Dick drew a weapon from his holster and fired.

After a barrage of shots was exchanged, two of Sheriff Boggs's deputies were injured. As the outlaws fled, the lawmen fired shots at them. One of the bullets hit Rattlesnake Dick in the chest. He almost toppled out of his saddle, but at the last minute straightened up and spurred his horse down the road and out of sight. With only two deputies to accompany him, Boggs decided not to follow Dick any farther. He chose instead to return to Auburn for help.

Several posses were dispatched to scour the countryside for Barter. One posse member spoke with a man who had seen two riders hurrying past his home and reported that one of the riders was reeling in his saddle and the other was supporting him. The following morning Sheriff Boggs received news that Dick's body had been found by a stage driver two miles outside of Auburn.

An affectionate letter from Dick's sister, pleading with him to reform, was found in one of the outlaw's coat pockets. It was dated March 14, 1859, and read, "I ask that you, my beloved brother, the guide of my infant joys, the long lost friend of my childhood, will allow a renewed correspondence to open between you and your good old home."

Rattlesnake Dick's lifeless body was taken to town and laid on the sidewalk in front of the Masonic Hall for a curious crowd to view. He was buried later at the Auburn Cemetery. He was twenty-six years old. The gold his gang stole from the Wells Fargo stage in the summer of 1856 and later buried has never been found.

JOAQUIN MURIETA

.👤.

The Bandito Who Lost His Head

In August 1853, a parade of stone-faced pioneers filtered into the lobby of a crowded, brick courthouse in Marysville, California. They talked among themselves in low, hushed tones as the line they waited in slowly advanced toward a table at the front of the corridor. Two large glass jars sat in the center of the table. Inside one of the containers was a human hand; in the other, a human head. The severed hand and head were bloated and floating eerily in a clear liquid. The morbidly curious onlookers gaped in astonishment at the sight, elbowing one another and pointing.

A slim, slip of a girl with long, dark hair shook with great sobs as she followed along behind the others. She blinked away the tears while forcing herself to look upon the disembodied face in the jar. For several minutes she stood frozen in one spot. The people behind her urged her on, but she wouldn't move.

Escorted by a deputy, Sacramento County judge O. P. Stridger, a thick, short-bodied man, strode over to the grieving woman. On their way they walked past a giant sandwich board sign that read, EXHIBITION: ONE DAY ONLY! THE HEAD OF THE BANDIT JOAQUIN AND THE HAND OF BANDIT THREE-FINGERED JACK.

"Young lady," Judge Stridger softly said, "Are you all right?" The distressed woman wiped her eyes with the shawl covering her shoulders and nodded. A slight smile of relief gradually spread over her tormented face. "That's not my brother," she sighed. "What?" the judge asked incredulously. He exchanged a troubled look with the deputy next to them. "Joaquin Murieta was your brother?" he further inquired. "Sí," she answered. "But that's not him." Her eyes looked from the judge to the deputy and back at the head in the jar. "Who is it?" the deputy quickly inquired. "It is Joaquin Gonzales," she told them.

The perplexed men watched the woman step out of the line and make her way through the eager viewers who continued to press in on the exhibit. "Captain Love swears this is the bandit Murieta," the deputy reminded Judge Stridger in a low voice. The judge stood thinking for a moment and then reached into his pocket, removed a cigar as fat as a baby's leg, and lit it. "Let's hope Captain Love is right," he said, taking a long puff off his stogie.

The judge glanced up in the direction of the door just as the woman was exiting the building. A blast of sunlight erased his view of her departure. For a split second he considered following her and questioning her further about her brother. The well-attended spectacle before him made him change his mind. He took another drag from his cigar and turned his attention back to the ill-fated deceased.

Joaquin Murieta was one of many bandits who drifted from mining camp to mining camp in the early 1850s. The seventy-five men who made up his gang helped him steal horses, hold up stages, raid farmhouses, and rob prospectors. They slit the throats of many of their victims and left settlements fearful of their violent return. Had it not been for the creative pen of journalist John Rollin Ridge, this man Murieta, known as the chief of bandits, would simply have been remembered as another ruthless Old West outlaw.

Ridge's fictionalized version of Joaquin Murieta transformed him into a folk hero. His book, entitled *The Life and Adventures of Joaquin Murieta,* was first published in 1854. Since that time, Murieta's actual wrongdoings and the motivation behind his criminal activity have been overshadowed by Ridge's romantic version of his dastardly deeds.

Most historians agree that Joaquin was born in Sonora, Mexico, in 1832, and that his surname was Carrillo. An 1855 edition of the *San Francisco Call* boasts that he grew to be a man of "refined appearance, with a high forehead crowned with a blanket of hair and endowed with gracious manners." His parents sent him to school in Mexico City. When his education was complete, Joaquin took a job in the country's president's stables and worked as a grooms-man. At seventeen he returned home and married a girl from his village named Carmen Rosita Feliz, and the two decided to build a life for themselves in Cali-fornia. Murieta had heard the cry of "gold" echoing from the riverbanks of the American River in the northern portion of the state and believed that that was where his future lay.

The prospectors who had already staked out sizeable claims for themselves resented one more miner vying for the gold in the area. Many white miners who wanted to see the native people in the region driven out particularly resented Mexicans and Indians panning or digging alongside them.

The unfriendly reception Joaquin and his bride, Carmen, experienced when they arrived in Stanislaus County had a strong impact. Time and time again the young couple were driven from the piece of earth where they decided to search for gold. When Murieta resisted his claim being jumped, it usually resulted in a serious beating. Bitter and angry, he abandoned his gold-mining venture and brooded over his unfortunate circumstances. He explained to his wife that his job opportunities were limited and that it seemed he was being forced to become a bandit. Deciding she would be better off without him, he left Carmen behind and headed off to the town of Murphy.

Before committing entirely to the lifestyle of an outlaw, he tried his luck at gambling. After losing all he had in a game of monte, he threw himself into the murky depths of crime. There were several disenfranchised men in the same situation as Murieta, Mexican natives and desperadoes of other nationalities deemed outcasts. Equipped with a strong personality and leadership ability, Murieta was able to unite these renegades.

In November 1851, Murieta and his gang held up a number of stages traveling between the mining camps of Calaveras and Tuolumne Counties. They also stole more than three hundred head of horses and drove them to Mexico to be sold. They left several dead bodies in the wake of each crime. Victims weren't just murdered, they were flogged, beaten, and had their throats cut. Oftentimes the outlaws would throw a lariat around the neck of a victim and drag the person around until the body was unrecognizable. Among the savage men who rode with the man many now referred to as Bloody Joaquin Murieta were Three-Fingered Jack, Reyes Feliz, and Joaquin Valenzuela. Valenzuela was one of three men named Joaquin who kept company with Murieta. Three-Fingered Jack is credited with killing six Chinese miners found tied together by their queues (long braids of hair that reached down their backs), with their heads nearly severed from their torsos.

In the winter of 1851, Murieta orchestrated a spree of robberies and raids on campsites that resulted in twenty-three murders in the area around Chico, California. Settlers were outraged by the brutal attacks and fearful for their lives. Posses and vigilante committees were formed, but Murieta was able to elude his pursuers by taking unknown routes and brush-covered pathways. He would split his men into small groups and travel under cover of darkness. He had contacts in various towns and mining camps, unsavory characters who would benefit monetarily if they let the bandit chief know the location of approaching law enforcement officers.

By the spring of 1853, Murieta's reign of terror had extended into the southern half of California. He invaded homesteads, stealing cattle and personal belongings; held up supply wagons making their way from one outpost to the next; and robbed some of the isolated saloons that dotted the territory.

Before robbing saloonkeepers of their nightly earnings, he would engage the gamblers on hand in a game of poker. On one particular occasion Murieta sat opposite a drunken dealer who was shuffling a deck and eyeing the menacing-looking desperado. With a hint of recognition in his voice, the gambler exclaimed, "I'd give $1,000 for a chance at that greaser Murieta." Murieta sneered and removed a knife from his pocket. He leaned over the man and placed the tip of the blade against his temple. "You damned gringo," he whispered in his ear. "I am Murieta." A panicked look twisted the inebriated man's face. He gently pushed himself away from the table and slowly backed out of the saloon.

Settlers and landowners tired of being held hostage by the lawless element that drifted unchallenged from county to county. California governor John Bigler was compelled to take serious action, and on May 11, 1853, he signed a legislative act creating the California State Rangers, whose reason for existence was to bring in the Murieta gang, known as the "Five Joaquins." The act specifically targeted the handful of men with that name who were either leaders or members of the gang.

Reward money was appropriated to apprehend the fugitives and wanted posters were circulated. The price on Joaquin Murieta's head was $5,000. The bandit noticed his wanted poster while passing through Stockton. He studied the petition, carefully reading the words aloud to himself: "$5,000 to the one who delivers Joaquin Murieta. Dead or Alive." In a cool, unflinching manner, the bandit removed a pencil from his pocket and scribbled a message on the bottom of the poster. Townspeople dared to inspect the poster only after Murieta and his gang had ridden off. The defiant outlaw had written, "I will give $10,000. Joaquin."

The mounted rangers were empowered to "arrest, drive out of the country, or exterminate the numerous gangs which continually placed in danger the life and property of all citizens." Captain Harry Love, a Texas army scout and the deputy sheriff of Los Angeles, was hired to lead the manhunt.

The twenty members of Love's California Rangers enlisted for a ninety-day period, were paid $150 a month, and promised $1,000 reward for apprehending the criminals. The majority of the Rangers had shady pasts. They were murderers and thieves hoping to make a name for themselves in law enforcement. Love had a reputation as a cowardly braggart and believed capturing any of the Joaquins would change the public's perception of him.

Murieta was aware of Love and his Rangers and had decided to return to Sonora with the thousands of dollars in cash he had illegally acquired, as well as the horses he had stolen. His plan was to stay ahead of the posse that was after him while organizing a series of raids on river schooners near Stockton before heading back to Mexico.

Love led a determined chase. Time and again he and his men were on the verge of overtaking Murieta when their efforts were thwarted by Mexican natives fearful of what Murieta might do to them if they did not protect the bandit. Murieta employed the same successful escape tactics he had always used. He divided his large band of thieves into smaller groups and had them go separate ways. Under these conditions, tracking the bandit down was an arduous task.

In July 1853, two months after Love's search began, the captain took seven of his men into the San Joaquin Valley to investigate a column of smoke they'd seen in the distance. According to Captain Love's account, they followed the smoke to a group of men seated around a campfire. Love asked the men where they were going.

"One of the bandits," Love later recounted, "replied that they were traveling to Los Angeles. At this juncture another member of the group addressed me, and insolently told me that if I had any further inquiries to make to address them to him, as he was the leader of the party. I replied that I was an American officer, and as such spoke when, how and to whom I pleased. The man made a quick move as if to reach for his gun, when I warned that a single move would provide him with a quick exit from this world."

The leader of the gang was identified by one of the California Rangers as Joaquin Murieta. Knowing they had been found out, Murieta and his men quickly scattered and rushed to their waiting horses. Joaquin made it to his horse, but the animal was shot out from under him. The bandit toppled over his mount and landed hard on the ground. The frantic and dazed outlaw got to his feet and started to run away. His body was hit with a volley of bullets. He fell again, and this time he was dead. Joaquin's followers were also killed. Three-Fingered Jack was chased for five miles before Love shot him in the head.

Captain Love anticipated that his dubious past might prompt skeptics to question whether the notorious outlaw Murieta was indeed dead. To prove the shooting took place, Love ordered Joaquin's head and Three-Fingered Jack's hand to be cut off and preserved in alcohol-filled jars. He returned to the state capital with his prize in tow. Love was immediately presented with a $1,000 reward, plus a bonus of $5,000. The bandits' remains were put on display at county jails and saloons. Visitors came from miles around to view the human trophies.

Not everyone agreed that the man Love killed was Murieta. The editor of the *San Francisco Alta* investigated the claim and determined that the ambitious captain had gunned down someone other than the outlaw in question.

"It affords amusement to our citizens to read the various accounts of the capture and decapitation of 'the notorious Joaquin Murieta.' The humbug is so transparent that it is surprising any sensible person can be imposed upon by the statements of the affairs which have appeared in the prints.

"A few weeks ago a party of native Americans and Sonorians started for Tulara Valley for the expressed and avowed purpose of running mustangs. Three of the party have returned and report that they were attacked by a party of Americans and the balance of their party, four in number, had been killed; that Joaquin Valenzuela, one of them, was killed as he was endeavoring to escape and that his head was cut off and taken as a trophy.

"It is too well known that Joaquin Murieta was not in the party nor was he the person killed by Captain Harry Love's party at the Panache Pass. The head recently exhibited in Stockton bears no resemblance to that individual, and this is positively asserted by those who have seen the real Murieta and the spurious head."

The *Alta* editor's article, which appeared on August 19, 1853, raised doubts among many readers about whether the remains of the man the Rangers brought in and displayed were those of Murieta. The controversy did not stop people from attending public viewings of the deceased, however. Murieta's sister, a resident of Marysville, openly objected to the barbaric display. She went to her grave insisting her brother had escaped to Mexico and lived out his days with his second wife and their children. Her claim was supported by a few who had seen Murieta years after his supposed death.

Captain Harry Love never deviated from his assertion that he had killed Joaquin Murieta. Love died on June 29, 1868, from a wound received in a gunfight with one of his employees.

Joaquin's head toured California for more than thirty years before being put on permanent display at Dr. Jordan's Museum of Horrors in San Francisco. The exhibit was destroyed in the great earthquake of 1906.

The life of Joaquin Murieta was a violent affair, accentuated by thievery, killings, and narrow escapes. A handful of sympathetic newspapermen in the mid-1850s suggested he was propelled by vengeance and the need to regain the dignity he felt the "blue-eyed gringos" stole from him.

Reporter, magazine writer, and poet John Rollin Ridge agreed. Ridge's own past had been mired by murders and prejudice, and he identified with the notion that Murieta was misunderstood and desperate for acceptance.

Ridge, a Cherokee Indian from Georgia, was struggling to find a way to make ends meet when he decided to write about the outlaw. Using the basic facts of Murieta's life, he created an intriguing story, built on the traditional Robin Hood tale. Ridge's main character was a man of "generous and noble nature, built like a tiger and unafraid to challenge mistreatment from white men."

Historians believe Ridge saw himself in the legend he'd created. The hopeful author expected to earn a great deal of money from the book, but his publisher was less than honest and he never made a dime. "After selling 7,000 copies," Ridge wrote in a letter to his cousin in Oklahoma, "he put the money in his own pockets; fled, and left me and a hundred others to whistle for our money."

Since the release of Ridge's book in 1854, numerous other authors have written about Joaquin Murieta. Many books and magazine articles merely reworked Ridge's original material, plagiarizing some of the dialogue. In 1938 Hollywood made a movie based on Ridge's book, aptly titled, *Joaquin Murieta*.

John Rollin Ridge died in 1867 at the age of forty. He is remembered as the Old West's first desperado image maker to turn legend into history. More than 150 years after his death, Joaquin Murieta—whatever his fate—is still recognized as one of California's most notorious outlaws.

JOHN WESLEY HARDIN

Family Man

On May 26, 1874, John Wesley Hardin joined his wife, Jane, and their fifteen-month-old daughter Mollie in Comanche, Texas, to celebrate his twenty-first birthday by watching the horse races. The Comanche County sheriff liked Hardin, a light-complected man with blue eyes who was five feet, ten inches tall. They enjoyed playing cards together in the local saloons. Deputy Sheriff Charles Webb of adjoining Brown County was also in Comanche that day, and friends warned Hardin that Webb wanted him dead or alive.

"Do you have papers for my arrest?" Hardin asked Webb.

"I don't know you," Webb lied. He had been studying Hardin's pictures for weeks.

"My name is John Wesley Hardin."

"So I know who you are, but I don't have arrest papers," Webb lied again.

"Then let's go in this saloon and take a drink."

When Hardin turned his back on Webb to enter the saloon, a friend shouted, "Look out, Wes!"

Later, Ranger N. A. Jennings would write that Hardin, with a six-shooter in each hand, could "with lightning rapidity put twelve bullets in a playing card at twenty yards." This time Hardin whirled, cross-drawing his revolvers from the holsters on his chest. Webb's bullet struck first, hitting Hardin in the side, but Hardin's killed Webb instantly with a head shot. Hardin, a careful counter, said Webb was the fortieth man he had killed.

Hardin fled, and irate citizens forgot that the deputy sheriff had tried to shoot Hardin in the back after denying that he had arrest papers. A vigilante mob then hanged Hardin's brother Joe, a completely innocent man.

Texas Rangers, Pinkerton detectives, and assorted gunmen seeking the $4,000 reward combed Texas for Hardin, but three years passed before the Rangers found him in Pensacola, Florida, and brought him back for trial. By that time he and Jane had a son, John Wesley Junior, and another daughter, Jennie, born eight days before the Rangers took her father away. The Comanche County jury found him guilty, and the judge gave him twenty-five years. Now Hardin sat in the Travis County jail in Austin, waiting for a decision from the Texas Court of Criminal Appeals.

Jane's brother, Brown Bowen, waited in the same jail for the appellate decision on his murder conviction in Gonzales County. Brown had killed Tom Halderman just before Christmas 1872 in a country store. Hardin was with him shortly before the killing, and he had helped his brother-in-law escape from the Gonzales County jail. The Rangers found Brown about the same time that they found Hardin, and his jury in Gonzales found him guilty at the same time that Hardin was found guilty in Comanche County.

The few meetings of the brothers-in-law, waiting in the Travis County jail, were not happy ones. First, Brown's carelessness had led to the Texas Rangers finding Hardin in Florida and Brown in Alabama. Jane's brother had betrayed Hardin's whereabouts in a letter to his (and Jane's) father, Neal Bowen, which the Rangers intercepted.

Second, Brown Bowen had the nerve to complain that Hardin only got twenty-five years for killing a sheriff while he got the death penalty for killing a no-account drunk. Halderman had just happened to be in the store that day, he had too much to drink, and he passed out behind the stove when Bowen, out of pure spite, shot him in the back.

Third, it had been Hardin who smuggled the iron file into the jail shortly after Brown's arrest, who pried off his handcuffs after Brown cut through the bars, and who helped him escape to Florida and Alabama where the Bowens had kinfolk. In spite of that assistance, Brown's carelessness had led to Hardin's arrest and Brown's turning against his brother-in-law.

Fourth, and even more invidious, Brown Bowen and his father tried to cast doubt on Brown's conviction by laying the blame on Hardin.

"Why not tell the Rangers you killed Halderman?" Brown asked. "You already got a twenty-five-year sentence to serve. One more conviction won't mean much."

"Besides," Neal added, "you've got a lot of friends down in Gonzales. You might get off."

"They had the eyewitness," Hardin said, looking at Brown with contempt. "He saw you shoot the sleeping drunk in the back."

"But don't forget," Brown insisted, "you know how to get out of that poor excuse for a jail in Gonzales. You even escaped from it once yourself."

Hardin tried to conceal his contempt of his brother-in-law. He had never trusted him. But Jane's father had never treated him badly. He'd do his best to keep harmony in the family, but he wasn't going to admit to a killing he had nothing to do with. God knows, Texas and some of those other places had enough killings that he did do if they just wanted another one to charge. He looked directly at his father-in-law.

"You can't ask me to make a false statement, Neal. It wouldn't be honorable. They'd see through it. They had the eyewitness, you know."

In his pleas to the governor and to the public through the newspapers, Brown Bowen still claimed innocence and that John Wesley Hardin had shot Halderman.

Later, in answering a question by a newspaper reporter, Hardin was more blunt. "I've never killed a man the way Tom Halderman was killed. He was asleep. He had no chance to defend himself."

Neal, embittered that Hardin wouldn't take the blame for his son's crime, went before the grand jury at Cuero and told about Hardin's 1873 killing of J. B. Morgan. Hardin had never denied that killing, claiming self-defense. He had never been charged, but now, on the complaint of his father-in-law, he was indicted for another murder.

Hardin kept Jane informed of the family struggles, and Jane had always stood by him. He wrote, "You can rest assured that Neal Bowen and Brown are not our friends but have done all they can against me. I am sorry for Brown's condition and yet it is only justice. . . . He has tried to lay his foul and disgraceful crimes on me."

Shortly before Brown's scheduled hanging, Neal and another daughter, Matt, visited Hardin in jail.

"Couldn't you make some statement, Wes," Neal pleaded, "something that would save Brown?"

"Not an honorable one. I don't think you'd want me to make a false one."

The day before the hanging, Matt came back to the jail, but Hardin refused to see her. She sent a note, pleading for some helpful statement. He replied: "For your sake, I would do anything honorable. I cannot be made a scapegoat. A true statement would do your brother no good and I won't make a false one."

On May 17, 1878, at the scheduled hour and before thousands of witnesses who packed the streets, Brown Bowen was hanged. Hardin wrote Jane that he had forgiven Brown for "his false and unfounded reports, and may God forgive him. Even after the cap (hood) was taken off, he said he was innocent, but that I had done it. Then he fell 7 feet and lived 7 seconds, witnessed by 4,500 people. May his poor soul be in peace and I hope that God forgives his sins. Kiss those darling babies for me once more and ever remember that I am ever your loving and true husband."

Old Neal Bowen took his son's body and buried it on the family farm in Coon Hollow. He didn't know that he dug the grave under the same oak tree where his daughter and Hardin had pledged their love five years before.

The appellate court affirmed Hardin's conviction, and he entered the Texas State Prison on October 5, 1878, to serve twenty-five years.

In spite of his pious statements about only telling the truth, even as a boy John Wesley Hardin had shown a callousness to some people, surprising in the light of his family and background. He was born in Bonham, Texas, on May 26,

1853, the second of eight children born to James and Elizabeth Hardin. His father, a circuit-riding Methodist preacher, named his son after the founder of his denomination. We know of nothing bad about his siblings, including the one killed by vigilantes.

When Hardin was eight, his father passed the bar examination and began teaching school and practicing law in Polk County. John Wesley's cold-blooded heartlessness showed up early. In 1868, the fifteen-year-old boy killed his first victim, a former slave. At that time in east Texas the community probably did not consider that the victim was a former slave, but Hardin fled, thinking he could not get a fair trial.

Later Hardin claimed that he had killed three soldiers who tried to arrest him and that neighbors and relatives helped him bury the evidence. Hardin always showed signs of intelligence, education, and fluency in language. His father sent him away in 1869 to teach school in Navarro County where other relatives lived. The sixteen-year-old soon left that for gambling and horse racing. By the end of that year he admitted that he had killed a freedman and four more soldiers.

In 1871, eighteen-year-old Hardin drove cattle to Abilene, Kansas. His cousin, Mannen Clements, was on the trail crew. On the drive up Hardin killed an Indian, who had shot an arrow toward him, and five Mexicans who were crowding the herd. When his cousin was jailed for killing two cowboys, Hardin arranged with Wild Bill Hickok for the cousin's escape. Later, after killing a man at his hotel, Hardin fled Abilene, fearing arrest by Hickok.

Eighteen-year-old Hardin married Jane Bowen on February 29, 1872, when he returned to Gonzales after the cattle drive. She would always be loyal to him, even though he was gone much of the time dodging arrest. Later in 1872, Hardin was arrested on a variety of indictments and lodged in the Gonzales County jail. This is when he broke out of jail with the help of Clements.

Hardin had killed Morgan in April 1873. That killing and the killing of Deputy Sheriff Webb were the only ones for which he was ever convicted.

After the Morgan killing, Hardin became embroiled in the Taylor-Sutton feud in south Texas as a leader in the Taylor faction, many of them his relatives. He helped kill Bill Sutton, the leader of the other side. Two months later came the shooting of Deputy Sheriff Webb in Comanche.

After Hardin's conviction for shooting Webb in October 1877, he was chained into a buggy with thirty pounds of iron around his neck, arms, and legs for transportation to Austin. A large crowd followed them out of town. Remembering what had happened to his brother Joe, Hardin was glad the Rangers had an armed escort for the first twenty miles. The crowd disappeared on the second day, and the prisoner breathed easier.

When the rangers reached Brushy Creek, fifty miles north of Austin, one of them rode down to the creek looking for a spring. He found one with a small, dark fortune-teller camped nearby. When the guard carried that news back to camp, Hardin told the Rangers that he believed somewhat in mystic powers and he would like to have his fortune told. They brought the gypsy up to their camp. He gazed into Hardin's eyes, turned Hardin's handcuffed hands up, and studied them carefully.

Finally the gypsy spoke in a low, quavering voice. "You've had a hard life, young man. You are going to the penitentiary for a long time. You will be a good man there and get out."

Then he paused as though finished.

"What then?" Hardin asked.

The dark little man closed his eyes as though not wanting to talk. Soon he continued, "I see grave trouble ahead for you. When you get out, you will kill two men. If you are not careful, you will be attacked from the back and killed."

A grim, gray look came to Hardin's eyes.

The Rangers openly admired Hardin and treated him well. He had daring and skill with guns and horses. Many Rangers were not very tamed themselves. Soon after his return to Austin, Hardin wrote Jane, who was now back in Texas, "Dear, I had an ice cream treat today by the Rangers. I thought of our ice cream visits in New Orleans."

Jane hurried to Austin with the children, and for a short time while waiting for the mandatory appeal the family had visits together in the Travis County jail. Jane's cheeks were pale and some sparkle had gone from her eyes, but both she and her husband remembered their pledges to stick together until death. That loyalty was severely tested by the conflict between Jane's husband and her father and brother. But Jane stayed true to her pledge and broke with her father.

Hardin tried several times to escape from prison. He never succeeded and drew severe punishment each time. Eventually he settled down, joined a debating society, began attending Sunday school, and studied law in prison. In 1888, ten years into his prison term, he wrote Jane, "I desire through you once more to make glad the hearts of our precious children by informing them that I, by the grace of God, still live. I still love them with that undying love that belongeth only to a true and devoted brave, but oppressed and exiled, father. I tell you that my deep, anxious solicitude for your welfare and their prosperity is unabating and that my love for you and them is so vast that it is boundless, so deep that it is unfathomable of that tenacious quality that neither time, vicissitudes, nor expatriation can impair, let alone sever. I but faintly outline the love that mel-lifluently flows from me to them to you that no vocabulary, no symbols, can describe, no sum of words define."

In January 1892, Hardin plea-bargained for a two-year concurrent sentence for the Morgan killing. Jane Hardin died the next November. The children went to live with Fred Duderstadt, a longtime friend of their father's who ranched nearby.

Hardin received a full pardon in February 1894. Although he had only served fourteen years and the early years had been marked with escape attempts and harsh punishments, his pardon recited that he had completed his sentence and was "behaving in an orderly manner." The gypsy on Brushy Creek had proved correct in one prediction: Hardin had been a good man in prison, at least after he gave up trying to escape.

Hardin joined his children in Gonzales, passed his bar examination, and began law practice there in October. He wished that Jane was with him to talk to Mollie when the twenty-one-year-old girl announced that she and Charley Billings were getting married. Hardin tried in vain to get them to wait, thinking that Mollie was in too much haste. In the November 1894 election for sheriff, Hardin supported the man who lost by eight votes out of almost five thousand cast. The campaign had been bitter, and Hardin decided to leave before he got into trouble.

He moved west to Junction, where his brother Jeff lived. Hardin's son Johnny and daughter Jennie remained with Duderstadt. Hardin opened another law office, and in January 1895 he married fifteen-year-old Callie Lewis, daughter of a prominent rancher in Junction. Callie, just a few months older than Hardin's Jennie, left him on their wedding night.

In April 1895, after Hardin had given up any hope of reconciliation with Callie, he heard what amounted to a call of the clan from Pecos in West Texas. There, Jim Miller, a close friend and son-in-law of Mannen Clements, who was Hardin's cousin and close friend, had been shot in an unprovoked attack by George Frazer, the former sheriff. Hardin began preparing Miller's defense on rustling charges and was also hired to prosecute a criminal case against the former sheriff for shooting his client. The sheriff's case was moved to El Paso, and Hardin went there to handle it and finish the autobiography he was writing.

El Paso at that time was a safe harbor for evil. A hunted man could cross the river into Mexico or travel a few miles north to hide in the raw and lawless territory of New Mexico. El Paso was so overloaded with killers that the city hired Jeff Milton—perhaps Texas's greatest lawman—as its police chief.

Hardin had pleaded with his son Johnny to stay away from such places as El Paso, but Hardin opened a law office there. Milton warned his policemen that Hardin was the most dangerous man in America. As Hardin made the rounds of the saloons, men set up drinks, lost to him in poker, and tried desperately for friendship with such a famous gunman. They knew nothing about his self-education and reform in prison, and his later attempts to lead a law-abiding life.

One day, Mrs. Helen Morose called at Hardin's office. The husband of the over-painted woman—a prostitute in her younger days—had fled to Juarez, and Chief Milton sent word that he would be killed or jailed if he tried to return.

Mrs. Morose wanted her husband back with protection from the law in El Paso. But she liked the looks of her new lawyer and soon forgot about Morose.

Jeff Milton didn't forget. When Morose tried to return, he was shot to death before reaching the Texas bank of the river. Mrs. Morose was soon known as "Wes Hardin's woman."

While Hardin was back in Pecos seeing about Miller's case there, Mrs. Morose went on a binge. Policeman John Selman Jr. arrested her, and she paid a $50 fine. Selman's father, an El Paso constable, had been a gunman in Fort Griffin thirty years before and a close associate of John Larn, another famous Texas outlaw.

When Hardin returned to El Paso and learned of the arrest of his new love, he became irate. "If I'd been here, you wouldn't have dared do that," he told the policeman. Brooding about the arrest of the faded blonde, Hardin put her on a train to Phoenix. She sent a telegram from Deming, New Mexico, that she was returning because she had just had a premonition that something terrible was about to happen to Hardin. The premonition troubled Hardin. Perhaps he remembered the prediction of the gypsy on the creek north of Austin.

Early in the evening of August 19, 1895, Hardin told friends that one more day would finish his book. A little later, while walking along San Antonio Street near the Acme Saloon, he saw young Selman and showered him with verbal abuse. The policeman had nerve, but he knew better than to draw against Hardin.

Later, Hardin strolled into the Acme Saloon, which had only a few customers that night. He drank a little and tried a few games. About eleven o'clock, in a good humor, he matched dice with an El Paso grocer. As he rolled the dice, he had his back to the front door.

Old John Selman walked in, drew his revolver, took careful aim, and shot Hardin in the back of the head. One of the West's most dangerous and efficient killers fell to the floor dead.

The Brushy Creek gypsy had missed one of his predictions. Hardin may have wanted to kill the Selmans, father and son, but during his seventeen months as a free man after his pardon, he had killed no one.

Hardin's life was a tragedy from a family point of view. His first wife opposed her own family to stick by him for many years. After she died and he won release from prison, he married a fifteen-year-old beauty, who left him after a few hours. His life ended in a brutal slaying brought on by his relationship with an ex-prostitute. Incidentally, Callie Lewis Hardin later married a physician and won respect from all in Mason and Kimble Counties, but she never wanted to talk about Hardin.

BILL LONGLEY

He Was a Man Before He Was Done Being a Boy

Believe-It-or-Not Robert Ripley may have exaggerated in claiming that Bill Longley had been hanged three times. Longley, of course, should have known, and the second time he had a noose around his neck he did say, "Hanging is my favorite way of dying. I'd rather die that way than any other way except a natural death."

When Sheriff J. M. Brown sprung the trap on October 11, 1878, in Giddings, Texas, the noose slipped, and Longley dropped to his knees. He was hoisted up and dropped again, so one can see why Ripley made the claim about three hangings. Nine years before, vigilantes had also tried to hang the man. Longley, finally doing his last dance in the air, was just six days past his twenty-seventh birthday.

Born October 5, 1851, William Preston Longley grew up on the family farm in what would become Lee County, a few miles from Giddings, and learned early to use guns. He would become one of the fastest draws in Texas.

The first of the nation's modern gunslingers, Longley differed from most Texas outlaws in that he was not a robber or cattle rustler, and was never part of a gang. He generally played a lone hand. His distinguishing mark seemed to be his pure enjoyment in the act of killing.

The reconstruction effort after the Civil War included the creation of a state police in Texas, made up mostly of freed slaves. Most Southerners, including Texans from the eastern part of the state, nursed bitterness about the war and hated reconstruction. In December 1866, shortly after his fifteenth birthday, Bill and his father were in town when a black policeman, waving his gun, insulted Bill's father. Perhaps the black man didn't know that Bill's father was a staunch Unionist—a clear minority in east Texas. The elder Longley's sterling record at the Battle of San Jacinto warded off criticism from his white neighbors.

Bill, carrying his usual pistol, stepped forward. "You put that gun down," he said.

The policeman pointed his gun at Bill, and Bill shot him dead. Bill joined other young men and began to terrorize the newly freed slaves. He was already six feet tall, with curly black hair and a high-cheekboned, angular face, and his small, fierce black eyes smoldered with hate. During 1867 Bill killed at least three and perhaps five black men.

In 1869, near Yorktown, Texas, Bill was mistaken for his brother-in-law and friend, Charley Taylor, one of the leaders in the Sutton-Taylor feud. Black army troops had been ordered into the area to put down violence. Some soldiers, thinking Bill was a Taylor, approached to make an arrest. Bill thought they wanted him for his most recent killing, and he fled. Bill Longley rode like a Comanche, and after six miles he had outdistanced all but the sergeant in charge, who was mounted as well as he. Longley had only one bullet left when the sergeant pulled abreast. He jammed his pistol into the sergeant's side and pulled the trigger. The soldier fell dead from his saddle, and Longley escaped.

Now Longley preyed on freed slaves and Union soldiers in black regiments who were traveling alone. One evening, vigilantes caught him and a horse thief named Tom Johnson, who had joined Longley at his campfire. Believing that birds of a feather flocked together, the vigilantes strung both men up. Longley, just sixteen with five notches already in his pistol, found himself face-to-face with death. But as the vigilantes rode away, they fired their pistols toward their victims in the customary celebration. One of the bullets struck Longley's rope before he died, his heavy body broke the rope, and he recovered from his first hanging. Johnson wasn't so lucky.

By this time Longley was Texas's most wanted outlaw. His aged parents begged him to leave the state. Later that year he joined a trail herd to Abilene, bossed by a man named Rector.

After they reached Indian Territory and Rector got his crew to pitch in and buy a keg of liquor, Rector got into a shooting scrape with one of the men, wounding him in the shoulder. The next day Longley remarked that Rector had better not treat him that way or he would regret it. Rector, hearing about the remark, rode up to face Longley.

"I understand, damn you," Rector said, "that you said I had better not run on to you. Is that so?"

"As sure as hell," Longley answered calmly, "I damn sure did say them very words." Rector went for his pistol, but Longley beat him to the draw. Longley had six bullets in Rector's body before the trail boss started to slide out of the saddle, dead.

The trail crew advised Longley to give himself up at Fort Sill, as the authorities would surely let him go on their evidence that Rector had started the fight. But Longley was afraid the authorities would discover that he was wanted in Texas, so he rode on, joined by a cowboy named Davis who volunteered to ride with him.

One night, five Osage Indians tried to steal horses from Longley and Davis. The men killed one Indian; the other four ran. After visiting Abilene, Kansas, for a few days, Longley went on to Fort Leavenworth, where he got into an argument in a saloon with a soldier who had asked him if he was from Texas.

"Yes, I'm from Texas," Longley answered.

"Well, now," the trooper snarled, "if I was from Texas I'd be damned ashamed of it and keep it to myself. I know from firsthand experience that there's not an honest man in Texas nor a virtuous woman either."

Later Longley would say, "Before the words were cold on his lips, I sent a bullet through his heart, and when several of his companions made a move as to interfere, I covered them and informed them that if they did not want to get a quick pass to hell, to keep quiet."

Bill took the train to St. Joseph, where two armed officers grabbed him and said he was under arrest for killing the soldier in the saloon. Three weeks later he bribed the sergeant in charge of the guardhouse with $50 and a violin he had carved out of soft wood and escaped.

Bill Longley spent the next two years as a miner, mountain man, gambler, and teamster in Wyoming. He killed a man at Camp Brown (later called Fort Washakie) and got a thirty-year sentence in federal prison. Again he escaped and rode south to Colorado, where he lived a year with the Ute Indians.

Lonesome now for Texas, Bill headed for the Kansas trail towns, hoping to find a way to ride back to his home. At Parkerville, Kansas, a small town near the Santa Fe Trail, he shot a man to death in a gambling hall. The victim's father offered a $1,500 reward. Bill and two others, also on the dodge, cooked up a scheme in which the two companions turned Bill in for the reward and then sprang him from the jail. They divided the money evenly and rode their separate ways, Bill going back to Texas.

By this time his parents had moved a short way north to Belton, and Bill spent some time with them. But he learned that a Lee County posse was coming to arrest him for a $1,000 reward, and he again hit the Owl Hoot Trail. Soon a black man who'd gotten drunk and insulted a white woman lay dead with two of Bill's bullets in his head. Bill continued riding west.

Five men caught up with him in the Santa Anna Mountains of Coleman County. After a short battle in which Bill killed one, the other four withdrew. It was now late in 1874, and Bill returned to Central Texas, took the name Jim Patterson, and went to work in a cotton gin. But he got into an argument with a George Thomas and shot him through the heart. He stopped in Bell County long enough to hug his old mother and shake the trembling hand of his father. Deeply conscious of the worry he had caused them, he rode southwest to a lonely ranch in the Frio Canyon of Bandera County. He was just beginning to think about settling down in that beautiful canyon when he learned that a recent friend, Lon Sawyer, was scheming with the sheriff back in Lee County to turn Bill in for half the offered reward.

At first Bill considered just shooting Sawyer, but he learned that a reward had been offered for Sawyer, and Bill decided to turn the tables on him. Bill got himself deputized by the Uvalde County sheriff to bring Sawyer in. Bill, in turn, deputized a youth named Hayes to help him capture Sawyer.

An unsuspecting Sawyer, still waiting to hear from the Lee County sheriff, cantered leisurely down a trail with Longley, Hayes, and a wagon to cut up a steer that Longley and Sawyer had recently stolen and killed. Suddenly Longley leveled his pistol at Sawyer and shouted: "Throw up your hands. You're my prisoner."

"I'll see you in hell, first," Sawyer shouted back, drawing his own weapon and spurring his horse forward.

Longley's first bullet hit Sawyer's shoulder, and Sawyer's bullet missed, as the two men began one of the West's wildest shooting rides. They rode through a cedar brake and burst into a glade about two hundred yards long. When they reached the end of the glade, both pistols were empty, Longley was still untouched, and Sawyer had three more bullets in his back. One of the two bullets fired by Longley, which missed Sawyer, disabled Sawyer's horse. Sawyer drew his shotgun, leaped to the ground, and killed Longley's horse. Then Sawyer disappeared into another dense cedar brake.

Bill had a second pistol, but the caps had gotten wet and wouldn't fire. He ran back toward the approaching wagon, where he knew the teamster had a gun. On the way he met Hayes and told him he could follow Sawyer's trail from the blood spurting out of his four back wounds.

Learning that the teamster only had a carbine with three cartridges, Longley unharnessed one of the wagon horses, jumped on its back, and plunged through the cedar brake to cut Sawyer off. In the meantime a pack of hounds, attracted by the noise, were assailing Longley.

Suddenly Sawyer, lying on the ground, fired his shotgun and barely missed Longley. Longley jumped to the ground and fired at Sawyer. He hit the man's shotgun stock and spun around to shoot two of the closest hounds. Then Longley took his time to reload his good pistol.

After Longley fired eight more times and Sawyer six, Sawyer called out that he wanted to talk things over.

"Not unless you throw your pistol out," Longley replied.

Sawyer did that, and Longley walked over to where he lay, weak from loss of blood. But Sawyer had another pistol that Longley didn't know about. He fired it but missed. Longley's shot, fired so simultaneously to his opponent's that they sounded like one roar, hit Sawyer above the eyes, killing him instantly.

Sawyer's last shot had hit Hayes in the leg as he arrived at the battle scene. Sawyer had fired fourteen shots, and only killed Bill's horse. Longley had fired eighteen times, hitting Sawyer thirteen times, besides killing his horse and five dogs. Longley said Sawyer was the bravest man he had ever fought. Longley's short career in Texas law enforcement was over.

Later in 1875, Longley learned that a boyhood friend, Wilson Anderson, had killed Bill's nephew, Cale Longley, in Bastrop County, near where Bill grew up. Joined by his brother James, Longley rode directly to Anderson's farm, found his old friend plowing in the field, and gunned him down with a shotgun. This was the murder that would result in Longley's eventual execution.

After the Anderson killing the Longley brothers fled to Indian Territory and then returned to Texas. James turned himself in and was acquitted of any part in Anderson's murder. Bill Longley stayed on the loose. He was captured in Edwards County by Sheriff Bill Henry. Henry took his prisoner to Austin to collect the reward, but when the governor refused to pay it, Sheriff Henry turned Longley loose.

On February 12, 1876, Bill Longley was riding through Delta County in northeast Texas when he met Louvenia Jack at a small farm near Ben Franklin. Falling in love for the only time in his life, he introduced himself as William Black of Missouri, saying he had lived in Texas about three years.

"We sat up late that night," Bill would write later from jail. "I never felt such feelings on earth as now seemed to take possession of me. I lay and thought of all my past life, and never before did I realize my true condition. I thought I would give all the wealth in the world, if I had it to give, if I was only a plain, civil, and pious man. I thought I would get up an excuse so I could stop and rest for a day or two, and perhaps in that time I could make up my mind what I should do."

Later Bill got out of bed in the Jack home, retrieved a nail from the fireplace, and hammered it into his horse's hoof. After breakfast he "discovered" that his lame horse could not travel, so Mr. Jack invited him to stay over a day or two. Then sixteen-year-old Louvenia suggested that Bill "Black" talk to a preacher, Roland Lay, who lived a mile away and needed someone to farm his place on shares. Jack thought the idea great, and the arrangements with Preacher Lay soon were worked out.

Bill had always enjoyed working the soil, and now he was only a mile from the love of his life. But he soon learned that the preacher's cousin also had designs on Louvenia. In fact, they had been engaged to be married when Mr. and Mrs. Jack opposed the match.

Bill had taken a great liking to the preacher, and he was shocked to learn that the preacher was the main one encouraging his cousin to resume his attempt to win Louvenia. Three months after he had been living in the preacher's cabin and farming the land, Bill found a note tied to the plow handles, warning him to leave the county. To a cold-blooded killer like Bill Longley, such a note was an invitation to violence. Yet Bill, for the first time in his life, did something noble: He rode away and found work on another farm, ten miles away in Lamar County.

Some days later, while Bill was visiting the Jacks, one of the Lay family killed a Jack dog, and Bill horsewhipped him. Preacher Lay responded by getting a warrant from Lamar County, saying Bill had threatened his life. Bill escaped from the Lamar County jail by burning it down. He reached the Jack cabin just before dawn, grabbed their shotgun from their mantel, rode to Lay's and found the preacher in the cow pen, milking. A double-barreled, heavy load of turkey shot left the community without a preacher. But this time Bill had killed an old, unarmed man, who had an infant daughter asleep in her crib inside the house. Bill knew he had to ride far away.

Bill crossed into Indian Territory, riding past the house where Jim Reed, outlaw husband of Belle Starr, had been killed two years before. He tried to stay away from people; sometimes he didn't see another person for a week at a time. Once, he traded his horse and shotgun to an Indian for the Indian's horse. The Indian changed his mind, caught up with Bill, and attacked him with a knife. Bill shot him in the forehead and again in the chest before the body hit the ground. Then Bill found two improved Colt's cartridge pistols under the Indian's blanket and took them, since they were no use to a dead Indian.

Bill kept thinking of Louvenia back in Ben Franklin, and sometimes cried himself to sleep. He rode through northeast and east Texas, always keeping to himself, and finally reached De Soto Parish, Louisiana. There he made another sharecropping deal, this time as Will Jackson. He became friends with another farmer, June Courtney, who had just been elected town constable. Courtney often asked his new friend to help make arrests. Bill was so efficient as a helper that Courtney began studying wanted posters from Texas. Then Courtney tipped off the Nacogdoches County, Texas, sheriff that he thought he had Bill Longley in his town.

Using a carefully planned approach, the Texas sheriff, his deputy, and the Louisiana constable were able to take Longley into custody on May 11, 1877, without getting hurt.

Longley was tried in Giddings in September for the Anderson killing. On Monday, September 3, 1877, he was arraigned on a grand jury indictment. He pled not guilty and asked for a continuance. The court denied his motion, and the trial began the next morning at 8:30. Later that day jury foreman J. S. Wade signed a verdict of guilty. The court still had time to take up other matters that day. Longley was removed to Galveston to await the decision on his automatic appeal. While there he complained to the governor that it was unfair to execute him as he had only killed thirty-two men, and John Wesley Hardin received a life sentence for killing many more.

Bill wrote a lot and told a lot to reporters while he was in jail waiting for execution. He had only regretted one of his thirty-two killings. That victim was a cowboy on the trail to Kansas who seemed to be watching Bill too closely.

"I wasn't going to sleep with that fellow watching," Bill said. "So I shot him and then went to sleep. The next day I learned that he was on the dodge, just like me."

Longley came back in court on September 5, 1878, for formal pronouncement of judgment, his execution having been affirmed. The judge ordered "that you be by the sheriff of Lee County hung by the neck until you are dead, dead, dead."

Some detested Bill Longley because he killed for the love of killing. Others saw him as a heroic figure resisting a reconstruction that had been inflicted by an insensitive victor in war. Another judgment is contained in an oft-quoted statement about Longley: He was a man before he was done being a boy.

Longley himself put it this way: "I have always known that I was doing wrong, but I got started when I was a fool boy, led off by older heads, and taught to believe that it was right to kill sassy Negroes, and then to resist military law."

When the noose was dropped over Bill's head in October 1878, just a few miles from where he had started as a fifteen-year-old killer, it was the second time he had felt the rope on his neck. This time, it still took two attempts to succeed.

JIM MILLER

Born to Hang

A fair description of John Wesley Hardin would be a juvenile punk who enjoyed killing blacks, Yankee soldiers, Mexicans, and Indians. Jim Miller, Hardin's cousin by marriage, is seldom mentioned in Texas history, but a fair description of him is worse. He killed his grandparents when he was eight and his brother-in-law when he was seventeen. Eventually he preyed on the world at large, demanding money for his services.

Miller, a slender five feet, ten inches tall and a dapper dresser, never swore, drank, or smoked. He had many friends and attended church so regularly that he was often called "Deacon Jim." He was usually soft-spoken, but his pale-blue cold, unblinking eyes gave some people goose bumps. When he killed his sister's husband John Coop on Sunday, July 30, 1884, he left during an evening worship service and galloped three miles to Coop's house, where his victim was sleeping on an outside porch. Miller crept up and shot Coop in the head and rode back to the church before the service ended. Despite his alibi about being in church at the time, the jury convicted him, and the judge gave him life in prison. But Miller appealed and got a new trial and an acquittal. The bizarre crime and its bizarre result became typical of Texas's leading assassin.

Miller was born in Van Buren, Arkansas, in 1866, one of nine children. His parents moved to Franklin, Robertson County, Texas, when Miller was a baby. When they died, he was sent to live with his grandparents in Coryell County. There was no other suspect for their murder in their own home, and Miller was arrested but released as too young to prosecute. Turned over to the custody of his sister, he soon clashed with her husband on their farm at nearby Gatesville.

Three years after Miller killed his brother-in-law he got a cowboy job with Mannen Clements, Hardin's cousin. He married Mannen's daughter, Sally, in February 1888, exactly twelve months after Sally's father had been killed by Ballinger City Marshal Joseph Townsend over a political dispute. Miller later avenged this killing by blasting Townsend out of his saddle from ambush as the marshal rode home at night.

Miller spent the next two years drifting around southeastern New Mexico Territory. Sometimes he gambled in saloons on the Mexican border; sometimes he rode into west Texas towns. One August afternoon in 1891 he rode into Pecos, seat of Reeves County. Oppressive heat hung heavy above the baked streets, and bystanders wondered why the stranger wore a black broadcloth coat.

Miller swung down in front of Juan's Saloon, and curious heads appeared in windows and doorways to watch. A half dozen cowboys from a rough cow outfit near Toyah and their ramrod, a man named Hearn, studied Miller carefully as he entered the saloon. After Miller ordered a glass of water, Hearn stepped up to the bar next to him.

"That big coat of yours sure makes me sweat," Hearn sneered. His cowboys felt duty bound to challenge someone every time they came to town.

Miller's eyes never changed, but his nose wrinkled in disgust at the dust-covered men with cow dung on their boots. "Your stink makes me sick," he said.

"Take it off," Hearn ordered, pointing with his left hand at Miller's coat.

Hearn's right hand moved too fast to see, and he had it on the butt of his revolver when Miller's revolver seemed to leap from under his coat into his hand, its muzzle against Hearn's belly.

"Drop it," Miller said softly. The room was suddenly silent.

Hearn's half-drawn six-shooter slid back into its holster. "Hell's bells," he muttered, his face suddenly ashen. "I was just a foolin'."

Miller stepped back, never taking his cold eyes off Hearn. "I like this town and figure to settle here. You have two minutes to get out, and take these jack-asses with you." He nodded at the other cowboys. "If you come back to raise more hell, I'll kill you."

When the dust of the departing cowboys had settled, Miller bought drinks for his wide-eyed audience and had another glass of water. The story swept through the small town, and its saloon soon filled. Even Sheriff Bud Frazer came in to order a round of drinks.

Other people had declined to ask about the coat, but Frazer inquired, "Would you mind telling me, sir, why you wear such a heavy coat in weather like this?"

The crowd tensed, but Miller smiled softly. "This coat is my life insurance. It belonged to an old friend of mine. He sheriffed on the border for years and never got a scratch." The crowd relaxed and Miller continued. "He gave credit to the coat, and he died in bed with his boots off." Miller stroked his worn coat. "He gave it to me. I figured it must be lucky."

"Well, a man's got a right to his own superstition," the sheriff said. "You say you're going to settle down here?"

"Thought I'd see about working in a hotel. I've done some of that."

"Let's go down to my office. I'd like to propose something you might be interested in."

Miller left the sheriff's office wearing a deputy's badge. Without knowing it, Frazer had deputized Texas's first hired assassin. He would soon become the most dangerous man in Texas, New Mexico, and Oklahoma.

Frazer and Miller worked well together and seemed to like each other. Then suddenly they had a falling out, and no one knew why. Some thought Frazer had stumbled onto evidence that Miller was running stolen cattle into Mexico. At any rate, Con Gibson told Frazer that Miller and Mannen Clements had tried to get him to help them kill Frazer. Then a Ranger captain came to town and arrested Miller.

Miller hired two fine lawyers (one would later be a district judge and the other a state senator), and he got an easy acquittal.

Gibson, the informer on Miller, left town in a hurry. When he reached Carlsbad, New Mexico, he got into an argument with John Denston, a cousin of Miller's wife. The argument ended with Gibson's funeral, and people considered it a revenge killing, but nothing implicated Miller. Only Bud Frazer seemed to be bitter.

On April 12, 1894, Miller, still wearing his frock coat, was talking to a rancher friend who noticed that Frazer kept walking back and forth near them. Miller, engrossed in the conversation, hadn't noticed.

"I wonder why the sheriff keeps walking by and looking at your back," the friend said.

"Well, I don't know." Miller turned around and stared into the muzzle of the sheriff's six-shooter.

"Jim, you're a cattle rustler and a murderer," Frazer shouted, opening fire. "Here's one for Con Gibson."

Frazer's gun roared, and the first bullet ricocheted off Miller's coat.

Frazer's second shot disabled Miller's gun arm. Miller got his pistol into his left hand and blazed away, but Frazer escaped unhit.

Frazer emptied his gun, but Miller stayed on his feet and kept shooting. When Miller finally fell, Frazer went back to his office, unhurt. By all rights, Deacon Jim Miller should have been dead.

The people who picked Miller up and carried him to his hotel discovered that three of Frazer's bullets had struck directly over Miller's heart. They had flattened against the steel plate he wore over his chest and under his coat. Then, for the first time, Miller's own friends learned why he wore that black coat even in the heat of summer.

When Miller regained consciousness, he smiled at his friends and said, "Tell Frazer he can't kill me and he can't run me out. Next time, I'll get him."

Miller took several months getting well, but he repeated his oath that he would kill Frazer if he had to crawl twenty miles on his knees to do it. In the meantime Frazer lost an election and moved to Lordsburg, New Mexico, to visit relatives.

Unfortunately Frazer returned in December. He rode into Pecos the day after Christmas and saw Miller standing in front of the blacksmith shop. Knowing of Miller's oath to kill him, Frazer drew his revolver and began shooting. His first bullet hit Miller's gun arm and the second hit his leg. Then he aimed for the heart. Miller, although again disabled, fired away with his left hand. Frazer again shot Miller over the heart and wondered why the man was still standing. He had never heard about the steel breastplate. Knowing that he was a good shot, the confused attacker turned and fled.

Miller's friends wanted to go after Frazer, but he smiled and said he'd try the legal way first. He swore out a complaint with the new sheriff.

Frazer's trial was moved to El Paso, and Miller hired his cousin, John Wesley Hardin, to assist in the prosecution. But Hardin was killed before it came to trial, and the jury disagreed. The trial was moved to Colorado City in Mitchell County, and Frazer won an acquittal in May 1896.

Miller, disgusted, determined to get Frazer once and for all. It took four months of waiting, while spies from each side reported on the other's movements, but Miller finally heard in September that Frazer was visiting relatives in Toyah, a tiny town eighteen miles from Pecos.

Knowing that Frazer would be advised of his every step, Miller got a friend, Bill Earhart, to wait outside Pecos with two horses. Then he sauntered out of town on foot to meet Earhart, and the two rode to Toyah. Earhart rented a hotel room across the street from the saloon on the night of September 13, and Miller slipped into the room by the back way.

The next morning, Frazer went to the saloon as usual and started playing cards with friends. Earhart signaled that all was clear, and Miller walked rapidly across the street with his shotgun. He pushed the swinging door open and fired both barrels. The double-barreled charge practically blew Frazer's head from his body.

One witness reported: "All of a sudden the room exploded like dynamite had hit the floor. I happened to be looking at Bud, and like to have fainted when I saw his whole head disappear in a clot of splashing blood and bone. That's all I took time to see. I dived through the window, taking glass and all with me. Next thing I remember I was under my bed three blocks away, shivering like hell."

Frazer's sister borrowed a gun and, with her mother, set out for Pecos. She confronted Miller when he arrived, covering him with the pistol.

"If you try to use that gun," Miller said softly, "I'll give you what your brother got. I'll shoot you right in the face."

She lowered the gun but gave Miller a vicious tongue-lashing. One of Frazer's friends, Barney Riggs, caught up with Earhart and killed him along with another of Miller's friends.

Miller's trial for murdering Frazer was transferred to Eastland, between Abilene and Fort Worth. Miller moved to Eastland well in advance of trial, went into business as a hotel operator, transferred his church membership, contributed to local charities, and did everything he could to make a good impression. Also, he had his wife and two sons—five and two years old—with him.

The three-week trial started in June 1897. Dozens of people came from Pecos to testify. One said Miller's conduct was as "exemplary as that of a minister of the gospel." Nevertheless, eleven jurors voted to convict. The one holdout made a second trial necessary. At the second trial Miller was acquitted on grounds of self-defense.

After keeping a saloon in Memphis in the Texas Panhandle, and even working for a time as a Texas Ranger, Miller went to Monahans, back in the Pecos area, where he apparently became a deputy U.S. Marshal. For the next eight years he killed sheepmen and farmers, both classes despised by some West Texas ranchers. His standard price was $150 per man. Once Miller said with pride, "I have killed eleven men that I know about; I've lost my notch stick on sheepherders I've killed out on the border."

In February 1908, Miller killed Pat Garrett, the legendary lawman who had killed Billy the Kid. Sheriff Garrett had killed the famous outlaw over twenty-five years before. The controversy over the killing—Garrett and Billy the Kid had been friends, and Garrett shot him without warning in a darkened room—made Garrett lose the next election, and he took up ranching. For the next twenty years Garrett ranched, served as a captain of the Texas Rangers, again as a New Mexico sheriff, and as a collector of customs appointed by President Theodore Roosevelt. For five years he raised racehorses in Uvalde, Texas, where John Garner, a young friend of his, would later become vice president of the United States.

By 1906 Garrett had a little ranch in the Organ Mountains east of Las Cruces, New Mexico. The land was coveted by W. W. Cox, a neighboring rancher, who could not get Garrett to sell. Somebody hired Miller to kill Garrett so Cox could get the land. Miller's price for this killing was $1,500.

Garrett was shot in the back of the head on February 29, 1908. He had been traveling toward Las Cruces in a buggy, accompanied by Carl Adamson. Wayne Brazil joined them on the way on horseback. Five miles from Las Cruces, the buggy stopped, and while Garrett was urinating someone shot him in the back of the head. He fell to the ground, dead, and he was shot again in the stomach. Brazil and Adamson went on to Las Cruces, where Brazil turned himself in to the sheriff, saying he had shot Garrett in self-defense. Adamson backed up his story.

Captain Fred Fornoff of the Territorial Mounted Police investigated the murder scene after the sheriff picked up the body. He found where a horse and rider had waited nearby for some time, leaving two .44 Winchester spent cartridges in the sand.

At a farce of a trial in which the jury heard only Brazil's story of shooting in self-defense—Garrett's heavy driving glove was still on his right (gun) hand and his fly was open—the jury acquitted Brazil. Captain Fornoff was never produced as a witness.

With the proof that the horse that waited beside the trail had been borrowed by Jim Miller and that the bullet that entered the back of Garrett's head came from his rifle, it is not surprising that most historians agree that Miller killed Garrett.

Miller spent the rest of 1908 back in Fort Worth gambling. Late that year he heard that his old friend Mannie Clements had been killed. He swore he would avenge the killing, but he had already been hired for another job, this time in Oklahoma. The fee was the highest he had ever been offered—$2,000.

Ada, Oklahoma, the scene of Miller's last killing and his own death, had a little over three thousand people and thirty-six murders in 1908. Gunfighters from two powerful factions had been feuding for years. Angus Bobbitt led one faction; Joe Allen and Jesse West led the other. Finally, Bobbitt forced Allen and West out. They moved their cattle herds to Hemphill County, Texas, and brooded like wounded rattlesnakes. The killing of Pat Garrett hastened their decision on how to strike back.

In late February 1909, a frock-coated man was seen riding near Bobbitt's home a few miles from Ada. In late afternoon on February 27, Bobbitt was driving home with a wagonload of meal cake for his cattle. A neighbor, Bob Ferguson, followed in his own wagon. Just before sundown, they met a lone rider who talked a few minutes with Bobbitt and then rode on, passing out of view as he crossed over a hill behind them.

Just after sundown, about a mile from Bobbitt's ranch, a double-barreled shotgun sounded twice. Bobbitt, struck twice, toppled from his wagon, dead. Ferguson recognized the man they had met earlier on the trail as he galloped away.

The sheriff followed the killer's tracks to the farm of young John Williamson. The shoes worn by the mare Williamson had rented had been removed, but were found under the kitchen floor. Williamson withstood a lot of pressure before he identified the rider who had rented his horse as his uncle from Fort Worth, Jim Miller. More investigation revealed that Berry Burrell, an old friend of Allen and West, was intermediary between them and Miller and had spotted Bobbitt for the killer. Miller was arrested on March 30 near Fort Worth. Burrell had already been arrested in Fort Worth. Afraid that Allen and West would fight extradition, the county attorney sent them this telegram at Canadian, Texas: "You and Joe come to Ada at once. Need $10,000, Miller."

The ruse worked, and Allen and West were arrested in Oklahoma City, just after stepping off the train to be greeted by their lawyer. The preliminary hearing was held on March 19. Some of Ada's citizens didn't wait for the trial.

At two o'clock in the morning of April 19, a group of vigilantes cut off Ada's electric current. In the darkness they overpowered the jailers and removed Miller, Allen, West, and Burrell. They took them to a livery stable and hanged all four. They saved Jim Miller for last. He refused to confess, merely saying, "Just let the record show that I've killed fifty-one men."

Miller was as unconcerned about his own death as he had been earlier about each of his many victims. The vigilantes stood him on a box, adjusted the noose around his neck, and told him to step forward to the edge of the box. Miller slipped a diamond ring from his hand, directing that it be given to his wife. He made other dispositions of his property.

"I'd like to have my coat," he said. "I don't want to die naked." He must have believed it would still make him invincible.

They refused, so he asked for his hat. They jammed his Stetson on his head.

Miller laughed. "Now I'm ready. I don't want this rope to knock my hat off. You sure you got it set right?"

The vigilantes looked on with amazement as they nodded their heads.

"I always knew I was born to hang," Miller continued. "They never was a bullet that could kill me."

He moved forward to the edge of the box. He looked down and laughed again.

"Let 'er rip," he shouted as he leaped forward.

Some people said Miller's conduct on the box showed his courage. Others said it showed his total depravity and inhumanity.

One of the vigilantes draped Miller's coat over his slumped shoulders as he hung there in the barn. "It won't do him no good, now," he said.

JOHN "BADEYE" SANTAMARAZZO

The Weston County Poisoner

In the 1814 book *Traité de Toxicologie,* Mathew J. B. Orfila wrote:

> *Revolted by the odious crime of homicide, the chemist's aim is*
> *to perfect the means of establishing proof so that the heinous*
> *crime (of poisoning) will be brought to light and proved to the*
> *magistrate, who must punish the criminal.*

In the Old West, deadly weapons of all types were readily available to anyone who wanted them. The most common weapons included rifles, shotguns, pistols, axes, and knives. Other dangerous weapons were available based upon a man's occupation, and miners had access to picks, shovels, sledges, and all sorts of tools and materials that could be used to kill another person. Therefore, with all of these readily available weapons, it was surprising when a man resorted to poison as a means to bring about another man's death.

Nonetheless, this seemed to occur about once every ten years between 1887 and 1906. In 1887 Frederick Hopt from Utah asked a druggist to supply him with strychnine "to kill the rats which are eating my grain at camp." The druggist refused to supply him with the poison, and so Hopt returned to camp and bludgeoned John F. Turner to death. Twenty years later in Montana, Miles Fuller put strychnine in Henry Callahan's sugar bowl in the hope that he would eat the poison and die, leaving his land vacant for Fuller to occupy. Callahan must have noticed the tampering and did not eat the poison. In his defense, Fuller would later claim, "I know too much about poison for that purpose and recommend arsenic." In another incident John Santamarazzo tried to use strychnine to kill a man with whom he had a dispute. Like the others, he too failed to kill his victim with poison.

John Santamarazzo was born in Italy in 1843. He came to America as a youth and traveled west, settling in Wyoming by the mid-1890s. He had been a miner all his life and found work in the coal mines of Weston County in northeast Wyoming. In August 1895 he was fifty-three years old. He was "married but without children" and described as "poorly educated, about five feet eight inches tall and weighing one hundred and sixty pounds, with long black hair and black eyes, 'white' but with a very dark complexion," according to Elnora L. Frye's work on the prisoners at Wyoming's Territorial Prison.

Santamarazzo's appearance was rugged, and he looked like a true outlaw. He had been injured in a mine explosion during his earlier mining days, and it had left him with powder burn discoloration on the left side of his face and ear. His left eyelid drooped over a blind eye, earning him the sobriquet "Badeye." He had led a somewhat violent life as evidenced by a cut scar in the middle of his forehead, another on his left arm, another large cut on his "short ribs," and an "ax mark" on his left arm.

In April 1895, Santamarazzo was working for the Cambria Mine. There he met Mike Dancy (sometimes spelled Dacy, Dacey, and Darcy), who was a teamster at the mine. Dancy and Santamarazzo had a heated argument on August 13, but it failed to escalate to violence; still, the ill-tempered and vindictive Italian swore he would kill Dancy.

The following afternoon Dancy took his dinner break with Santamarazzo, Theodore Shaw, Freeman Fossler, Charles Isem, and Henry Sulzner. He opened his meal bucket and took a large bite of bread, and then remarked to his companions that it had a "strong bitter taste to the first mouthful." Immediately, Dancy's neck began to stiffen in an awkward position. Before he could speak another word, he collapsed and was immediately overcome by violent spasms. His body jackknifed back and forth, and he groaned in agony. The slightest noise or vibration on the floor aggravated the symptoms and caused the convulsions to become even more severe.

Once summoned, Dr. George Garrison Verbryck rushed Dancy to the nearby hospital for treatment. Dancy's dinner bucket was also collected and turned over to the doctor, because there appeared to be foul play. Upon examination Verbryck found a colorless, crystalline powder sprinkled throughout the food. The doctor identified the substance as strychnine and determined there was enough of the poison present to kill a hundred men.

Fortunately for Dancy, the bitter taste had caused him to pause in eating his meal and have a conversation with his fellow workers. This had prevented him from ingesting a fatal dose. The doctor managed to pump his stomach and administer activated charcoal, which soon revived the patient. Still, it took a short while before the victim could talk. When he was able to speak, he stated that he did not know who could have tried to kill him. He knew of no enemy who would want to take his life, "unless it was that Italian who I argued with yesterday. He said he would kill me."

Sulzner, who was at the meal table that day, would later testify that he observed Santamarazzo "when Dancy first took ill and saw actions and expressions of the Itallion [sic] . . . and believed M. Dancy received poison at the hands of Santamarazzo." Others said they had seen Santamarazzo lurking around the meal buckets earlier in the day.

On the afternoon of August 14, 1895, Weston County Sheriff John Owens filed a criminal complaint before Justice of the Peace P. J. Welsh. The complaint charged that "J. Santamarazzo . . . [tried] to take the life of Mike Daucey [sic] by distributing poison in his lunch and victuals with the intention of poisoning the same." Dancy also filed a criminal complaint charging that Santamarazzo " . . . did willfully, maliciously and unlawfully administer poison with the intent to kill the said Mike Dancy." The judge issued a warrant based upon the complaints and, upon receiving it, the sheriff immediately served it on the suspected poisoner, arresting him and lodging him in the Weston County jail in Newcastle.

On April 4, 1896, Sheriff Owens took Santamarazzo from jail to the court, where counsel was appointed. Since the defendant could not adequately speak or understand the English language, the court provided an interpreter. On April 20, 1896, Wyoming's Fourth Judicial District Court convened and heard the testimony of several witnesses, including the four men that were present and Dr. Verbryck.

Theodore Shaw testified, "I was present and witnessed the condition of M. Dacey [sic] and saw that he had spasms and that I examined the dinner pail and contents and could see something resembling strychnine in the bread, and Dr. Verbryck made an examination of the food and found strychnine freely distributed in the food"; Freeman Fossler testified next and stated that Dancy "had spasms resembling that of a man having taken poison" and said he believed it was "administered by the hands of the accused prisoner." Charles Isem swore that "I was present . . . and saw the condition and action of M. Dancy after he had eaten his dinner and saw the food containing strychnine." Lastly, Henry Sulzner testified to the same and to the guilty appearance of Santamarazzo's countenance and demeanor. The doctor testified to the type of poison, its presence in the food, the symptoms of Dancy, and the treatment for strychnine poisoning that had been successful in reviving the victim.

An indictment charged the defendant with two counts. The first stating that: "Santamarazzo . . . unlawfully, willfully, maliciously and feloniously . . . administered poison—to wit: strychnine—to one Mike Dacy [sic], with intent to kill him . . . death not ensuing there from, contrary to the form upon the Statute in such case made and provided, and against the peace and dignity of the State of Wyoming." The indictment's second count read, ". . . and the said L. T. Griggs, County and prosecuting attorney . . . informs the Court and gives the Court to understand, that the same (Santamarazzo) did unlawfully, willfully, maliciously, feloniously . . . mingle poison—to wit: strychnine—with food of one Mike Dacy [sic], with intent to kill him . . . death not ensuing there from."

Santamarazzo was arraigned, and a jury was quickly empanelled. The same counsel that had represented him at the arraignment was appointed to represent him at trial. The case began before noon on the April 19, and the presentation of evidence occupied the remainder of that day and the next. The case went to the jury shortly before 9:00 p.m. The jury could not arrive at a verdict and remained in the jury room overnight, but in the morning the foreman told the judge that they were hopelessly deadlocked—eight for conviction and four for acquittal. The jury was dismissed, and a second jury empanelled.

Santamarazzo was then arraigned on a charge of "the crime of attempt to kill with poison," which was a slight change in the wording from the first trial. The testimony was again taken on April 21; the case went to the jury late on the second day, but again this jury could not arrive at a swift verdict and spent the night in the jury room. Deliberations continued throughout the following day. At 4:00 p.m. John P. Ost, jury foreman, announced, "We the jury . . . do find the defendant . . . guilty as charged in the Information." The prisoner was then remanded to the county sheriff to be held in the jail until sentence was passed.

Within a few days, on April 28, 1896, the prisoner was brought into court again. The former coal miner was sentenced to serve nine years in the penitentiary near Laramie. On May 5, 1896, the prisoner was delivered from the Newcastle jail to the prison by Weston County's Sheriff John Owens. He was registered in the Bertillon Book as convict #258.

Santamarazzo was at the Laramie prison, known as the Territorial Prison, when the new state prison, called the Frontier Prison, was opened in Rawlins. He was in the fourth group of convicts transferred there on December 21, 1901. On June 23, 1904, by reason of "expiration of sentence," authorities released Santamarazzo on his earliest release date, having awarded him 460 days of good time credit as required under the Goodwin Act. His release date would have been April 27, 1905, without the credit for good time.

Good police work and the willingness of witnesses to testify led to the arrest, trial, and conviction of John Santamarazzo before he could commit another crime. His disdain for the life of another man suggests that if he had succeeded in killing Mike Dancy, he would not have hesitated to commit another crime. He may have again chosen the diabolical and unique method of poisoning.

GEORGE A. BLACK

A "Black Day" for Ol' Tanglefoot

George A. Black was born in Indiana in 1862. When but a boy he moved with his parents and five siblings to Ryan County, Missouri. After his father died, the family moved to Davis County. He was a sickly child unable to attend school. When he turned eighteen years old, he left home for Laramie, Wyoming. There his health improved, and he married a fifty-three-year-old widow with several children. The marriage lasted only four years, and after that Black moved onto a small piece of land not far from Laramie, located next to the far superior claim of Robert Burnett.

Burnett, who was known as "Ol' Tanglefoot," had lived near Meridian, Missouri, during the Civil War, where he lost everything, including his wife. After the war he started westward, settling at several places for a while. After a decade of wandering, he finally stopped in Wyoming. Though quite peculiar he was a likable sort. His friends described him as an "eccentric." He wore gunnysacks, tied with wire, on his feet. He ate only with his hands and threw the scraps on the floor of his cabin, and had not been known to bathe in many years.

Burnett was feebleminded and terribly superstitious, but he was also a litigious old man. Burnett sued his neighbor, George A. Black, for harvesting the old man's hay. Burnett won the suit, and when Black could not pay the judgment, the plaintiff was awarded Black's buildings, some hay land, and a few cows. With no place to live, and the better part of his poor land gone, Black had no choice but to vacate his property.

Black wanted Burnett's land and held a grudge when he lost his property. He tried to drive the old man off the land and played upon Burnett's superstitious nature by posting White Cap notices—crude drawings of skulls, crossbones, and coffins—on his cabin door. Once, he hid in a clump of sagebrush and fired on Burnett, but missed his mark. The old man, instead of turning and running, charged and captured Black. Black insisted that he had mistaken Burnett for an elk, so the old man released him without charges being filed.

When Black failed to drive Burnett off the property, he moved to Medicine Bow, but soon returned to the Pole Mountain area near Laramie to live with his brother Benjamin. There Black found a willing accomplice to help him in his ongoing battles with Burnett. Black first met twenty-eight-year-old Dwight

"Roxy" Rockwell at the JD Ranch in Wyoming's Silver Crown mining district. Black and Rockwell became reacquainted in Laramie, where Black explained how Burnett had "stolen" his land. Rockwell agreed to go with Black to Burnett's land to help him reclaim "his" property. Black filed a mining claim on Burnett's property in Laramie, and then the two men stocked their wagon with supplies and started out.

They arrived at Burnett's cabin on May 28, 1889, and found the old man seated on an overturned pail cutting seed potatoes inside his cabin. Rockwell stood nearby while Black talked with Burnett. Black asserted that the land belonged to him and asked, then commanded, that Burnett vacate the property, but the old man refused. Suddenly Black pulled his six-shooter and shot Burnett in the back. When Burnett reached for his rifle, Black shot him in the head and then fired one more ball into the dead body.

The two men wrapped the head and then the entire body of Burnett, hauled it up a remote canyon, and placed it at the end of a huge log. They piled pitch pine onto Burnett's remains and set it afire before returning to the cabin to sleep. In the morning they scrubbed the wagon and smeared grease on the tarp to cover the bloodstains before returning to the body. They raked what remained of Burnett into a pile and, with a new pile of tinder, again set it afire. Then they returned to the cabin and replaced the bloodstained floorboards. That night they returned to Burnett's remains, gathered up the larger bones and remnants, and buried them in a gopher hole. Black and Rockwell took possession of the cabin, but Rockwell soon left for North Park, Colorado.

Burnett was not missed for several weeks. When friends finally noticed his absence, Black explained that the old man had sold out to him and gone east to spend his final days with his daughter. That story was soon discredited, but there was no evidence of foul play, so no action could be taken. There was talk of organizing a search, but this was abandoned when Black threatened to kill any organizer of an investigative committee.

The Pullman family, Charles, Mattie, and teenage daughter Mary, had recently arrived from Missouri. On August 6, 1889, Mattie and Mary were berry picking when they saw a strange pile of ashes covering an area nearly 8 feet in diameter, certainly no campfire. They investigated and found small human bones, bits of wire, and small remnants of clothing. They hurried home and told Charles. The next day the three returned to the site. Charles Pullman examined the remains, gathered every bit of evidence he could find into two pails, and carried them to Laramie.

Pullman gave the pails to the Albany County attorney, who called in Dr. John W. Harris. The doctor and his associate identified the remains as human finger bones, part of a skull, teeth, and a rib bone. They also found rivets from overalls (like those always worn by Burnett), hobnails, and bits of baling wire.

Coroner Dr. J. H. Hayford convened a jury and over five days of testimony and investigation found the remains to be Burnett's. The Black brothers and Rockwell were charged with the murder.

George Black and his brother Benjamin were arrested and jailed. At the preliminary hearing before Justice Charles E. Carpenter on August 22, George was held and Benjamin was released. The evidence against Black, though circumstantial, was very strong. Two weeks after the discovery of Burnett's remains, Sheriff Charles Yund learned that a check payable to Burnett had been endorsed by Rockwell and cashed in North Park, Colorado. Yund deputized J. J. Moore, and the two men went in search of the fugitive. Rockwell was working in a field on George Fletcher's ranch when the two officers found and arrested him. He willingly returned to Wyoming and confessed all the details, first to the officers and then under oath at Black's trial.

In mid-October Black was indicted for first-degree murder while Rockwell was indicted as an accessory after the fact. The trial in the district court commenced on Saturday, November 2. Five days later Black was found guilty. On November 16 Judge M. C. Saufley sentenced Black to hang on January 15, 1890.

Rockwell was tried after Black and received a light sentence, in consideration of turning state's evidence, and two years later was living in Montana. The appeals process, financed by his brother Benjamin, began for Black. The execution was stayed while the state's supreme court considered the matter, but the respite was only six weeks in duration. The supreme court denied the bill of exemption and upheld the lower court's decision. Governor Francis E. Warren quickly denied the petition for commutation of sentence, and the date for Black's execution was rescheduled for February 26, 1890.

Black had been a Baptist, but a week before the hanging he was baptized into the Catholic faith. On Tuesday evening, February 25, the prisoner was talking with his deathwatch guards when the reporter from the *Leader* was escorted to his cell by the sheriff. In the cell were papers and books read to him by the guards, a bouquet of flowers, and a potted plant. The reporter offered to print whatever the condemned man wanted to disclose and encouraged him to confess, but he professed his innocence and persisted in saying Rockwell committed the crime and that he was denied a fair trial. Just before the visitor left at 9:50 p.m., Black ordered his last breakfast of fried chicken.

Black retired at 12:50 a.m. and spent a restless night. He arose at 6:00 a.m. when he was awakened by the changing of the guard. Father Hugh Cummiskey arrived next and was with Black a good part of the morning, and Benjamin Black and their three sisters joined them for a while. Deputy Sheriff Alex McKay visited and pleaded with Black, for the sake of his soul, to tell the truth, but the condemned man continued to insist that he was innocent. The prisoner had his breakfast at 9:30 a.m. and this seemed to brace him for the ordeal. He dressed in a new black suit and kept his derby hat at hand. Special deputies were then admitted in small groups, and Black's last visitors, three women, came and went.

The scaffold had been erected within a twenty-by-twenty-foot shed at the rear of the jail. At 11:00 a.m. Father Cummiskey started from the cell with the prisoner, a metal cross firmly gripped in Black's right hand, and Sheriff Yund following closely behind. The distance to the trap was only one hundred feet. The procession ascended but stopped a few feet from the trapdoor, where the priest offered a prayer, shook hands with Black, presented a cross for him to kiss, and then quickly retired. Fifty people watched as Black stepped onto the trapdoor, unassisted, and then Deputy McKay pinioned his arms and legs with straps. The sheriff placed, cinched, and adjusted the noose. He asked the prisoner if he had anything to say to the witnesses, but Black declined except to say, "I am not the one who did it." Sheriff Yund pulled the black cap from his pocket and placed it over the prisoner's head at 11:12 a.m. and in the next moment turned toward the release, gave the twine a firm tug, and the trap fell. The body dropped 8 feet, breaking the prisoner's neck.

Dr. T. Getty Ricketts of Carbon and Drs. J. H. Finfrock and Henry L. Stevens of Laramie stood on chairs; one monitoring the heartbeat while the other two each held a wrist and counted the pulse of the hanging figure. The condemned man's pulse ceased at six minutes, and life was pronounced extinct. Black's body was cut down at 11:39 a.m., twenty-seven minutes after he fell. Black's remains were placed in a cheap coffin provided by the county and slid into a one-horse hearse. He was buried in a potter's field at county expense that afternoon.

Black had tried for months to murder Robert Burnett, or drive him off his land, and he finally succeeded in committing one of the most cold-blooded murders in Wyoming history. He coveted another man's land and was willing to do anything to get it.

GEORGE COOKE

He Had His Man for Thanksgiving

Mary Ann Cooke (sometimes spelled Cook) gave birth to son George in Worces-
tershire, England, on October 18, 1854. Four years later her husband died, and
Mary Ann spent the next eighteen years raising her seven children—four boys
and three girls. One son, upon reaching adulthood, found employment in the
East Indies, but the remaining six children immigrated to America with their
mother in 1876. The family settled in Laramie, Wyoming.

George's brother Albert and sister Mary Ann, named for her mother, settled in Laramie while his brother James moved to Rock Creek. One sister moved
to Fort Russell, and the other sister moved to Denver, Colorado. In 1883 Mary
Ann married James Blount, a large, forty-year-old man who spent a good deal
of his time in the many saloons of Laramie. He worked as a janitor at a public school building, but relied upon his wife for a substantial portion of their
income. They had a son they named Samuel, and on November 25, 1883, Mary
Ann gave birth to a second child, a daughter.

George, who had little education, first found work as a cowpuncher at various ranches near town. Later he found more permanent employment as an ostler
and coal-heaver with the Union Pacific Railroad at their Medicine Bow round-
house. George was considered a good worker, but it was obvious that he had a
wild streak.

On the evening of Wednesday, November 28, 1883, George hopped a
freight train from Medicine Bow to Laramie. His purpose was to see his new
niece and spend Thanksgiving with his family. The train arrived before daybreak. It was too early to disturb his family, so Cooke, who had developed a
fondness for liquor while a cowpuncher, went to a nearby saloon for a few beers.
From there he moved on to another saloon and had several drinks while waiting
for the gunsmith to open his shop, then picked up the .45 caliber six-shooter he
had left for repair during a previous visit to town. George continued his rounds
of the saloons and by midmorning had crossed paths with his brother-in-law
and brother Albert. The three men continued their drinking at one place after
another with no further thought of family or Thanksgiving dinner.

George was an inoffensive man when not indulging but became rude and
contentious when under the influence of liquor. His brother-in-law Blount was

always a bully, but especially so when he was drunk. During the course of the day, Blount threatened several times to pummel George, who had never hidden his displeasure at his sister's choice of a mate. George threatened to kill Blount if he tried.

The three men parted company about noon, before any trouble developed, with George and Blount continuing their sprees in separate saloons while Albert went his own way. After nearly a dozen hours of hard drinking, George was ready to initiate, rather than fend off, trouble. He went to the railroad's oil room and robbed the workers of their loose change, then went to another saloon to spend his windfall.

At 6:30 p.m. George was in Cleveland's Saloon, where he announced that he would kill Blount the next time he saw him. A half hour later he was in J. Fred Hesse's Saloon on Front Street. He left the saloon with two men to eat dinner. George stepped onto Front Street and nearly collided with Blount, who was coming out of Abrams' Saloon two doors away. George loudly insulted and threatened Blount, who tried his best to calm the situation and offered to buy George a drink, but finally threatened to beat George if he continued his harangue. Without warning or further provocation, George drew his pistol and pointed it at Blount's head, then fired a single shot. The ball entered Blount's left cheek just below his eye, the blast burning and blackening the skin around the wound. The ball ranged through Blount's brain and lodged against the back of his skull. He died instantly.

George fled west on Front Street, threatening pedestrians as he went, and vanished into the darkness. A posse was organized and went out in every direction in search of the murderer. After 8:00 p.m. George was seen near the rolling mills at the foot of North B Street. There he went inside and tried to sleep, but he was too restless and had moved on before he could be arrested. He made his way to the railroad tracks and threw away his pistol, which was later found by the city marshal during the night. At 7:30 a.m. George was found skulking around the railroad tracks trying to find a boxcar in which to hide.

He was arrested by Harry Smith, a railroad worker, and Cooke said that if he could have made it to Medicine Bow he would have gotten a horse, never to be seen again. He was lodged in an eight-by-ten-foot cage in the Albany County jail.

On December 1, 1883, an inquest was held, and George Cooke was charged with murder. On December 3 he was indicted, and four days later his trial commenced. He did not deny the killing, but said he could remember nothing. As his defense he stated that he was too intoxicated to have formed "malice aforethought" or to premeditate the murder, as required for a finding of murder in the first degree. Nevertheless, the jury found him guilty of first-degree murder, and within a few days Justice Jacob B. Blair sentenced him to hang.

An appeal followed, which delayed the execution, and during that period George spent his time in jail singing, telling obscene stories, and reading every newspaper and periodical he could obtain. During the early days of his confinement he made one feeble attempt to escape, but then settled in to await the outcome of his appeal. The Supreme Court spent nearly a year considering the request for a new trial before upholding the lower court's decision to deny one. The date of George's execution was then scheduled for December 12, 1884. An application for commutation of sentence to life in prison was submitted and just as quickly denied.

George's mother, infirm and unable to bear up, returned to England. Three days before his execution George wrote to Blount's widow, his sister Mary Ann, to ask her forgiveness. At first she refused but then reconsidered and forgave him. However, she would not visit him.

The night before his execution George spent time conversing with his death-watch guard William Tatham before retiring after 11:00 p.m. He slept soundly even though a bright light burned in his cell all night. Upon arising he made his toilet and then dressed in his burial clothes—a white collarless shirt, blue suit pants, and new shoes, but set aside his suit jacket. He ate a hearty breakfast and then received Reverend Father Hugh Cummiskey, who heard his confession and blessed him. After the priest left, the doors of the jail were flung open and more than two hundred curious people filed through to have their last look at the condemned man and bid him farewell.

George was described as five foot ten, one hundred sixty pounds, with sandy hair and a light sandy beard he had grown since being incarcerated. His time in jail had left him pale, but he had gained a little weight during the previous year. The doors to the jail were closed when Father Cummiskey returned at 10:00 a.m., and the priest spent those last hours with Cooke.

A temporary board structure had been attached to the rear of the courthouse building to house the gallows and obstruct public view of the execution. At 11:00 a.m. Sheriff Louis Miller called together the five reporters and escorted them into the execution building. A photographer was already in place with his camera set up. The priest, wearing a cassock and stole, led the procession to the scaffold a few minutes later, with the prisoner at his side. Sheriff Miller and Deputy James Sterling followed closely behind, and then came the jurors and witnesses walking two by two. In all, fifty men assembled within the execution building.

Father Cummiskey continued his prayers for two minutes after the condemned man was upon the trap. The prisoner had taken his position facing the scaffold. The priest turned him to face the crowd, took his hand and said, "Good-bye, George," and the prisoner responded in kind.

As soon as the priest left the platform, the sheriff stepped forward and asked, "George Cooke, have you anything to say why the sentence of the law should not be passed upon you?" George replied, "Nothing." The prisoner's hands were tied behind his back with a piece of rope, one strap was tightly bound about his chest to hold his arms, another was buckled just below his hips to secure his wrists, and a third strap was secured about his ankles. The sheriff produced a black velvet bag. The rope was put over Cooke's head, cinched and positioned, and the black bag was pulled over his head. Both lawmen stepped back, and at 11:20 a.m. the supporting post was jerked out and the trap was sprung.

City physician Dr. J. H. Finfrock, and Drs. Newell K. Foster, P. F. Guenster, and Lewis S. Barnes monitored Cooke's pulse. Just before the drop his pulse was at two hundred beats per minute; at one minute after it was eighteen; at two minutes, thirty-two; at three, forty; at four, twenty-five; at five, eighteen; at six, sixteen; at seven and eight, fifteen; at nine, ten; and at ten minutes after the drop George Cooke's heart ceased to beat. He was pronounced dead.

The coroner's jury of six men was summoned, and they delivered a verdict in accordance with the circumstances. The body hung a total of fifteen minutes before being cut down and placed in its coffin. Examination of the body revealed that the deceased's neck had been broken in the fall, but he never lost his grip on the crucifix in his right hand. The black bag was removed, and Cooke appeared more asleep than dead, except for a deep red contusion about his neck. The lid was fastened on the coffin and just after noon he was buried in the city cemetery at the county's expense.

And this is where George Cooke's story ends. He participated in activities of robbery and murder with no remorse. A cold-blooded killer, Cooke chose to become an outlaw. Perhaps most characteristic of how bad to the bone this outlaw was is that he perpetrated his worst crimes on Thanksgiving Day, a day set aside for peaceful family gatherings.

SOURCES

Outlaw Tales of Oklahoma
Old Tom Starr
The Undistinguished Career of Bill
    Dalton
Bob Rogers

Outlaw Tales of New Mexico
Jessie Evans
"Dirty" Dave Rudabaugh
Billy the Kid

Outlaw Tales of South Dakota
Charles Brown
Bud Stevens

Outlaw Tales of Missouri
William Quantrill
Frank and Jesse James

Outlaw Tales of Nevada
Sam Brown
John Moriarty
Milton Sharp

Outlaw Tales of Washington
William Frederick Jahns
Harry Tracy
John Tornow
Frank Leroy

Outlaw Tales of Colorado
Jack Slade
James Gordon
Alfred Packer

Outlaw Tales of Utah
Butch Cassidy
The Sundance Kid
Dart Isom

Outlaw Tales of Oregon
Black Bart
Dave Tucker

Outlaw Tales of Arizona
Frank Nashville "Buckskin Frank"
    Leslie
James Addison Reavis
The Apache Kid

Outlaw Tales of California
"Rattlesnake Dick" Barter
Joaquin Murieta

Outlaw Tales of Texas
John Wesley Hardin
Bill Longley
Jim Miller

Outlaw Tales of Wyoming
John "Badeye" Santamarazzo
George A. Black
George Cooke

BIBLIOGRAPHY

Old Tom Starr

Foreman, Grant. *The Five Civilized Tribes.* Norman: University of Oklahoma Press, 1989.

Shirley, Glenn. *Belle Starr and Her Times.* Norman: University of Oklahoma Press, 1982.

The Undistinguished Career of Bill Dalton

Indian-Pioneer Papers. Interview with Mike Gorman. University of Oklahoma Western History Library.

Nix, Evett Dumas. *Oklahombres: Particularly the Wilder Ones.* Lincoln: University of Nebraska Press, 1993.

Preece, Harold. *The Dalton Gang: End of an Outlaw Era.* New York: Hastings House, 1963.

Samuelson, Nancy. "Bill Dalton: The Most Mysterious of the Dalton Brothers." *Wild West* (June 2004).

———. *The Dalton Gang Story: Lawmen to Outlaws.* Eastford, CT: Shooting Star Press, 1992.

San Francisco Chronicle, May 24, 1894. "Loot of a Texas Bank."

Shirley, Glenn. *Six Gun and Silver Star.* Albuquerque: University of New Mexico Press, 1955.

———. *West of Hell's Fringe: Crime, Criminals, and the Federal Peace Officer.* Norman: University of Oklahoma Press, 1978.

Bob Rogers

Shirley, Glenn. *Law West of Fort Smith: A History of Frontier Justice in the Indian Territory.* Lincoln: University of Nebraska Press, 1968.

Jesse Evans

Bartholomew, Ed. *Jesse Evans: A Texas Hide-Burner.* Houston: Frontier Press of Texas, 1955.

Hough, Emerson. *The Story of the Outlaw: A Study of the Western Desperado.* New York: Copper Square Press, 2001.

Jacobsen, Joel. *Such Men as Billy the Kid: The Lincoln County War Reconsidered.* Lincoln and Norman: University of Nebraska Press, 1994.

L'Aloge, Bob. *The Code of the West.* Las Cruces: B & J Publications, 1992.

———. *Knights of the Sixgun: A Diary of Gunfighters, Outlaws and Villains of New Mexico.* Las Cruces: Yucca Tree Press, 1993.

McCright, Grady E., and James H. Powell. *Jesse Evans: Lincoln County Badman.* College Station, TX: Early West Series, Creative Publishing Co., 1983.

"Dirty" Dave Rudabaugh

Bryan, Howard. *Robbers, Rogues and Ruffians: True Tales of the Wild West.* Santa Fe: Clear Light Publishers, 1991.

———. *Wildest of the Wild West: True Tales of a Frontier Town on the Santa Fe Trail.* Santa Fe: Clear Light Publishers, 1988.

"Chronology of the Life of Billy the Kid and the Lincoln County War." www .angelfire.com/mi2/billythekid/chronology.html.

Fulton, Maurice G. *History of the Lincoln County War: A Classic Account of Billy the Kid.* Tucson: University of Arizona Press, 1968.

Hough, Emerson. *The Story of the Outlaw: A Study of the Western Desperado.* New York: Cooper Square Press, 2001.

L'Aloge, Bob. *The Incident of New Mexico's Nightriders: A True Account of the Socorro Vigilantes.* Sunnyside: BJS Brand Books, 1992.

Rickards, Colin. *Mysterious Dave Mather.* Santa Fe: The Blue Feather Press, 1968.

Stanley, F. *Desperadoes of New Mexico.* Denver: World Press, Inc., 1953.

Billy the Kid

Bartholomew, Ed. *Jesse Evans: A Texas Hide-Burner.* Houston: Frontier Press of Texas, 1955.

Bryan, Howard. *Robbers, Rogues, and Ruffians: True Tales of the Wild West.* Santa Fe: Clear Light Publishers, 1991.

———. *Wildest of the Wild West: True Tales of a Frontier Town on the Santa Fe Trail.* Santa Fe: Clear Light Publishers, 1988.

"Chronology of the Life of Billy the Kid and the Lincoln County War." www .angelfire.com/mi2/billythekid/chronology.html.

"The Death of Billy the Kid, 1881." www.eyewitnesstohistory.com/billythe kid.htm.

Fulton, Maurice G. History *of the Lincoln County War: A Classic Account of Billy the Kid.* Tucson: University of Arizona Press, 1997.

Hough, Emerson. *The Story of the Outlaw: A Study of the Western Desperado.* New York: Cooper Square Press, 2001.

L'Aloge, Bob. *The Code of the West.* Las Cruces: Yucca Tree Press, 1992.

———. *The Incident of New Mexico's Nightriders: A True Account of the Socorro Vigilantes.* Sunnyside: BJS Brand Books, 1992.

———. *Knights of the Sixgun: A Diary of Gunfighters, Outlaws, and Villains of New Mexico.* Las Cruces: Yucca Tree Press, 1991.

————. *Riders along the Rio Grande: A Collection of Outlaws, Prostitutes & Vigilantes.* Las Cruces: RCS Press, 1992.

Metz, Leon Claire. *The Shooters.* New York: Berkley Books, 1976.

Myers, Amanda Lee. "2 digging for Billy the Kid face legal woes." *Arizona Daily Star,* Sunday, May 14, 2006.

"Pioneer Oral History." Center for Southwest Research, Collection MSS 123 BC, Transcripts 22, 113, 123. Universities Libraries, University of New Mexico.

Sharp, Jay W. "The Night Pat Garrett (Probably) Shot Billy the Kid." www .desertusa.com/mag04/july/billy.html.

Simmons, Marc. *When Six-Guns Ruled.* Santa Fe: Ancient City Press, 1990.

Trachtman, Paul. *The Old West: The Gunfighters.* New York: Time-Life Books, 1974.

Charles Brown

Black Hills Daily Times, February 6, 1886; June 17, 1897.

Crisler, Frank. "Killer Halves Woman's Head with Meat Cleaver, Hanged Two Months Later." *Arlington Sun,* August 24, 2006.

Dakota Republican, July 22, 1897.

Deadwood Weekly Pioneer, May 20, 1897.

Watertown Public Opinion, July 23, 1897.

Bud Stevens

Corson County News, September 14, 1939.

Griffith, Rose. "The Trading Post of LeBeau." *True West Magazine* (date unknown).

Mobridge Tribune, December 18, 1909; March 25, April 1, 1910; May 28, 1981; April 30, 2003.

Philip Weekly Review, December 16, 1909.

Potter County News, December 16, 1909.

South Dakota Historical Collections (vol. 30). Pierre: South Dakota State Historical Society, 2007.

Walworth County Record, December 18, 25, 1909; January 1, March 26, 1910.

Ziebach County Historical Society. South Dakota's Ziebach County: History of the Prairie. Dupree, SD: Author, 1982.

William Quantrill

Brownlee, Richard S. *Gray Ghosts of the Confederacy: Guerrilla Warfare in the West, 1861–1865.* Baton Rouge: Louisiana State University Press, 1984.

Christensen, Lawrence, et al. *Dictionary of Missouri Biography*. Columbia: University of Missouri Press, 1999.

Kansas City Star, May 23, 1926.

Leslie, Edward. *The Devil Knows How to Ride: The True Story of William Clarke Quantrill and His Confederate Raiders*. New York: Da Capo Press, 1996.

Yeatman, Ted. *Frank and Jesse James: The Story Behind the Legend*. Nashville, TN: Cumberland House, 2000.

Frank and Jesse James

Beights, Ronald. *Jesse James and the First Missouri Train Robbery*. Gretna, LA: Pelican Publishing, 2002.

Brownlee, Richard S. *Gray Ghosts of the Confederacy: Guerrilla Warfare in the West, 1861–1865*. Baton Rouge: Louisiana State University Press, 1984.

Christensen, Lawrence, et al. *Dictionary of Missouri Biography*. Columbia: University of Missouri Press, 1999.

Croy, Homer. *Last of the Great Outlaws: The Story of Cole Younger*. New York: Duell, Sloan and Pearce, 1956.

Kansas City Times, September 27 and 29, 1872, and October 15 and 20, 1872.

Koblas, John. *The Great Cole Younger and Frank James Historical Wild West Show*. St. Cloud, MN: North Star Press of St. Cloud, 2002.

Parrish, William. *A History of Missouri. Volume III: 1860 to 1875*. Columbia: University of Missouri Press, 1973.

Settle, William A. *Jesse James Was His Name*. Columbia: University of Missouri Press, 1966.

Yeatman, Ted. *Frank and Jesse James: The Story Behind the Legend*. Nashville, TN: Cumberland House, 2000.

Sam Brown

Brown, George R., ed. *Reminiscences of Senator William M. Stewart*. New York: Neale Publishing, 1908.

Sacramento Daily Union, July 8, 10, 1861.

Van Sickle, Elona. "The Death of Sam Brown," 1932 manuscript, ND 161, Nevada Historical Society, Reno.

Van Sickle, H. "Utah Desperadoes," dictated manuscript in Bancroft Library, Berkeley, California. Filed in Nevada Historical Society papers, 1913-1914, v. 1.

Van Sickle, Henry. 1883 Manuscript, Nevada Historical Society, Reno.

Virginia City Territorial Enterprise, March 3, 1860.

John Moriarty

Gracey, Charles. "Early Days in Lincoln County," in First Biennial Report of the Nevada Historical Society, Carson City: State Printing Office, 1909.
Pioche Daily Record, September 22, 24, 1872; August 2, 3, 5, 1873.
Reese River Revielle, August 4, 1873.
Virginia City Territorial Enterprise, November 15, 1868.

Milton Sharp

Dillon, Richard. *Wells Fargo Detective, A Biography of James B. Hume.* Reno: University of Nevada Press, 1986.
Drury, Wells. *An Editor on the Comstock Lode.* Palo Alto: Pacific Books, 1936.
Reno Evening Gazette, September 6, 1880.
Virginia Chronicle, September 11, 1880.
Weekly Nevada State Journal, September 11, 18, 1880.

William Frederick Jahns

Fultz, Hollis B. *Famous Northwest Manhunts and Murder Mysteries.* Elma, WA: Fulco Publications, 1955.
Spokesman Review, October 30, 1909–October 31, 1909.
Spokesman Review, November 4, 1909–November 7, 1909.
Spokesman Review, January 2, 1910–January 4, 1910.
Spokesman Review, January 9, 1910.
Spokesman Review, January 12, 1910–January 22, 1910.

Harry Tracy

Centralia News-Examiner, July 18, 1902.
Chehalis Bee Nuggett, July 11, 1902.
Davenport Times-Tribune, July 8, 1954.
Dullenty, Jim. *Harry Tracy: The Last Desperado.* Dubuque, IA: Kendall/Hunt Publishing Company, 1996.
Fultz, Hollis B. *Famous Northwest Manhunts and Murder Mysteries.* Elma, WA: Fulco Publications, 1955.
Lewis County Advocate (Chehalis), July 18, 1902.
Gulick, Bill. *Manhunt: The Pursuit of Harry Tracy.* Caldwell, ID: Caxton Press, 1999.
History of the Big Bend Country. Spokane: Western Historical Publishing Co., 1904.
Horan, James D. *The Outlaws.* New York: Random House, 1977.
Lucia, Ellis. *Tough Men, Tough Country.* Englewood Cliffs, NJ: Prentice Hall, 1963.

Raine, William MacLeod. *Famous Sheriffs and Western Outlaws.* New York: Doubleday & Company, Inc., 1929.

Sifakis, Carl. *Encyclopedia of American Crime.* New York: Facts on File, Inc., 1982.

Wismer, F. D., and Douglas W. Ellison, eds. *The Life of Harry Tracy, The Convict Outlaw.* Medora, ND: Dacotah Publishing Company, 1990. Reprint of the 1902 edition.

John Tornow

Aberdeen Daily World, September 8, 1911–September 9, 1911.

Aberdeen Daily World, August 14, 1912.

Aberdeen Daily World, May 30, 1987.

Aberdeen Herald, March 21, 1912.

Bristow, Allen P. "Phantom of the Forest." *True West Magazine.* Stillwater, OK: Western Publications, August 1999.

Fowler, Ron. *Guilty by Circumstance.* Steilacoom, WA: Fowler Freelance, 1997.

Fultz, Hollis B. *Famous Northwest Manhunts and Murder Mysteries.* Elma, WA: Fulco Publications, 1955.

Hillier, Alfred J. "John Tornow, the Outlaw Hermit." *Pacific Northwest Quarterly.* Seattle: University of Washington, July 1944.

Lindstrom, Bill. "John Tornow: The legend lives after 75 years, but many questions are still unanswered." *Aberdeen Daily World,* April 16, 1988.

———. "John Tornow: The manhunt begins: In the next 19 months only the woods knew the real story." *Aberdeen Daily World,* April 17, 1988.

———. "Wildman of the Wynooche." *Peninsula Magazine.*

Lucia, Ellis. *Tough Men, Tough Country.* Englewood Cliffs, NJ: Prentice Hall, 1963.

Shields, Mike. "Terror in the Mist." *True West Magazine.* Austin: Western Publications, Inc., January/February 1967.

Unpublished transcription of interview of Dan McGillicuddy, from shorthand notes taken by Anne Cotton, August 23, 1971, courtesy Aberdeen Public Library.

Van Syckle, Edwin. *The River Pioneers, Early Days on Grays Harbor.* Seattle: Pacific Search Press, 1982.

Frank Leroy

Getty, Mona. "Fred Thorp, Sheriff of Okanogan County." Okanogan County Heritage. Okanogan, WA: Okanogan County Historical Society, Inc., March 1966.

Okanogan Independent, November 12, 1909.

Okanogan Independent, November 17, 1909.

Okanogan Independent, November 26, 1909.

Okanogan Record (Conconully), November 26, 1909.

Wilson, Bruce A. *Late Frontier, A History of Okanogan County, Washington (1800–1941).* Okanogan, WA: Okanogan County Historical Society, Inc., 1990. 61 Wash. 405, State v. Leroy.

Jack Slade, Gunslinger

O'Dell, Roy Paul and Kenneth C. Jessen. *An Ear in His Pocket.* Loveland, CO: J.V. Publications, 1996.

Scott, Robert. *Slade! The True Story of the Notorious Badman.* Glendo, WY: High Plains Press, 2004.

Southworth, Dave. *Feuds on the Western Frontier.* Round Rock, TX: Wild Horse Publishing, 1999.

Twain, Mark. *Roughing It.* Hartford, CT: American Publishing Company, 1872.

James Gordon, Murderer

Casey, Lee, ed. *Denver Murders.* New York: Duell, Sloan, and Pearce, 1946.

Jessen, Kenneth. *Colorado Gunsmoke.* Boulder, CO: Pruett Publishing Company, 1986.

Perkin, Robert L. *The First One Hundred Years.* New York: Doubleday & Co., 1959.

Smiley, Jerome C. *History of Denver.* Denver: Old Americana Publishing Co., 1901.

Alfred Packer, Cannibal

Gantt, Paul H. *The Case of Alfred Packer, the Man-Eater.* Denver: University of Denver Press, 1952.

Kushner, Ervan F. *Alferd G. Packer, Cannibal! Victim?* Frederick, Colorado: Platte 'N Press, 1980.

———. *Otto Mears, His Life and Times with notes on Alferd Packer Case.* S. Platte: Jende-Hagan Book Corp., 1979.

Shores, Cyrus Wells. *Memoirs of a Lawman.* Denver: Sage Books, 1962.

Butch Cassidy

Association Journal. "Where Lies Butch Cassidy?" Old West, Fall 1991.

Betenson, Lula, and Dora Flack. *Butch Cassidy, My Brother.* Provo, UT: Brigham Young University Press, 1975.

Drago, Gail. *Etta Place: Her Life and Times with Butch Cassidy and the Sundance Kid*. Plano, TX: Republic of Texas Press, 1996.

Dullenty, Jim. *The Butch Cassidy Collection*. Hamilton, MT: Rocky Mountain House Press, 1986.

——. "The Farm Boy Who Became a Member of Butch Cassidy's Wild Bunch."

Hayden, Willard C. "Butch Cassidy and the Great Montpelier Bank Robbery." *Idaho Yesterdays*, Spring 1971.

Patterson, Richard. *Butch Cassidy: A Biography*. Lincoln: University of Nebraska Press, 1998.

——. "Did the Sundance Kid Take Part in the Telluride Robbery?" *Western Outlaw-Lawman History Association Journal*, Summer 1994.

Slatta, Richard W. "The Legendary Butch and Sundance." *The Mythical West: An Encyclopedia of Legend, Lore, and Popular Culture*. Santa Barbara, CA: ABC-CLIO, 2001.

Walker, Herb. *Butch Cassidy*. Amarillo: Baxter Lane Company, 1975.

The Sundance Kid

Patterson, Richard. "Did the Sundance Kid Take Part in the Telluride Robbery?" *Western Outlaw-Lawman History Association Journal*, Summer 1994.

Slatta, Richard W. "The Legendary Butch and Sundance." *The Mythical West: An Encyclopedia of Legend, Lore, and Popular Culture*. Santa Barbara, CA: ABC-CLIO, 2001.

Black Bart

Collins, William, and Bruce Leven. *Black Bart: The True Story of the West's Most Famous Stagecoach Robber*. Mendocino, CA: Pacific Transcriptions, 1992.

Hoeper, George. *Black Bart: Boulevardier Bandit*. Fresno, CA: World Dancer Press, 1995.

Frank Nashville "Buckskin Frank" Leslie

Bailey, Lynn R., and Don Chaput. *Cochise County Stalwarts: A Who's Who of the Territorial Years*. Vols. 1 and 2. Tucson: Westernlore Press, 2000.

Breakenridge, William M. *Helldorado: Bringing the Law to the Mesquite*. Lincoln: University of Nebraska Press, 1992. Originally published 1928.

Chafin, Carl, ed. *The Private Journals of George Whitwell Parsons*. Vol. 2. Tombstone, AZ: Cochise Classics, 1997.

Chaput, Don. *"Buckskin Frank" Leslie*. Tucson: Westernlore Press, 1999.

Martin, Douglas D. *Silver, Sex and Six Guns: Tombstone Saga of the Life of Buckskin Frank Leslie.* Tombstone, AZ: Tombstone Epitaph, 1962.

Rickards, Colin. *"Buckskin Frank" Leslie: Gunman of Tombstone.* El Paso: Texas Western College Press, 1964.

Traywick, Ben T. *The Chronicles of Tombstone.* Tombstone, AZ: Red Marie's Bookstore, 1986.

James Addison Reavis

Burgess, Glenn, ed. *Mount Graham Profiles: Volume 2, Ryder Ridgeway Collection.* Safford, AZ: Graham County Historical Society, 1988.

Cookridge, E. H. *The Baron of Arizona.* New York: Ballantine Books, 1967.

Farrell, Robert J., ed. *They Left Their Mark.* Phoenix: Arizona Department of Transportation, 1997.

Powell, Donald M. "The 'Baron of Arizona' Self Revealed: A Letter to His Lawyer in 1894." *Arizona and the West* 1, no. 2 (summer 1959): 161–73.

_____. The *Peralta Grant: James Addison Reavis and the Barony of Arizona.* Norman: University of Oklahoma Press, 1960.

Tipton, Will M. "The Prince of Imposters." *Land of Sunshine* 8, nos. 3 & 4 (February and March 1898): 106–18, 161–70.

The Apache Kid

Forrest, Earle R. and Edwin B. Hill. *Lone War Trail of Apache Kid.* Pasadena, CA: Trail's End Publishing Co., Inc., 1947.

Freeman, Dr. M. P. *The Dread Apache: That Early-Day Scourge of the Southwest.* Tucson: n.p., 1915.

Garza, Phyllis de la. *The Apache Kid.* Tucson: Westernlore Press, 1995.

Genung, Dan B. Genung Reminscences manuscript collection. Tucson: Arizona Historical Society.

Genung Jr., Dan B. "The Death of the Apache Kid." *Arizona Highways Magazine.* November 1995: 32–35.

Pool, Frank M. "The Apache Kid." *The Sheriff* 6, no. 2 (March 1947): 18–24.

Ringgold, Jennie Parks. *Frontier Days in the Southwest: Pioneer Days in Old Arizona.* San Antonio, TX: The Naylor Company, 1952.

Robinson, Sherry. *Apache Voices: Their Stories of Survival As Told to Eve Ball.* Albuquerque: University of New Mexico Press, 2000.

Sparks, William. *The Apache Kid, a Bear Fight and Other True Stories of the Old West.* Los Angeles: Skelton Publishing Company, 1926.

Wharfield, H. B. "Footnotes to History: Apache Kid and the Record." *The Journal of Arizona History* 6, no. 1 (spring 1965): 37–46.

Williamson, Dan R. "The Apache Kid: Renegade of the West." *Arizona Highways Magazine* 15, no. 5 (May 1939): 14–17.

"Rattlesnake Dick" Barter

McLeod, Norman. "Rattlesnake Dick." *Sierra Heritage Magazine* (August 1972).

Joaquin Murieta

Block, Eugene B. *Great Stagecoach Robbers of the West.* New York: Doubleday, 1962.

Henshall, John A. "A Bandit of the Golden Age." *Overland Monthly* (July 1963).

Ridge, John R. *The Life & Adventures of Joaquin Murieta.* Norman: University of Oklahoma Press, 1855.

John Wesley Hardin

El Paso Times, April 17 and April 24, 1895.

Hardin, John Wesley. *Life of John Wesley Hardin as Written by Himself.* Norman: University of Oklahoma Press, 1961.

Jennings, N. A. *A Texas Ranger.* New York: Charles Scribner's Sons, 1899.

John Wesley Hardin Collection, Southwestern Writers Collection, Texas State University, San Marcos, Box 174, Folders 1, 2, and 4.

Bill Longley

Bartholomew, Ed. *Wild Bill Longley: A Texas Hard Case.* Giddings, Texas: privately published by Woodrow Wilson, 1953. Reprint, 1969.

Cunningham, Eugene. *Triggernometry: A Gallery of Gunfighters.* Caldwell, ID: The Caxton Printers, 1952.

Killen, Mrs. James C., ed. *History of Lee County, Texas.* Quanah, TX: Nortex Press, 1974.

State of Texas v. William P. Longley, Case No. 100, Criminal Minutes Book A, District Court for Lee County, Texas, 1877, 1878.

Jim Miller

Shirley, Glenn. *Shotgun for Hire.* Norman: University of Oklahoma Press, 1970.

Sonnichsen, C. L. *Ten Texas Feuds.* Albuquerque: University of New Mexico Press, 1957.

———. *Tularosa.* New York: The Devin-Adair Company, 1961.

John "Badeye" Santamarazzo

Frye, Elnora L. *Atlas of Wyoming Outlaws at the Territorial Penitentiary.* Cheyenne: Wyoming Territorial Prison Corporation, 1990.

Newcastle (WY) *Democrat:* August 15, 1895; April 23, 1896.

Stevens, Serita D., and Anne Klarner. *Deadly Doses, a writer's guide to poisons.* Cincinnati: Writer's Digest Books, 1990.

Weston County Court. Case file A-121.

George A. Black

Albany County Criminal Court. Case file #464.

Brown, Larry K. "Fingered by the Fire." NOLA Quarterly; October–December 1995, p. 29.

———. *You Are Respectfully Invited to Attend My Execution.* Glendo, WY: High Plains Press, 1997.

Cheyenne (WY) *Daily Leader*: February 26–27, 1890.

Frye, Elnora L. *Atlas of Wyoming Outlaws at the Territorial Penitentiary.* Cheyenne: Wyoming Territorial Prison Corporation, 1990.

Wyoming Territorial Supreme Court. Docket 2–76.

George Cooke

Albany County Criminal Court. Case file #181.

Beery, Gladys B. "He Died Game." *Real West,* Yearbook, Fall 1984, p. 31.

Brown, Larry K. *You Are Respectfully Invited to Attend My Execution.* Glendo, WY: High Plains Press, 1997.

Cheyenne (WY) *Daily Leader:* December 1, 1883; December 8–9, 1883; December 6, 1884; December 12–13, 1884.

Frye, Elnora L. *Atlas of Wyoming Outlaws at the Territorial Penitentiary.* Cheyenne: Wyoming Territorial Prison Corporation, 1990.

Laramie (WY) *Weekly Sentinel:* December 1, 1883.